*Desk Reference on*
# AMERICAN GOVERNMENT

CONGRESSIONAL QUARTERLY'S

# *Desk Reference on*
# AMERICAN
# GOVERNMENT

BRUCE WETTERAU

Congressional Quarterly Inc.
Washington, D.C.

Copyright © 1995 Congressional Quarterly Inc.
1414 22nd Street, N.W., Washington, D.C. 20037

Printed in the United States of America

Cover and interior design: Anne Masters Design, Inc., Washington, D.C.

Library of Congress Cataloging-in-Publication Data

Wetterau, Bruce.
    CQ's desk reference on American government / Bruce Wetterau.
       p.   cm.
    Includes bibliographical references and index.
    ISBN 0-87187-956-5
       1. United States—Politics and government—Handbooks, manuals, etc. 2. Federal government—United States—Handbooks, manuals, etc. I. Title. II. Title: Congressional Quarterly's desk reference on American government. III. Title: Desk reference on American government.
    JK274.W449 1994
    320.473—dc20
                                                                            94-44948
                                                                              CIP

# CONTENTS

# PREFACE

Within the pages of *CQ's Desk Reference on American Government* the reader will find the otherwise complex subject of American government presented in an easy-to-understand, question-and-answer format. The more than six hundred questions and their brief, fact-filled answers range across all three branches of government. Many focus on how the government works, while others highlight notable firsts and present useful lists for reference purposes. All the material has been specially selected and written to be as accessible as possible to general readers—insider jargon and technical procedural matters, for example, are not within the scope of this book.

Nevertheless, *CQ's Desk Reference* presents a wealth of information in a well-organized fashion. To help readers navigate through the governmental maze, for example, most entries are fully cross-referenced to other, related entries. The extensive index will help readers who want to know about a specific person or fact but who don't necessarily have a question in mind. Furthermore, each entry has bibliographic notes on the sources used to write the answer. Most of the sources are available at local libraries, and so can be used for further research as needed.

Though designed primarily as a ready reference for librarians, *CQ's Desk Reference* will be both interesting and useful for anyone involved with the federal government, as well as for those who are simply curious about it. The questions were culled from various sources, beginning with those frequently asked of CQ's library.

The first section of *CQ's Desk Reference* features questions on the Constitution, finances, war, and the seemingly ever-present government scandals. The presidency, Congress, and campaigns and elections are the focus of the middle sections. The fifth and final section covers the Supreme Court. Overall the book contains material from about 1789, when the present federal government was formed, up to events as recent as late 1994. Only the federal government is covered; there are no questions about state governments.

While the focused, question-and-answer approach reduces to manageable proportions a large and unwieldy subject like government, the reader also must be made aware of additional information appearing in other questions. Within the presidency section, for example, questions have been grouped into subsections, such as "Presidential Powers and Privileges" and "Getting into and out of the White House." Considerable time and effort have gone into putting closely related questions immediately after one another in the subsections.

Still, some questions could easily fit in three places or contain information related to other entries. That is where the two types of cross-references come in. First, there are free-standing cross-references. These are not attached to a question, but simply refer the reader to an entry in another section. Second, and more numerous are the cross-references after the bibliographic notes at the end of many answers. These references tell the reader which other questions contain related information.

Sources for the answers were generally the most up-to-date available on the particular subject covered. Many are Congressional Quarterly publications, which are updated regularly. For some facts and figures that seem to change with the seasons, such as statistics on the budget and government employment, the latest available government publications are cited. Readers who consult the sources referred to in the bibliographic notes will find a wealth of current information about the federal government. The bibliography at the end of the book provides full publication information for the works cited in abbreviated form in the notes at the end of the entries.

I thank my editor, Jeanne Ferris, and the copy editor, Christopher Karlsten, for all their help in pulling this manuscript together. The government documents staff at the University of Virginia Alderman Library also deserves thanks for helping untangle some knotty research problems.

—Bruce Wetterau

# THE GOVERNMENT

## IN GENERAL

**Q 1. When was the name *United States* first used?**

A The name *United States of America* was first used officially in the Declaration of Independence (adopted July 4, 1776). Later, on September 9, 1776, the Continental Congress formally resolved to replace the name *United Colonies* with *United States.* For a time, the country was officially called United States of North America, but in 1778 the Continental Congress shortened it to the present United States of America.

(*Dict. of Amer. Hist.,* vol. 7, 153; *Encyc. of Amer. Facts & Dates,* 92; *I Hear America Talking,* 6)

**Q 2. Who designed the flag and when was it officially adopted?**

A Contrary to popular belief, Betsy Ross probably did not sew the first United States flag. Her grandson, William J. Canby, first made the claim in 1870 that she had, at George Washington's request. But there is no recorded reference to a national flag until a year after Ross, a Philadelphia seamstress and flagmaker, supposedly made it. Though we may never know who actually designed the first flag, the most likely candidate is Francis Hopkinson, a Pennsylvania judge, artist, poet, and composer who also designed emblems for various states and nations. The Continental Congress officially adopted the Stars and Stripes on June 14, 1777.

(*Dict. of Amer. Hist.,* vol. 3, 34; *Encyc. Americana,* 352)

**Q 3. How did the bald eagle become a national symbol?**

A Long known as a symbol of strength and military might in other countries and cultures, the eagle was adopted as an American symbol during the Revolution. Apparently the first use was on copper pennies minted in 1776, but the American bald eagle gained official status in 1782, when Congress proclaimed it the national emblem and included it on the Great Seal of the United States.

(*Dict. of Amer. Hist.*, vol. 2, 384; *PAZ*, 379)

(*See 2 Who designed the flag and when was it officially adopted?*)

**Q** **4. Where was the nation's first capital?**

**A** New York City, already the capital under the Articles of Confederation, also served briefly as the nation's first capital after the Constitution was ratified. The first Congress met in New York City on March 4, 1789, and George Washington was inaugurated there as the first president on April 30th. But in 1790 Congress approved the building of a new capital city, and that same year temporarily moved the seat of government to Philadelphia, pending construction of Washington, D.C.

(*Encyc. of Amer. History,* 147)

**Q** **5. When did Washington, D.C., become the capital?**

**A** When construction of Washington, D.C., began in 1791, the projected completion date was 1800. But carving a new capital city out of the wilderness proved a bigger task than expected, with financial problems and infighting creating ever longer construction delays. Congress transferred the capital from Philadelphia to Washington as originally scheduled, even though construction had barely begun. President John Adams and about 130 government officials arrived in October 1800 to find Washington's broad avenues ankle-deep in mud, just one wing of the Capitol Building finished, the presidential mansion nearing completion, and the government office building still under construction. Congress convened its first session in Washington on November 17, 1800, but construction continued for another ten years before the city finally took shape.

(*CAZ*, 56; *RD Encyc. of Amer. Hist.*, 1205–6, 1237)

**Q** **6. Why is the District of Columbia not a state?**

**A** The Framers of the Constitution originally envisioned the District as separate from any state, believing it would provide a symbolic center for the new federal government and allow it to function free of outside intimidation. The Constitution even empowered Congress to govern the District. However, from 1800 to 1874, and more recently since 1973, the District of Columbia has been allowed limited self-rule. In recent years moves for statehood, and full representation in Congress, have encountered substantial opposition, including arguments that the District was never intended to have the same authority as the states. In 1990 District voters sent two nonvoting shadow senators and one nonvoting shadow representative to Congress to lobby for statehood.

(*CAZ*, 109–10)

(*See 272 What is a shadow senator or representative?; 382 What do delegates to the House do?*)

## Q 7. How can a state join the Union?

A First, the legislature of a territory, republic, or other entity must petition Congress for admission. Congress must then authorize the legislature to draft a constitution. If the constitution is acceptable, Congress then passes legislation approving statehood. The president's signature on the act completes the new state's admission to the Union. Apart from the original thirteen states, thirty-seven new states have been admitted, and of them thirty were U.S. territories before statehood. Admitted in 1959, Hawaii was the last state to join the Union.

(*SOW*, 19–20)

(*See 251 How many seats did each state have on entering the Union?*)

## Q 8. What is federalism?

A The organizing principle of the United States government, federalism provides for a strong central government while also preserving the states as political entities. During the nineteenth century, the Supreme Court evolved a doctrine called "dual federalism," which held that the federal government and states were each supreme within their own well-defined spheres. The effect was to prevent expansion of federal powers into the state sphere. But the Court shifted direction in 1937, when it began ruling in favor of New Deal legislation that infringed on state powers. Since then, the Court has allowed vast expansion of federal powers at the states' expense.

(*SCAZ*, 163)

(*See 497 What did the Court rule in* Cooley v. Board of Wardens of Port of Philadelphia?)

**9. What do political parties do?**

A  Political parties provide an important link between citizens and government leaders. The parties' most important function is nominating, and then working for the election of, candidates at the federal, state, and local levels. They also help define issues, propose solutions consistent with the party's basic beliefs, and seek to implement those solutions after their candidates have been elected. At the federal level, for example, the majority party in Congress may try to enact certain laws, or the president may propose a bill favored by his party. Though elected officials still appoint party members to some government posts, the number of such patronage jobs has been sharply reduced in this century.

(*PAZ*, 339)

(*See 109 What is patronage?*)


Q  **10. When has the same party controlled the White House and both houses of Congress?**

A  Surprisingly, this has been the case in all but 34 of the 103 Congresses through 1994. In the first fifty years under the Constitution, the president's party dominated both houses in all but two Congresses—1793–1795, during Washington's second term, and 1827–1829, during the second half of John Quincy Adams's term. The president's party has been out of power in one or both houses most often in the second halves of both the nineteenth and twentieth centuries—13 Congresses in each half-century, from 1849–1853, 1855–1857, 1859–1861, 1865–1867, 1875–1881, 1883–1889, 1891–1893, 1895–1897, 1955–1961, 1969–1977, and 1981–1993. Democrats controlled the presidency and both houses from 1993 to 1995. But midterm elections during Bill Clinton's presidency gave Republicans the majority in both houses for the 1995 to 1997 term.

(*CAZ*, 468–70)


Q  **11. How many people work for the federal government?**

A  The federal government employs 3.03 million civilian workers, including postal workers. Federal employment peaked at 3.8 million during World War II, after mushrooming from just a million or so in the late 1930s. As of mid-1993, the biggest single employer of civilian workers was the Defense Department, with just over 933,000. The Veterans Affairs Department ranked second with about 266,000 civilian employees.

(*Fed. Civ. Workforce Stats.*, 14–17; *SOW*, 270–2)

## HISTORIC DOCUMENTS

**Q** **12. Who wrote the Declaration of Independence?**

**A** On June 10, 1776, the Second Continental Congress appointed a committee of five delegates—including Thomas Jefferson, John Adams, and Benjamin Franklin—to write the Declaration. They in turn named the thirty-three-year-old Jefferson to produce the rough draft. Though the committee members (including Jefferson himself) made changes to the draft, the document was largely Jefferson's own work, and he is considered its author. Adopted by the Continental Congress on July 4, 1776, the Declaration ranks among the most important U.S. state documents.

(*PAZ*, 251; *RD Encyc. of Amer. Hist.*, 330–1)

**Q** **13. Who were the signers of the Declaration of Independence?**

**A** Fifty-six delegates to the Second Continental Congress signed the declaration. They were, with the states they represented:

| Delegate | State | Delegate | State |
|---|---|---|---|
| John Adams | MA | Lyman Hall | GA |
| Samuel Adams | MA | John Hancock | MA |
| Josiah Bartlett | NH | Benjamin Harrison | VA |
| Carter Braxton | VA | John Hart | NJ |
| Charles Carroll of Carrollton | MD | Joseph Hewes | NC |
| Samuel Chase | MD | Thomas Heyward Jr. | SC |
| Abraham Clark | NJ | William Hooper | NC |
| George Clymer | PA | Stephen Hopkins | RI |
| William Ellery | RI | Francis Hopkinson | NJ |
| William Floyd | NY | Samuel Huntington | CT |
| Benjamin Franklin | PA | Thomas Jefferson | VA |
| Elbridge Gerry | MA | Francis Lightfoot Lee | VA |
| Button Gwinnett | GA | Richard Henry Lee | VA |

| Delegate | State | Delegate | State |
|---|---|---|---|
| Francis Lewis | NY | Benjamin Rush | PA |
| Philip Livingston | NY | Edward Rutledge | SC |
| Thomas Lynch Jr. | SC | Roger Sherman | CT |
| Thomas McKean | DE | James Smith | PA |
| Arthur Middleton | SC | Richard Stockton | NJ |
| Lewis Morris | NY | Thomas Stone | MD |
| Robert Morris | PA | George Taylor | PA |
| John Morton | PA | Matthew Thornton | NH |
| Thomas Nelson Jr. | VA | George Walton | GA |
| William Paca | MD | William Whipple | NH |
| Robert Treat Paine | MA | William Williams | CT |
| John Penn | NC | James Wilson | PA |
| George Read | DE | John Witherspoon | NJ |
| Caesar Rodney | DE | Oliver Wolcott | CT |
| George Ross | PA | George Wythe | VA |

(*New Columbia Encyc.*, 733; *Webster's Biog. Dict.*, 1671)

**Q 14. What were the Articles of Confederation?**

**A** Approved by the Continental Congress on November 15, 1777, and ratified by the states on March 1, 1781, the Articles of Confederation created the first U.S. government by establishing a loose confederation of the original thirteen states. Congress formed the sole branch of the national government, and each state delegation to Congress, comprising from two to seven appointed delegates, had only one vote. Congress could make treaties, raise an army and navy, declare war, borrow money, and assess states for needed funds, but real power resided with the states themselves. This arrangement reflected American leaders' distrust of any central government with powers like those of the British monarchy. By 1786, however, Americans had recognized the need for a stronger central government, especially one with powers to tax and to force the states to comply with its laws. The Constitutional Convention was called the following year (see next question).

(*RD Encyc. of Amer. Hist.*, 61–2; *SOW*, 6–7; *WHAD*, 60)

**15. What was the Constitutional Convention?**

A Congress called the convention to deal with serious political and economic problems facing the nation. Originally the convention was held to amend the Articles of Confederation, which had been in effect just six years. But after the meeting convened at Philadelphia's Independence Hall on May 25, 1787, convention president George Washington and the other delegates decided the weak government set up by the Articles of Confederation had to be replaced. They immediately set about writing a new constitution, one that would establish a strong central government. After months of sometimes heated debate, delegates completed the proposed Constitution, signed it on September 17, 1787, and formally ended the convention that same day. Washington, James Madison, and others played an important role in the subsequent public debate over ratification of the Constitution.

(*Encyc. Britannica,* vol. 3, 575–6; *SOW,* 7–12)

Q **16. What was the "Great Compromise" made by the Framers of the Constitution?**

A Early in 1787, the Constitutional Convention considered Edmund Randolph's "Virginia Plan" for a two-chambered legislature. The small states balked, though, because both the House and Senate would have had proportional representation based on each state's population. Small states feared their larger neighbors, having more votes, would ignore their interests, and the convention suddenly deadlocked. A month of bitter debate followed until Connecticut delegates Roger Sherman and Oliver Ellsworth finally won approval for their "Great Compromise": House membership would be proportional based on each state's population, but the Senate would have equal representation for each state. House members would be elected by popular vote; senators, by the state legislatures. (The Seventeenth Amendment to the Constitution, ratified April 8, 1913, provided for the popular election of senators.)

(*CAZ,* 342; *RD Encyc. of Amer. Hist,* 286–7)

(See 349 When were senators first elected by popular vote?)

## Q 17. What does Article I of the Constitution say, in brief?

A Consisting of ten sections, Article I says the following:

Section 1: Grants Congress all legislative powers; specifies Congress will be composed of two chambers, the House and Senate.

Section 2: Sets qualifications and the two-year term for directly elected House members; provides a formula for apportionment; mentions the Speaker; grants the House sole power of impeachment.

Section 3: Describes qualifications and the six-year term for senators; grants each state two senators, to be selected by the state legislatures; names the vice president as president of the Senate and gives him a tie-breaking vote; mentions the president pro tempore; grants the Senate the sole right to try impeachment cases; discusses impeachment.

Section 4: Gives Congress the power to regulate procedures in the states for electing representatives and senators; requires that Congress meet at least once a year.

Section 5: Requires each house to keep a journal of its proceedings; allows each to establish its own rules for conducting legislative business but requires approval from both for an adjournment longer than three days.

Section 6: Discusses congressional immunity and pay; bars members of Congress from simultaneously holding office in any other branch of government.

Section 7: Grants the House the right to originate revenue bills; requires the president's approval of all measures passed by Congress for them to become law; describes the president's veto power, the pocket veto, a veto override, and the requirement that the president sign or veto a bill within ten days (otherwise it automatically becomes law).

Section 8: Empowers Congress to raise and spend money for the common defense and welfare of the nation; grants Congress the following specific powers: (1) to borrow money, regulate commerce, and establish uniform laws of naturalization and bankruptcy; (2) to coin money, set uniform weights and measures, establish the post office, establish patents and copyrights, create lower courts, and punish piracy; (3) to declare war, raise and support armies and a navy, and provide for a militia; (4) to establish and control a district [the District of Columbia] that will serve as the seat of government and to control all forts, arsenals, and other structures built by the federal government; and (5) to "make all Laws which shall be necessary and proper for carrying into Execution the foregoing Powers . . ." [the so-called elastic clause].

Section 9: Bars Congress from ending the slave trade before 1808; forbids suspension of the writ of habeas corpus (except during rebellion or invasion); prohibits passage of a bill of attainder, passage of an ex post facto law, and taxation of goods exported from a state; bars the granting of titles of nobility; gives Congress the sole power to withdraw money from the treasury (by appropriation).

Section 10: Limits the powers of states, barring such specific actions as making war, entering into treaties or alliances with other states or foreign powers, coining money, passing any law impairing obligation of contracts, or imposing duties on imports and exports.

(*SCAZ*, 481–3)

(*See also the full text of the Constitution, including the list of signers, in the appendix.*)

**Q 18. What does Article II of the Constitution say, in brief?**

**A** Consisting of four sections, Article II says the following:

Section 1: Describes the executive branch and office of the president, the Electoral College, and the election of the president; gives the House the right to select the president if no candidate wins a majority of electoral votes; gives the Senate the right to select the vice president; sets qualifications for the president; grants Congress the power to establish the line of succession for the president (after the vice president); specifies the president's oath of office.

Section 2: Names the president as commander-in-chief of the armed forces; grants the president the power to pardon; gives the president treaty-making powers and the power of appointing ambassadors, Supreme Court justices, and other officials (all with Senate approval).

Section 3: Requires the president to report periodically on the state of the Union; gives the president the power to call extraordinary sessions of Congress.

Section 4: Describes offenses warranting impeachment and removal from office.

(*SCAZ*, 483–5)

(*See also the full text of the Constitution, including the list of signers, in the appendix.*)

**Q** **19. What does Article III of the Constitution say, in brief?**

**A** Consisting of three sections, Article III says the following: Section 1: Establishes the federal court system, including the Supreme Court, and sets the standard of behavior for judges. Section 2: Defines the jurisdiction of federal courts; establishes trial by jury (except for impeachment). Section 3: Discusses treason and its punishment.

*(SCAZ, 485)*

*(See also the full text of the Constitution, including the list of signers, in the appendix.)*

**Q** **20. What does Article IV of the Constitution say, in brief?**

**A** Consisting of four sections, Article IV says the following:

Section 1: Requires that each state give full faith and credit to the public acts, records, and judicial proceedings of other states.

Section 2: Grants the privileges and immunities of all citizens to the citizens of each state; provides for extradition of criminals.

Section 3: Provides for admission of new states and limits the ability of states to divide or join with other states. Section 4: Requires the federal government to protect states against invasion and to provide aid against rebellions within their borders.

*(SCAZ, 485)*

*(See also the full text of the Constitution, including the list of signers, in the appendix.)*

**Q** **21. What does Article V of the Constitution say, in brief?**

**A** Article V provides for amending the Constitution either by congressional act or by constitutional convention.

*(SCAZ, 486)*

*(See also the full text of the Constitution, including the list of signers, in the appendix.)*

**Q** **22. What does Article VI of the Constitution say, in brief?**

**A** Article VI guarantees that the Constitution, federal laws, and treaties are binding upon the states as the supreme law of the land; requires that public officials (federal and state) take an oath to uphold the Constitution.

*(SCAZ, 486)*

*(See also the full text of the Constitution, including the list of signers, in the appendix.)*

**Q 23. What does Article VII of the Constitution say, in brief?**

**A** Article VII provides for ratification of the Constitution (by nine states).

*(SCAZ, 486)*

*(See also the full text of the Constitution, including the list of signers, in the appendix.)*

**Q 24. What were the first nine states to ratify the Constitution?**

**A** They were: Delaware (December 7, 1787), Pennsylvania (December 12, 1787), New Jersey (December 18, 1787), Georgia (January 2, 1788), Connecticut (January 9, 1788), Massachusetts (February 6, 1788), Maryland (April 28, 1788), South Carolina (May 23, 1788), and New Hampshire (June 21, 1788).

*(SCAZ, 486)*

*(See also the full text of the Constitution, including the list of signers, in the appendix.)*

**Q 25. Where can you see the original Constitution?**

**A** The Constitution, the Declaration of Independence, and the Bill of Rights are on display at the National Archives in Washington, D.C. Original copies of each document are encased in a movable display platform for public viewing. After closing time each day, the platform is lowered twenty feet into a special vault designed to withstand a nuclear blast.

*(SOW, 5)*

**Q 26. How can the Constitution be amended?**

**A** An amendment must first be formally proposed, either by two-thirds majority votes in both the House and Senate or by approval of a constitutional convention. The amendment must then be ratified by three-fourths (now thirty-eight) of the states. Congress can set a deadline for ratification (usually seven years) and determine whether ratification will be by the state legislatures or by state conventions. Only the Prohibition Amendment was ratified by state conventions. All twenty-seven amendments have originated with Congress.

(*CAZ,* 88–90)

(*See 29 What do the amendments to the Constitution say, in brief?*)

**Q** **27. How can a constitutional convention be convened?**

**A** The Constitution specifies that Congress must convene a constitutional convention if requested by two-thirds—now thirty-four—of the state legislatures. No convention has ever been called, no procedures exist for running one, and there is no current limit on what could be debated. Because the format is unstructured, many fear a convention might get carried away and amend more of the Constitution than originally intended. Nevertheless, nearly successful drives for calling a constitutional convention have been mounted. In the early 1900s, the Senate finally approved a proposed amendment for direct election of senators when a convention on that issue seemed likely. More recently, the campaign for a convention on a balanced budget amendment fell just two states short of the required thirty-four.

(*CAZ,* 88–90)

(*See 49 Has the United States ever had a budget surplus?*)

**Q** **28. What is the Bill of Rights?**

**A** The first ten amendments to the Constitution make up what is called the Bill of Rights. Originally proposed by supporters of the Constitution to counter fears that the new federal government might threaten personal liberty, the original Bill of Rights was approved by Congress in 1789 and contained twelve amendments. The states ratified the ten now considered the Bill of Rights by 1791. Another of the original twelve amendments, the one barring members of Congress from voting themselves midterm pay raises, was belatedly ratified two centuries later in 1992. The other unratified amendment would have added members to the House as the U.S. population grew, instead of reapportioning seats.

(*SCAZ,* 37–8)

(*See 29 What do the amendments to the Constitution say, in brief?*)

**Q** **29. What do the amendments to the Constitution say, in brief?**

**A** The first ten amendments listed below are called the Bill of Rights, ratified on December 15, 1791. Seventeen other amendments have been ratified since.

Amendment I: Guarantees freedoms of religion, speech, and the press, as well as the right to peaceful assembly and to petition the government.

Amendment II: Guarantees the right to bear arms.

Amendment III: Restricts quartering of soldiers in private homes.

Amendment IV: Forbids unreasonable searches and seizures of private property; warrants may not be issued without probable cause.

Amendment V: Protects the accused from being tried more than once for the same crime, from being forced to testify against themselves, or from being deprived of life, liberty, or property without due process of the law.

Amendment VI: Grants accused criminals the right to a speedy trial by jury, as well as other rights, including the right to counsel.

Amendment VII: Sets forth rights in civil suits.

Amendment VIII: Prohibits excessive bail and "cruel and unusual punishment."

Amendment IX: Grants the people rights not specifically enumerated in the Constitution.

Amendment X: Grants the states or the people powers not delegated to the federal government by the Constitution.

Amendment XI: Restricts federal court jurisdiction; ratified February 7, 1795.

Amendment XII: Changes electoral college procedures, mandating separate votes for the president and vice president; ratified June 15, 1804.

Amendment XIII: Abolishes slavery; ratified December 6, 1865.

Amendment XIV: Guarantees due process of law and equal protection of the laws for all citizens, and establishes the new basis for apportioning representatives; ratified July 9, 1868.

Amendment XV: Prohibits denial of the right to vote based on race, color, or previously having been a slave; ratified February 3, 1870.

Amendment XVI: Establishes the income tax; ratified February 3, 1913.

Amendment XVII: Sets up direct election of senators; ratified April 8, 1913.

Amendment XVIII: Establishes Prohibition; ratified January 16, 1919.

Amendment XIX: Guarantees women the right to vote; ratified August 18, 1920.

Amendment XX (Lame Duck Amendment): Fixes the start of terms for the president, vice president, senators, and representatives in January (instead of March) and defines the presidential line of succession; ratified January 23, 1933.

Amendment XXI: Repeals Prohibition; ratified December 5, 1933.

Amendment XXII: Sets the presidential term limit; ratified February 27, 1951.

Amendment XXIII: Gives residents of the District of Columbia the right to vote; ratified March 29, 1961.

Amendment XXIV: Abolishes poll taxes; ratified January 23, 1964.

Amendment XXV: Provides for succession in the event that the president is incapacitated, and when the vice presidency is vacant; ratified February 10, 1967.

Amendment XXVI: Lowers the voting age to eighteen years of age; ratified July 1, 1971.

Amendment XXVII: Bars Congress from voting itself a midterm pay raise; ratified May 7, 1992.

(*CAZ*, 504–9; *WHAD*, 266)


Q **30. Which amendment took the longest to ratify?**

A When Congress originally approved the Bill of Rights in 1789, it sent twelve amendments to the states for ratification, but only ten were finally adopted in 1791. One of the other two, barring members of Congress from voting themselves midterm pay raises, was nearly forgotten after being ratified by just six states. But a new ratification effort, begun in the 1980s, finally won approval of the amendment by the required thirty-eighth state in 1992. At just over two centuries, the amount of time needed to ratify the Twenty-seventh Amendment is the longest ever, far ahead of the previous record of three years, eleven months needed for ratification of the Twenty-second Amendment. Proposed amendments now usually include a time limit on the ratification process.

(*CAZ*, 10; *PAZ*, 415)

(*See 125 How long do the president and vice president serve?*)

**Q** **31. What is separation of powers?**

**A** Separation of powers is a fundamental principle underlying our system of government. The Constitution seeks to prevent abuses of power by separating government functions into independent branches—legislative, executive, and judicial. The separation is not complete, however. Because of the system of "checks and balances" (see next question), there are enough overlapping powers to prevent any one branch from acting arbitrarily. Furthermore, dividing up authority is only part of the original plan. Also important is the strict limit on membership to just one branch at a time (the vice president excepted). Senators can become cabinet members and judges but they must resign their seats in Congress. That keeps any one individual from accumulating excessive power and also prevents the president from using powerful jobs and extra salaries as incentives to win key votes from members of Congress. While the fragmentation of power has prevented arbitrary government, it is sometimes inefficient (as when one party controls Congress and another the White House). It also diffuses responsibility, allowing officials to evade criticism for failed policies.

(*PAZ*, 382; *SCAZ*, 370–6; *CAZ*, 353–5; *Encyc. Britannica*, vol. 9, 657)

(*See 106 What is executive privilege?; 163 What experience have presidents had before being elected?; 171 Who is the only president to serve on the Supreme Court after leaving the White House?; 172 Which president served in the Senate after leaving the White House?; 173 Which president served in the House after leaving office?; 196 What does the vice president do?; 219 Which vice presidents have also been senators?; 221 Which vice president served longest in Congress?*)

**Q** **32. What are checks and balances?**

**A** The Constitution does not rely solely on the separation of powers to prevent abuses by government. As a further safeguard, it also institutes "checks and balances," by which the powers of one branch overlap with one or both of the others. For example, the president recommends legislation to Congress, can veto bills passed by Congress, and implements the laws passed by Congress. Also, the vice president serves as president of the Senate, though this is largely a ceremonial post. Congress, in turn, passes laws to create executive agencies and programs, allocates funding, can override presidential vetoes, and can impeach the president. Congress also must confirm appointments to posts in the executive branch, and though the president commands the armed forces, only Congress can declare war.

The president influences the judicial branch by appointing judges, but Congress also becomes involved by confirming the nominations. Congress was empowered to create the district and appeals courts and can reorganize the federal court system as needed. But the judicial branch holds a powerful tool of its own. The courts can declare unconstitutional both laws passed by Congress and actions of the executive branch.

(*CAZ*, 353–5; *Encyc. Britannica*, vol. 3, 146; *PAZ*, 382, *SCAZ*, 370–6)

*(See 97 How many bills have presidents vetoed?; 100 How many vetoes have been overridden?; 105 What are executive orders, and how many have various presidents signed?; 108 How are judges and ambassadors chosen?; 145 Which president was impeached?; 151 Who was the first president to ask Congress to declare war?; 245 Who failed to be confirmed by the Senate for a cabinet post?; 266 What is impeachment?; 269 Who has been impeached by Congress?; 463 How many acts of Congress have been declared unconstitutional?; 547 Who has failed to be confirmed by the Senate?)*

**Q 33. Who can appoint and remove officials in the executive branch?**

**A** The president appoints and removes executive branch officials, but his power is subject to limitations. For example, the Senate confirms the president's executive branch appointments. Officers of the armed forces, every one of whom receives a presidential appointment, also are subject to Senate confirmation. The president's sole power to remove executive branch officials, challenged in the past, was confirmed in a 1926 Supreme Court decision. However, the Court later ruled the president could not, on his own, remove officials from independent regulatory commissions, which were deemed quasi-judicial bodies.

(*SCAZ*, 17)

**Q 34. What are implied powers?**

**A** After enumerating the specific powers of Congress in Article I, Section 8, the Framers of the Constitution added a final clause giving Congress the power to pass all laws "necessary and proper for carrying into Execution the foregoing Powers. . . ." Called the "elastic clause," it became the basis for the Supreme Court doctrine of "implied powers," or powers that the Constitution does not specifically mention but that the government needs to carry out its duties. Chief Justice John Marshall articulated the doctrine of implied powers in the Court's 1819 ruling in *McCulloch v. Maryland*. The case set a key precedent that eventually led to the far-reaching expansion of federal government powers.

(*CAZ*, 382; *RD Encyc. of Amer. Hist.*, 542; *SCAZ*, 246–7)

(*See 514 What did the Court rule in* McCulloch v. Maryland?)

**Q 35. What is the oversight power?**

**A** Congress retains "oversight power" over programs and agencies it creates, though it delegates to the executive branch the job of actually running them. Congress exercises oversight power by conducting hearings and investigations, by controlling the budget, and by working directly with agencies. Congress also uses informal legislative vetoes to overrule executive actions.

(*CAZ*, 281)

(*See 278 What is a legislative veto?*)

**Q 36. What is the supremacy clause?**

**A** The supremacy clause is Article VI, Section 2 of the Constitution, which establishes the Constitution, the laws of the United States, and all treaties as "the supreme Law of the Land." The Framers of the Constitution wrote the clause to create a stronger national government than had been possible under the Articles of Confederation. Since the late 1930s, the clause has provided a basis for expansion of federal government control over commerce and over other economic affairs formerly regulated by the states.

(*SCAZ*, 406–7)

(*See 14 What were the Articles of Confederation?*)

**Q 37. What is the Lame Duck Amendment?**

**A** Until ratification of the Twentieth ("Lame Duck") Amendment in 1933, presidents and members of Congress defeated in a November election served several more months before their terms ended. But these lame duck officials could accomplish little during that time. The Twentieth Amendment shortened the lame duck interval by moving the day of the president's inauguration from March 4 to January 20, and, similarly, by changing the start of new sessions of Congress from March 4 to January 3.

(*CAZ*, 392; *PAZ*, 273)

(*See 338 When was the last lame duck session of Congress?*)

**Q** **38. Where did the term** *lame duck* **originate?**

**A** Americans borrowed this English term for a bankrupt businessman, applying it instead to politically "bankrupt" politicians from the 1830s onward. Lame ducks are presidents, members of Congress, and other elected officials who have been defeated in November elections but who still have some months left to serve before leaving office. Even presidents near the end of their second term become lame ducks because they cannot be reelected for a third term. Lame ducks usually can accomplish little because they will soon be out of office and so have lost their political clout.

(*PAZ*, 273)

**Q** **39. Where is the right of privacy mentioned in the Constitution?**

**A** The Constitution nowhere mentions privacy specifically, but Supreme Court rulings have established it as a Constitutional right. The Court first limited the government's power to interfere with personal liberty in the 1920s, when it overturned a Nebraska state law banning the teaching of foreign languages in public schools. The law, the Court said, deprived children, parents, and even teachers of a measure of personal liberty. The notion of an individual's right to make decisions affecting his or her private life eventually expanded to include such areas as child rearing, marriage, contraception, abortion, and suicide (examined in the right-to-die cases). The 1973 *Roe v. Wade* decision explicit recognized the right to privacy. However, the Court refused to decide whether the right was based on the Fourteenth Amendment (personal liberty) or on the Ninth Amendment (unenumerated individual rights).

(*SCAZ*, 313–15)

(*See 523 What did the Court rule in* Roe v. Wade?*)

**Q** **40. What is a treaty?**

**A** A treaty is a formal written agreement between nations or other sovereign entities. Treaties usually are major agreements assigning rights and duties to the nations involved and may deal with international concerns such as regulating commerce, providing for mutual defense, and adjusting national boundaries. Documents called protocols, conventions, executive agreements, and the like are less formal international agreements than treaties.

(*Encyc. Britannica,* vol. 11, 907; *New Columbia Encyc.,* 2779)

(*See 104 What are executive agreements?*)

## Q 41. Who must agree to treaties between the United States and other countries?

A The president has the power to negotiate treaty terms with foreign powers, but the Senate must approve the final agreement by a two-thirds majority. The Senate cannot prevent the president from entering into negotiations with any foreign power, and by tradition the president is not required to consult the Senate before negotiating terms. But because the Senate can amend the treaty, forcing renegotiation of the terms, Senate opposition must be considered. Once the Senate has approved the treaty, the president must ratify the final version.

(*CAZ,* 393; *PAZ,* 97, 431–2)

(*See 31 What is separation of powers?*)

## Q 42. Has the Senate ever rejected a treaty?

A The Senate has rejected twenty treaties, though presidents have withdrawn others before an unfavorable vote. The first treaty rejection came on March 9, 1825, when the Senate voted unanimously against a treaty with Colombia for suppression of the African slave trade. The most important rejection was the Senate's refusal, in 1920, to approve the Treaty of Versailles, which ended World War I and established the League of Nations. The Senate objected to collective security requirements and other aspects of U.S. membership in the League of Nations. Since 1920, presidents have increasingly relied on executive agreements, which do not require Senate approval.

(*CAZ,* 395; *The Senate,* 730)

(*See 104 What are executive agreements?*)

## Q 43. Where can you find copies of treaties?

A Treaties are reprinted in *United States Treaties and Other International Agreements* (UST) and in *Treaties and International Acts Series* (TIAS). Important treaties that directly involve federal laws also may be found in the *United States Code.* All three are available through the Government Printing Office.

(*Legis. Drafter's DR,* 297)

## FINANCES

**Q 44. Where does the government get the money it needs to operate?**

**A** The federal government's two main sources of spending money are taxes and borrowing. According to estimates for fiscal 1995, about 39 percent of all revenue needed to keep the government running will come from personal income taxes. Social Security taxes will generate another 32 percent, corporate taxes 9 percent, excise taxes (federal taxes on gasoline and telephone service, for example) about 5 percent, and other taxes and receipts (estate and gift taxes and customs duties, for example) about 4 percent. The government will borrow 11 percent more to make up the difference between revenue and what it will spend. The actual dollar amounts for fiscal 1993 are as follows:

|  | FISCAL 1993 |
| --- | --- |
| *Source of income* | *(In billions of dollars)* |
| Personal income tax | $509.7 |
| Social Security tax | 428.3 |
| Corporate tax | 117.5 |
| Excise tax | 48.1 |
| Estate & gift taxes | 12.6 |
| Customs duties | 18.8 |
| Miscellaneous receipts | 18.6 |
| Total | $1,153.6 |

(*Budget of the U.S. Govt., Analyt. Perspectives,* 236; *CAZ,* 313–16)

(*See 52 How was federal money allocated in a recent budget?*)

**Q 45. When was the income tax first enacted?**

**A** Congress passed the first income tax in August 1861 to help pay Civil War costs, and the law remained in effect until 1872. Then a depression in 1893 forced Congress to levy a new income tax in 1894 to make up for lost revenue. The tax was limited, affecting only the wealthiest 2 percent of the population, but the Supreme Court later ruled against imposing such taxes. The ruling prompted passage of the Sixteenth Amendment, ratified in 1913, which granted Congress the right to tax income. Congress enacted the income tax later in 1913.

(*Encyc. of Amer. Facts & Dates*, 273; *SCAZ*, 199–200)

(*See 29 What do the amendments to the Constitution say, in brief?*)

### Q 46. When did the federal government get its first budget?

A The government has operated under a budget since 1921. Congress previously handled appropriations in a haphazard way, but by the close of World War I, the government had grown far too complex. In 1921 Congress passed the Budget and Accounting Act, setting up the Bureau of the Budget to oversee the budget-making process and the General Accounting Office to improve congressional oversight of spending. The Bureau of the Budget was reorganized as the Office of Management and Budget in 1970.

(*PAZ*, 37–8)

(*See 60 What does the General Accounting Office do?*)

### Q 47. How is the budget prepared?

A The president proposes a budget for the coming fiscal year, which begins October 1, and submits it to Congress on the first Monday in February. By April 15 the House and Senate are supposed to agree on a budget resolution, setting congressional guidelines for spending and taxes. Congress then begins work on specific appropriations while keeping within guidelines set by the budget resolution. Each year, thirteen major appropriations bills—ranging from agriculture to veterans' affairs— must be passed to keep the government running. Ideally, House and Senate conferees will resolve differences between versions of these bills during the summer and early fall, and all taxing and spending legislation will be enacted by October 1.

(*CAZ*, 39–42; *SOW*, 145)

(*See 48 Why does the government's fiscal year begin in October?; 284 What are continuing resolutions? How often are they used?; 281 What is the difference between an authorization bill and an appropriations bill?*)

**Q 48. Why does the government's fiscal year begin in October?**

**A** Congress moved the start of the government's fiscal year from July to October because it needed more time to draft, debate, and pass the various appropriations bills required to fund the annual budget. The change, enacted in 1974, went into effect for fiscal 1977, which began October 1, 1976, and ended on September 30, 1977. Among other budget reforms passed in 1974, Congress set itself a timetable for enacting the annual appropriations.

(*CAZ,* 146; *PAZ,* 36)

(*See 47 How is the budget prepared?*)


**Q 49. Has the United States ever had a budget surplus?**

**A** The federal government has halted the annual tide of red ink only eight times since 1931, the last time being 1969, when the Nixon administration took in $3.2 billion more than it paid out. After a huge runup in the public debt to pay for World War II, the government enjoyed an all-too-brief flurry of budget surpluses between 1947 and 1949, the first such surpluses since 1930. The government eked out surpluses again in 1951, 1956–1957, 1960, and 1969, but never managed to dent the ever-increasing public debt. For ten years up to 1930, there were consecutive budget surpluses. But between 1900 and 1920, the government posted deficits most years due to World War I and other factors.

(*Budget Baselines,* 278–9; *World Almanac 1993,* 127–8)


**Q 50. Where can you find current and historical statistics on the budget? The deficit and the debt?**

**A** *Vital Statistics on American Politics,* by Harold W. Stanley and Richard G. Niemi, gives past (post-1940), present, and estimated future budget figures, as well as those for the deficit and debt. For budget data prior to 1940 as well as deficit and debt statistics, consult *Budget Baselines, Historical Data and Alternatives for the Future* or *Historical Tables, Budget of the United States Government.* Both are published by the Government Printing Office.

(*Budget Baselines,* 278–9, 346–7; *VSAP,* 421, 426)

### Q 51. What is the difference between the deficit and the debt?

A When the federal government spends more than it takes in during any given year, the shortfall is called the budget deficit. To make up for this red ink, the government simply borrows money, which then adds to the national debt. Because the government has posted budget deficits in all but eight years since 1931, the debt has grown to alarming proportions—it passed $3 trillion in fiscal 1990. Interest on the national debt is over $200 billion a year, making it the third largest budget item after defense and Social Security. The current estimate for the 1994–1995 deficit is about $176.1 billion.

(*Budget of the U.S. Govt., Analyt. Perspectives*, 13; *SOW*, 141–2)

### Q 52. How was federal money allocated in a recent budget?

A For fiscal 1993, the actual federal spending was as follows:

| SPENDING SOURCE | EXPENDITURE (IN BILLIONS) |
| --- | --- |
| *Executive department* | |
| Health and Human Services | $ 586.7 |
| Treasury | 300.5 |
| Defense (military) | 267.4 |
| Agriculture | 67.9 |
| Labor | 46.9 |
| Transportation | 40.0 |
| Veterans Affairs | 36.0 |
| Education | 31.5 |
| Housing and Urban Development | 26.5 |
| Energy | 17.7 |
| Justice | 10.5 |
| Interior | 6.9 |
| State | 5.3 |
| Commerce | 3.2 |
| Total | $1,447.0 |
| | |
| *Major agency* | |
| Office of Personnel Management | $ 39.3 |

| | |
|---|---|
| Corps of Engineers, military retirement & other defense | 29.9 |
| Funds appropriated to the president | 24.8 |
| NASA | 14.3 |
| Environmental Protection Agency | 6.7 |
| Judicial branch | 2.6 |
| Legislative branch | 2.6 |
| Small Business Administration | 1.2 |
| General Services Administration | 0.6 |
| Executive Office of the President | 0.2 |
| Total | $122.2 |
| | |
| *Other agencies* | 24.1 |
| | |
| *Undistributed offsetting receipts* | |
| (fees and other miscellaneous charges collected | |
| by the government) | ($119.7) |
| Total | $1,473.6 |

(*Budget of the U.S. Govt., Analyt. Perspectives*, 252)

## Q 53. What is an entitlement?

A Entitlements are federal programs like unemployment compensation, Social Security, Medicare, and farm price supports. These programs guarantee certain benefits by law and must be fully funded each year by Congress, unless it passes legislation mandating cutbacks. Congress has been reluctant to make cuts because so many individuals benefit from the programs. As a result, entitlements have absorbed an increasing budget share in recent years. In an effort to control entitlement growth, Congress in 1990 instituted the pay-as-you-go policy, requiring revenue increases for new entitlement programs, and for changes to existing programs that would raise costs.

(*CAZ*, 121)

## Q 54. What part of the total budget goes to entitlements?

A The federal government estimated that about 48 percent of the total federal outlay for fiscal 1995 would go to entitlements. That amounted to $763.7 billion. Another 15 percent went to states and localities in the form of direct grants. Budget outlays for entitlements for 1993 are as follows:

| Entitlement | 1993 Expenditure (in billions) |
|---|---|
| Social Security | 302.0 |
| Medicare | 127.8 |
| "Means tested" benefits (food stamps, family support, Supplemental Security Income, child nutrition, veterans pensions, etc.) | 80.8 |
| Medicaid | 75.8 |
| Federal retirement benefits | 59.8 |
| Other | 50.7 |
| Unemployment benefits | 35.5 |
| Deposit insurance | (28.0) |
| Undistributed offsetting receipts[1] | (37.4) |
| Total | 667.0 |

[1]. Fees and other miscellaneous charges collected by the government.

(*Budget of the U.S. Govt., Analyt. Perspectives*, 12, 235)

### Q 55. What is impoundment?

A When a president refuses to spend money appropriated by Congress, the action is called impoundment. First used by President Thomas Jefferson, the tactic aroused a major controversy when President Richard M. Nixon impounded billions to combat inflation. Congress responded by passing the Congressional Budget and Impoundment Control Act of 1974, establishing procedures for impoundment. Presidents now must get congressional approval for a "rescission," the name for a partial or complete cutoff of spending for a program or agency.

(*CAZ*, 191)

### Q 56. What is rescission?

A Included in the Congressional Budget and Impoundment Control Act of 1974, a rescission cuts or entirely eliminates funds already budgeted for a program or agency. The president requests the rescission in a written message to Congress, which then must approve the funding cut within a specified period. If Congress takes no action or votes the measure down, the president must release the funds. The U.S. comptroller general can sue for release of the funds if the president continues to withhold them after Congress has rejected the rescission request.

(*Amer. Cong. Dict.*, 235)

**Q** **57. What does sequestration do?**

**A** Sequestration automatically cuts the federal budget when Congress and the president fail to keep spending within specified budget limits. The procedure was first set by the 1985 Gramm-Rudman-Hollings antideficit law, revised in 1987 and again in 1990. The president's Office of Management and Budget estimates the annual budget deficit and decides how much money to cut, or sequester, if federal spending threatens to go above the prescribed limit. Cuts are made across-the-board in the category exceeding the limit (domestic, defense, and international). About two-thirds of the budget is exempt from sequestration. Automatic cuts were imposed on a limited scale in October 1989. Congress and the White House narrowly avoided a massive $106 billion sequestration by concluding the 1990 budget deal.

(*CAZ*, 44; *CQ Almanac 1990*, 176; *CQ Almanac 1991*, 74)

**Q** **58. What does the Congressional Budget Office do?**

**A** The congressional equivalent of the president's Office of Management and Budget, the Congressional Budget Office (CBO) provides Congress with economic forecasts and alternatives to the president's proposed budget. Created in 1974 to help Congress control the budget process, the CBO also develops five-year cost projections for proposed bills and tracks appropriations bills through the legislative process.

(*CAZ*, 83; *SOW*, 154)

**Q** **59. What does the Federal Reserve System do?**

**A** The Federal Reserve formulates and administers the federal government's monetary policy and also regulates the banking industry. A board of seven governors directs the Federal Reserve and determines how best to alter interest rates and money supply to achieve such goals as low inflation, low unemployment, and good economic growth.

Because the board so directly influences the country's economic future, its chair ranks among the most powerful government officials.

(*PAZ*, 174–5)

## Q 60. What does the General Accounting Office do?

A Called "Congress's watchdog," the General Accounting Office (GAO) reviews how the executive branch spends money appropriated by Congress. The 5,000 accountants and other investigators who work for the GAO do not perform routine audits, but instead focus on uncovering poor management, waste, and outright fraud. In that capacity the GAO has exposed various improprieties, including weapons systems cost overruns and the House Banking scandal.

(*CAZ*, 159; *SOW*, 153–4)

*(See 71 What was the banking scandal in the House about?)*

## Q 61. What does the Office of Management and Budget do?

A An important agency within the president's executive office, the OMB helps the president prepare the annual budget request, which when approved by Congress provides funding for the entire government. The OMB's responsibilities go beyond helping to prepare the national budget, though. In order to control spending, the OMB reviews all executive branch proposals to Congress as well as all legislation passed by Congress and sent to the president for his signature. It even recommends whether the president should sign or veto a bill. Another of its responsibilities affects millions of Americans in an unusual way: The OMB determines the content of all blank forms used by government agencies.

(*SOW*, 79)

## WAR

## Q 62. How many times has the United States declared war?

A The federal government has formally declared war five times—in the War of 1812, Mexican War, Spanish-American War, World War I, and World War II. Undeclared wars are discussed in the next entry.

(*Encyc. of Amer. Hist.,* 169, 243, 342; *PAZ,* 154)

(*See 151 Who was the first president to ask Congress to declare war?*)

**Q 63. How many other wars has the United States fought in?**

**A** In addition to the five declared wars and the Civil War, the United States has played a major role in conflicts not formally declared wars, including the Korean, Vietnam, and Persian Gulf Wars. U.S. military forces also have been used in various, more limited, engagements—either to enforce policy or to act as peacekeepers—and in wars against American Indians during the eighteenth century.

(*VSAP,* 354)

**Q 64. What states were in the Confederacy, and when did each secede?**

**A** 

| Confederate state | Date of secession |
| --- | --- |
| Alabama | January 11, 1861 |
| Arkansas | May 6, 1861 |
| Florida | January 10, 1861 |
| Georgia | January 19, 1861 |
| Louisiana | January 26, 1861 |
| Mississippi | January 9, 1861 |
| North Carolina | May 20, 1861 |
| South Carolina | December 20, 1860 |
| Tennessee | June 8, 1861 |
| Texas | February 1, 1861 |
| Virginia | April 17, 1861 |

(*SOW,* 21)

**Q 65. How many Americans have died in various wars?**

**A** The following figures include both those killed immediately in battle and those who died later of wounds sustained in battle. Figures for the declared and major undeclared wars were:

| War of 1812 | 1,877 |
| Mexican War | 1,721 (disease killed over 11,000 others) |
| Civil War | 234,000 (140,000 Union; 94,000 Confederate) |
| Spanish-American War | 379 (disease and other causes killed over 5,000 others) |
| World War I | 53,000 |
| World War II | 292,000 |
| Korean conflict | 34,000 |
| Vietnam conflict | 47,000 |
| Persian Gulf War | under 500 |

(*Encyc. of Amer. Hist.,* 182, 247, 292, 345, 373; *VSAP,* 354)

## Q 66. What is the War Powers Act?

A Congress passed the 1973 War Powers Act to limit the president's war-making powers. One provision called on the president to consult with Congress whenever possible before committing U.S. troops to combat. Another required the president to report to Congress within forty-eight hours after a troop commitment. It also provided that, in an undeclared war, Congress could by a majority vote in both houses force the president to withdraw troops from the fighting, and unless Congress specifically approved the military action, troops had to be withdrawn within sixty to ninety days. Critics have questioned the law's constitutionality, and presidents from Nixon onward have largely ignored it while continuing to commit troops to combat they believed necessary. The act has had little real effect, but it did force President Ronald Reagan in 1983 to accept a limit on the deployment of U.S. peacekeeping troops in Lebanon. At other times Congress has been either unwilling or unable to enforce compliance.

(*PAZ,* 98–9, 469)

## Q 67. Has martial law ever been declared in the United States?

A Martial law has been imposed a few times, but only in certain parts of the country. President Abraham Lincoln declared martial law in several areas during the Civil War, but no president has declared it since that time. Other officials have imposed it in specific locales with presidential approval, though. After the Japanese attacked Pearl

Harbor in 1941, for example, the territorial governor proclaimed martial law in Hawaii with President Franklin Roosevelt's approval.

(*PAZ*, 297)

**Q** **68. Were there ever any internment camps in the United States?**

**A** After the Japanese attack on Pearl Harbor, the federal government forcibly relocated to internment camps in the U.S. interior about 120,000 Japanese Americans living on the West Coast. The internees, many of whom lost their homes and businesses as a result, were regarded as a possible threat to security. However, no similar action was ever taken in Hawaii, where a large Japanese American population lived, and no Japanese American was ever convicted of espionage. Though the Supreme Court had upheld the order in 1944 as a legal use of the president's wartime powers, Congress in 1988 formally apologized to the surviving internees and authorized tax-free payments of about $20,000 apiece.

(*Harvard Encyc.*, 566; *PAZ*, 250–1)

## SCANDALS

**Q** **69. What was Abscam?**

**A** FBI agents posing as wealthy Arabs offered bribes to various members of Congress in the 1980 undercover "sting" operation called Abscam. A highly publicized scandal followed the arrest of six representatives and one senator who took bribes, and by May 1981 all were convicted. Six defendants either resigned or lost election campaigns before being convicted. The House expelled the seventh, Rep. Michael J. "Ozzie" Myers of Pennsylvania, who became only the fourth representative expelled since the Civil War and the first ever ousted for corruption.

(*CAZ*, 3–4)

(*See 262 Which members of Congress have been expelled?; 363 Which sitting senators have been indicted?*)

## Q 70. How did the Bobby Baker scandal come about?

A friend and protégé of President Lyndon B. Johnson, Robert G. "Bobby" Baker ranked among the most powerful congressional staff members of his time. But Baker reportedly used his position as secretary of the Senate to further his personal business ventures and pocketed about $100,000 in campaign contributions donated by business interests. Forced to resign his Senate post in 1963, Baker was convicted in 1967 of income tax evasion, theft, and conspiracy to defraud the government. He served seventeen months in prison before being paroled in 1972.

(*CAZ*, 336, 364; *Dict. of Amer. Hist.*, 243–4; *Encyc. of Amer. Facts & Dates*, 672)

## Q 71. What was the banking scandal in the House about?

The House banking scandal erupted in 1991 when the public learned that many of their representatives regularly wrote thousands of bad checks on the bank—8,331 in one year alone—without paying any penalty. Strictly speaking, the House bank was a convenience for members, not a true bank, but angry voters saw the interest-free loans on overdrafts—the largest being $60,625—as an abuse of privilege. After shutting down the bank, the House released a list of check kiters, including 269 sitting members. By the close of the 1992 election campaign, 77 of them had either retired or been defeated for reelection.

(*CAZ*, 176; *SOW*, 150–1)

## Q 72. What happened in the Belknap scandal?

Just one of the scandals to rock the Grant administration, this affair linked Grant's secretary of war, William Belknap, with bribery charges. Belknap, who was war secretary from 1869 to 1876, was charged with receiving tens of thousands of dollars in bribes for granting rights to trading posts on Indian reservations. Belknap's wife received the money until she died, and after that Belknap collected it himself. Belknap resigned the day the House voted to impeach him in 1876. The Senate held the impeachment trial anyway, but doubts about its jurisdiction over a resigned official resulted in a vote for acquittal. Belknap never faced criminal charges in the matter.

(*Encyc. of Amer. Hist.*, 300; *RD Encyc. of Amer. Hist.*, 98–9)

(See *73 What was the Black Friday scandal?*; *74 What was the Crédit Mobilier affair?*; *80 What happened in the Whiskey Ring scandal?*)

**Q** **73. What was the Black Friday scandal?**

**A** Financial speculators James Fisk and Jay Gould developed a plan to corner the U.S. gold market in 1869, and that plan involved preventing the treasury from dumping gold on the market. Fisk and Gould hired President Ulysses S. Grant's brother-in-law, drew in the New York subtreasury head, tried (but failed) to enlist Grant's private secretary, and finally entertained Grant himself aboard Fisk's steamboat. Believing Grant would not intervene (he had not agreed to anything), Fisk, Gould, and many other financial operators began buying gold in September 1869. The price rose sharply until finally on Friday, September 24, Grant ordered the government to sell $4 million in gold. The resulting market collapse ruined many speculators and the scandal deeply embarrassed Grant. Gould and Fisk, by getting out quickly, netted an $11 million profit.

(*Dict. of Amer. Hist.,* vol. 1, 311; *RD Encyc. of Amer. Hist.,* 115)

(*See 72 What happened in the Belknap scandal?; 74 What was the Crédit Mobilier affair?; 80 What happened in the Whiskey Ring scandal?*)

**Q** **74. What was the Crédit Mobilier affair?**

**A** Construction of the Union Pacific Railroad, the last link in the transcontinental railroad, gave birth to this scandal during the late 1800s. After receiving government loans and land grants, Union Pacific officials used Crédit Mobilier of America, a phony construction company they controlled, to skim off huge profits while building the railroad. Rep. Oakes Ames, a major Crédit Mobilier stockholder, tried to head off an official inquiry by selling $33 million of Crédit Mobilier stock to various people in Congress and in the Grant administration. After the scandal finally broke in 1872, the House censured Ames and another representative. Vice President Schuyler Colfax and Rep. James A. Garfield (the future president) were implicated but not disciplined.

(*CAZ,* 196–7; *Encyc. of Amer. Hist.,* 299; *RD Encyc. of Amer. Hist.,* 309; *SOW,* 149)

(*See 263 Which members of Congress have been censured or reprimanded?*)

**Q** **75. What happened in the Iran-Contra affair?**

**A** This scandal arose from a dispute between President Ronald Reagan and Congress over U.S. policy in Central America. Around 1984 Congress cut off government funding for the Contras, CIA-backed rebels against Nicaragua's leftist government.

White House officials sought other, apparently legal, means to unofficially support the Contras, however. National Security Council (NSC) staffer Lt. Col. Oliver North directed the aid network, while other officials sought money from foreign governments. Meanwhile, the NSC also orchestrated secret arms sales to Iran in exchange for cash and their help in freeing Americans kidnapped by pro-Iranian terrorists in Lebanon. But about $3.5 million from the sales was illegally diverted to the Contras in 1986, apparently just before Congress dropped its ban against Contra funding. Reagan was roundly criticized, but his direct involvement was never proved. Both North and his boss, Vice Admiral John Poindexter, had their convictions on criminal charges reversed outright or dismissed because Congress had earlier granted them immunity from prosecution during its own investigation of the scandal. In 1992 President George Bush pardoned six others implicated in the scandal.

(*CAZ*, 199–202)

(*See 92 What is the National Security Council?; 110 Who have presidents pardoned?*)


### Q 76. Who were the Keating Five, and what did they do?

A The Keating Five were senators accused of intervening with federal regulators to help Charles Keating, Jr., head of the failing Lincoln Savings and Loan Association. Keating, it turned out, had channeled some $1.5 million to the senators' campaigns or favorite political causes. The five senators, including Alan Cranston (D-Calif.), met with regulators during the mid-1980s on Keating's behalf. The S&L remained open until collapsing in 1989, at a cost of $2 billion to taxpayers. The Senate Select Ethics Committee in 1991 criticized the "poor judgment" of four accused senators—Dennis DeConcini (D-Ariz.), John McCain (R-Ariz.), John Glenn (D-Ohio), and Donald Riegle, Jr. (D-Mich.)—and officially reprimanded Senator Cranston for his conduct.

(*CAZ*, 211)

(*See 263 Which members of Congress have been censured or reprimanded?*)


### Q 77. What was the Teapot Dome scandal?

A This scandal is remembered chiefly as an example of the blatant corruption during President Warren G. Harding's administration. In return for bribes totaling $400,000, Interior Secretary Albert Fall secretly leased federal oil reserves—at Teapot Dome, Wyoming, and Elk Hills, California—to oilmen Harry F. Sinclair and Edward L.

Doheny. President Harding died soon after this and other scandals emerged in 1923. Secretary Fall was sentenced to a year in jail, but both Sinclair and Doheny were acquitted on a technicality. Sinclair later served time for attempted jury tampering and contempt of the Senate.

(*PAZ*, 412–13)

**Q 78. What happened in the Watergate scandal?**

A Perhaps the greatest political scandal in U.S. history, Watergate forced President Richard M. Nixon's resignation and put top White House officials behind bars for criminal wrongdoing. The scandal began the night of June 17, 1972, when the five "Watergate burglars" were caught trying to bug a telephone in the Democratic National Committee headquarters, at the Watergate complex in Washington, D.C. Investigators eventually linked the burglars to the White House and, despite denials, proved President Nixon and top advisors directed a cover-up involving deliberate efforts to obstruct justice. In late July 1974, the House Judiciary Committee voted to impeach Nixon. Days later on August 5, after a long court battle, Nixon released secret Oval Office tapes of conversations that showed he indeed had been involved in the cover-up. The first president to do so, Nixon resigned on August 9, 1974, rather than face impeachment and removal from office. His successor, President Gerald R. Ford, officially pardoned him on September 8.

(*CAZ*, 421–6; *SOW*, 76)

(*See 106 What is executive privilege?; 110 Who have presidents pardoned?; 143 Who became president without having been elected to that office or to the vice presidency?; 146 Which president resigned?*)

**Q 79. How many Nixon officials went to jail as a result of Watergate?**

A Among those jailed were seven high-ranking officials: Nixon campaign manager and former attorney general John N. Mitchell, and Nixon aides John D. Ehrlichman, H. R. Haldeman, John W. Dean III, Charles W. Colson, Jeb Stuart Magruder, and Egil Krogh, Jr. In all, over 30 people were convicted as a result of Watergate or the cover-up, including the Watergate burglars, Nixon White House officials, campaign officials, and even some campaign contributors.

(*Encyc. Americana*, 467; *SOW*, 76)

**Q 80. What happened in the Whiskey Ring scandal?**

**A** A conspiracy to defraud the government of liquor tax revenues, the Whiskey Ring proved the most damaging scandal of President Grant's scandal-plagued administration. Between about 1870 and 1875, distillers, tax revenue officers, and treasury officials conspired to divert millions in federal liquor taxes, first to the Republican Party and then to themselves. In all, about 240 prominent Republicans and officials, including President Grant's personal secretary, Orville E. Babcock, were arrested. Babcock and most of the officials were acquitted after Grant used his influence on their behalf.

(*PAZ, 480–1; RD Encyc. of Amer. Hist., 1233*)

(*See 72 What happened in the Belknap scandal?; 73 What was the Black Friday scandal?; 74 What was the Crédit Mobilier affair?*)


**Q 81. Which cabinet members have taken the Fifth Amendment?**

**A** During congressional investigations following the 1923 Teapot Dome scandal, Interior Secretary Albert B. Fall and Navy Secretary Edwin Denby both invoked the Fifth Amendment protection against self-incrimination. Secretary of Housing and Urban Development Samuel R. Pierce, Jr., also resorted to the Fifth Amendment at a congressional investigation of corruption during his tenure under President Ronald Reagan.

(*SOW, 75*)


**Q 82. Which cabinet members have been convicted of crimes?**

**A** In 1876 President Ulysses S. Grant's secretary of war, William Belknap, nearly became the first convicted cabinet member, but he resigned to avoid impeachment and prosecution on bribery charges. The first cabinet officer actually convicted of crimes was Albert Fall, President Warren G. Harding's secretary of the interior. A key figure in the Teapot Dome scandal, Fall served almost a year in prison. Since then, presidential staff members have been convicted, but no other cabinet officer has gone to jail for crimes committed while in office.

(*CAZ, 196–7, 389–90; SOW, 77–9*)

(*See 72 What happened in the Belknap scandal?; 75 What happened in the Iran-Contra affair?; 77 What was the Teapot Dome scandal?; 78 What happened in the Watergate scandal?*)

# II

# THE PRESIDENCY

## IN GENERAL

**Q 83. Who thought of the names *president* and *vice president*?**

**A** A South Carolina delegate to the Constitutional Convention, Charles Pinckney, proposed a plan on May 29, 1787, that first mentioned the title *president*. It was a familiar term, having been used before for the presiding officer of various legislative bodies. Two months passed, during which various other titles were tried—*national executive, supreme executive,* and *governor. President* won out, though, after the August 6, 1787, report of the Committee on Detail used the title, and the Convention accepted it without debate. Delegates also adopted the title of *vice president,* vice being the Latin word for "in place of."

(*PAZ*, 420–1)

**Q 84. Which presidents and vice presidents served when?**

**A** Forty-two presidents and forty-five vice presidents have been in office since 1789. (President Grover Cleveland is counted twice, once for each of his two noncon-secutive terms.) In the list below, unless otherwise specified, terms began and ended on March 4 before 1937, and on January 20 thereafter.

| | President | Term | Vice president | Term |
|---|---|---|---|---|
| 1 | George Washington | April 30, 1789–1797 | John Adams | 1789–1797 |
| 2 | John Adams | 1797–1801 | Thomas Jefferson | 1797–1801 |
| 3 | Thomas Jefferson | 1801–1809 | Aaron Burr | 1801–1805 |
| | | | George Clinton | 1805–1809 |
| 4 | James Madison | 1809–1817 | George Clinton | 1809–April 12, 1812 |

| | | | | |
|---|---|---|---|---|
| | | | Elbridge Gerry | 1813–November 23, 1814 |
| 5 | James Monroe | 1817–1825 | Daniel D. Tompkins | 1817–1825 |
| 6 | John Q. Adams | 1825–1829 | John C. Calhoun | 1825–1829 |
| 7 | Andrew Jackson | 1829–1837 | John C. Calhoun | 1829–December 28, 1832 |
| | | | Martin Van Buren | 1833–1837 |
| 8 | Martin Van Buren | 1837–1841 | Richard M. Johnson | 1837–1841 |
| 9 | William H. Harrison | 1841–April 4, 1841 | John Tyler | 1841–April 6, 1841 |
| 10 | John Tyler | April 6, 1841–1845 | | |
| 11 | James K. Polk | 1845–1849 | George M. Dallas | 1845–1849 |
| 12 | Zachary Taylor | 1849–July 9, 1850 | Millard Fillmore | 1849–July 10, 1850 |
| 13 | Millard Fillmore | July 10, 1850–1853 | | |
| 14 | Franklin Pierce | 1853–1857 | William R. King | March 24, 1853–April 18, 1853 |
| 15 | James Buchanan | 1857–1861 | John Breckinridge | 1857–1861 |
| 16 | Abraham Lincoln | 1861–April 15, 1865 | Hannibal Hamlin Andrew Johnson | 1861–1865 1865–April 15, 1865 |
| 17 | Andrew Johnson | April 15, 1865–1869 | | |
| 18 | Ulysses S. Grant | 1869–1877 | Schuyler Colfax Henry Wilson | 1869–1873 1873–November 22, 1875 |
| 19 | Rutherford B. Hayes | 1877–1881 | William Wheeler | 1877–1881 |
| 20 | James A. Garfield | 1881–September 19, 1881 | Chester A. Arthur | 1881–September 20, 1881 |
| 21 | Chester A. Arthur | September 20, 1881–1885 | | |

| President | Term | Vice president | Term |
|---|---|---|---|
| 22 Grover Cleveland | 1885–1889 | Thomas Hendricks | 1885–November 25, 1885 |
| 23 Benjamin Harrison | 1889–1893 | Levi P. Morton | 1889–1893 |
| 24 Grover Cleveland | 1893–1897 | Adlai Stevenson | 1893–1897 |
| 25 William McKinley | 1897–September 14, 1901 | Garret A. Hobart | 1897–November 21, 1899 |
| | | Theodore Roosevelt | 1901–September 14, 1901 |
| 26 Theodore Roosevelt | September 14, 1901–1909 | Charles Fairbanks | 1905–1909 |
| 27 William H. Taft | 1909–1913 | James S. Sherman | 1909–October 30, 1912 |
| 28 Woodrow Wilson | 1913–1921 | Thomas Marshall | 1913–1921 |
| 29 Warren G. Harding | 1921–August 2, 1923 | Calvin Coolidge | 1921–August 3, 1923 |
| 30 Calvin Coolidge | August 3, 1923–1929 | Charles G. Dawes | 1925–1929 |
| 31 Herbert Hoover | 1929–1933 | Charles Curtis | 1929–1933 |
| 32 Franklin Roosevelt | 1933–April 12, 1945 | John N. Garner | 1933–1941 |
| | | Henry A. Wallace | 1941–1945 |
| | | Harry S. Truman | 1945–April 12, 1945 |
| 33 Harry S. Truman | April 12, 1945–1953 | Alben W. Barkley | 1949–1953 |
| 34 Dwight Eisenhower | 1953–1961 | Richard M. Nixon | 1953–1961 |
| 35 John F. Kennedy | 1961–November 22, 1963 | Lyndon B. Johnson | 1961–November 22, 1963 |
| 36 Lyndon B. Johnson | November 22, 1963–1969 | Hubert H. Humphrey | 1965–1969 |
| 37 Richard M. Nixon | 1969–August 9, 1974 | Spiro T. Agnew | 1969–October 10, 1973 |

| | | Gerald R. Ford | December 6, 1973–August 9, 1974 |
|---|---|---|---|
| 38 Gerald R. Ford | August 9, 1974–1977 | Nelson Rockefeller | December 19, 1974–1977 |
| 39 Jimmy Carter | 1977–1981 | Walter F. Mondale | 1977–1981 |
| 40 Ronald Reagan | 1981–1989 | George Bush | 1981–1989 |
| 41 George Bush | 1989–1993 | Dan Quayle | 1989–1993 |
| 42 Bill Clinton | 1993– | Al Gore | 1993– |

(*PAZ,* 503–6)

**Q 85. Who are considered the greatest presidents?**

**A** Abraham Lincoln, George Washington, Franklin D. Roosevelt, and Thomas Jefferson are almost uniformly considered the greatest, usually in that order. Theodore Roosevelt, Woodrow Wilson, Andrew Jackson, and Harry S. Truman often are ranked among the best presidents, too.

(*PAZ,* 210–11; *VSAP,* 260–1)

(*See 540 Who are considered the greatest justices?*)

**Q 86. What is the presidential oath of office?**

**A** The Constitution spelled out the presidential oath of office, the only official oath it set down in detail. The oath, usually administered by the chief justice of the Supreme Court on inauguration day, reads simply: "I do solemnly swear (or affirm) that I will faithfully execute the Office of President of the United States, and will to the best of my ability preserve, protect, and defend the Constitution of the United States." The president-elect may choose either *swear* or *affirm,* as some Christian sects prohibit swearing. Only Franklin Pierce has used *affirmed* (1853).

(*PAZ,* 327–8)

(*See 257 What is the oath of office for a member of Congress?; 543 What is the Court's oath of office?*)

**Q  87. What does the president get paid?**

**A** The president's salary has remained the same since 1969, $200,000 a year. Presidents enjoy various perks as well, including a bullet-proof limousine; free use of the presidential plane, *Air Force One,* or other government aircraft; a $50,000 expense account; and the presidential retreat, Camp David. The president's White House office receives a $100,000 allowance to cover travel, among other things, and a $19,000 entertainment allowance. The first family lives rent-free in the 132-room White House, though the president pays for family food and other incidentals. The government covers expenses for all official White House functions, security, maintenance, domestic help, and other costs, which together amounted to about $8 million in 1992.

(*SOW,* 92–3)

(*See 157 Who was the first president to get a pension?; 195 What does the vice president get paid?*)

**Q  88. How is the executive branch organized?**

**A** The president, of course, heads the executive branch. Under the president are the vice president, the Executive Office of the President (including the White House Office, Office of Management and Budget, and National Security Council), and the fourteen executive departments. Also considered part of the executive branch are dozens of independent regulatory agencies, such as the Federal Reserve System. These agencies usually are headed by a bipartisan board or commission and are not under the president's direct control. Similarly, government corporations, such as the U.S. Postal Service, are considered part of the executive branch, though they also operate independently of the president.

(*PAZ,* 533)

(*See 59 What does the Federal Reserve System do?; 61 What does the Office of Management and Budget do?; 89 How many people work in the Executive Office of the President?; 92 What is the National Security Council?; 107 What is a presidential commission?; 223 What is the cabinet?; 247 When did the post office become a government-run corporation?*)

**Q 89. How many people work in the Executive Office of the President?**

**A** As of January 1993, hundreds of advisors and staffers worked in the Executive Office of the President (EOP), including 600 in the Office of Management and Budget, 388 in the White House, and 252 in the Office of Administration. The Council of Economic Advisors, National Security Council, and other EOP offices had relatively small staffs. Taken together, these and other EOP staffers totaled 1,836 in early 1993.

(*VSAP*, 267–9)

**Q 90. What is the budget for the Executive Office of the President?**

**A** For fiscal 1995, the budget allowed about $200 million for the president's executive office, and that figure was expected to remain roughly the same through 1999. Expenses for that office, of course, represent just a small part of the vast sums allocated to the many departments and agencies within the executive branch.

(*Budget of the U.S. Govt., Analyt. Perspectives,* 252)

(*See 52 How was federal money allocated in a recent budget?*)

**Q 91. Who are the Joint Chiefs of Staff?**

**A** The Joint Chiefs of Staff (JCS) are the country's five top military officers—the army and air force chiefs of staff, the chief of naval operations, the Marine Corps commandant, and the chairman of the JCS. Together they advise the president on military matters and plan unified military strategy. The president appoints all five joint chiefs for four-year terms, subject to Senate approval. The chairman of the JCS, considered the president's supreme military advisor, serves a two-year term.

(*PAZ,* 116–17; 259–60)

**Q 92. What is the National Security Council?**

**A** Created in 1947, the National Security Council (NSC) advises the president and helps coordinate the foreign policy efforts of various agencies. By law, the president, vice president, secretary of defense, and secretary of state are NSC members, while the chairman of the Joint Chiefs of Staff and the CIA director serve as NSC advisors. A more focused group than the full cabinet, the NSC has proved effective in developing policy, notably during international crises. The NSC staff, headed by the president's national security adviser, serves the president and other NSC members. The president's national security adviser is not an NSC member.

(*PAZ*, 165; 317–18)

## PRESIDENTIAL POWERS AND PRIVILEGES

**Q 93. What does the president do?**

**A** The president is the nation's chief executive and the head of the executive branch. As such, the president "wears many hats": in addition to being responsible for the executive branch and its many agencies, the president is also head of state and chief diplomat; commander-in-chief of the armed forces; legislative leader and economic policy maker; and law enforcer. Moreover, the president acts as chief spokesman for his party. The president and vice president are the only elected members of the executive branch.

(*SOW,* 68)

*(See 66 What is the War Powers Act?; 88 How is the executive branch organized?; 151 Who was the first president to ask Congress to declare war?; 249 What does Congress do?; 466 What does the chief justice do?)*

**Q 94. Which presidents have not delivered State of the Union addresses to Congress in person?**

**A** Presidents George Washington and John Adams delivered their annual addresses in person. But our third president, Thomas Jefferson, objected to the elaborate formal ceremony and in 1801 decided a written report was more dignified. Presidents after Jefferson all did likewise until 1913, when President Woodrow Wilson delivered his State of the Union message before Congress. Since then, only President Herbert Hoover has not delivered his message in person. Today the address has become an important way for presidents to influence the national agenda.

(*CAZ,* 368; *PAZ,* 400)

**Q 95. What is a veto?**

**A** From the Latin for "I forbid," the veto is the president's power to reject legislation passed by Congress. It is one of the constitutional checks and balances between the executive and legislative branches. Once Congress approves a bill, the president has three options: he can sign the bill into law, veto it, or do nothing (in which case the bill automatically becomes law after ten days, unless Congress adjourns before then). To veto a bill, the president simply sends it back to the house that originated it, along with a "veto message" explaining what parts of the bill caused the rejection. Congress can do nothing (and let the bill die), rewrite it to remove the objectionable parts, or override the president's veto. Winning an override is usually difficult, though, because two-thirds of those present and voting in each chamber (a quorum being present) must vote for it. (See also the next question and those following.)

(*PAZ*, 446–7)

(*See 32 What are checks and balances?; 278 What is a legislative veto?; 296 What is a quorum?*)

### Q 96. What is a pocket veto?

A Ordinarily the president must either sign a bill or veto it and return it to Congress within ten days. But if Congress has adjourned in the interim, the president can simply "pocket" a bill he wants to veto, since he has no way to return it. President James Madison used the pocket veto first, but the practice did not become common until after the Civil War. In the twentieth century, Congress has limited pocket vetoes by appointing "agents" to receive vetoed bills during some recesses and adjournments.

(*PAZ*, 450)

(*See 301 How does Congress adjourn?*)

### Q 97. How many bills have presidents vetoed?

A Between 1789 and early 1994, presidents vetoed 2,513 bills. All but 52 were cast after 1860, when the veto emerged as a powerful tool in political battles between the president and Congress. President Franklin Roosevelt had the most vetoes, 635, followed by President Grover Cleveland with 414 (in his first term; 170 in his second), and President Harry S. Truman with 250. President Dwight Eisenhower vetoed 181 bills.

(*CAZ*, 402–4; *CQ Almanac 1992*, 6–7; *CQ Almanac 1993*, 31; *SCAZ*, 442; *SOW*, 87; *The Senate*, 497–8; *VSAP*, 278)

(*See 276 How does a bill become law?*)

**98. Who pocket vetoed the most bills?**

A Franklin Roosevelt pocket vetoed 263 bills, more than any other president, though he also served longer than any other president, too—three terms and part of a fourth. President Grover Cleveland was not far behind, however, with 238 pocket vetoes during his two terms (110 first, 128 second). The only other president to pocket veto over one hundred bills was Eisenhower (108).

(*CAZ*, 402; *SOW*, 87)

(*See 96 What is a pocket veto?*)

**99. Have any presidents not vetoed bills?**

A Seven presidents have not used either a regular veto or a pocket veto during their administrations: John Adams, Thomas Jefferson, John Q. Adams, William H. Harrison (died after one month in office), Zachary Taylor (died after sixteen months in office), Millard Fillmore, and James A. Garfield (assassinated after a few months in office). In the twentieth century, Presidents Warren G. Harding (6) and John F. Kennedy (21) had the fewest vetoes. President Bill Clinton did not veto a single bill during his first two years in office.

(*The Senate*, 497–8; *VSAP*, 278)

**100. How many vetoes have been overridden?**

A Because a veto cannot be overrideen without a two-thirds vote in both houses, vote overrides are extremely rare. Of the thousands of bills vetoed between 1789 and early 1994, Congress has overridden only 104.

(*SCAZ*, 442; *CAZ*, 403; *CQ Almanac 1992*, 6–7)

**101. Who had the most vetoes overridden?**

A President Andrew Johnson had the most, with fifteen overrides. He vetoed a total of twenty-nine bills. Johnson, a Democrat on the Republican presidential ticket in 1864, faced radical Republicans in Congress who were determined to impose a harsh reconstruction plan on the South after the Civil War.

(*SOW*, 87)

**Q** **102. What is the line-item veto?**

**A** The power to selectively veto just part of an appropriations bill is called a line-item veto. Most state governors have had this power since the early 1900s, but at the federal level, the president must either veto the whole bill or sign it as written by Congress. Line-item veto supporters argue the president often must sign appropriations bills that contain wasteful spending provisions. But critics claim the veto would usurp Congress' power of the purse by giving the president a way to pressure legislators into voting his way on a bill. They also argue that the line-item veto would not cut spending because much of the budget already goes to entitlements, which have mandatory funding.

(*CAZ,* 405; *PAZ,* 450–1)

(*See 53 What is an entitlement?; 274 What is pork-barrel politics?*)

**Q** **103. Who was the first president to call for a line-item veto?**

**A** Ulysses S. Grant became the first president to ask for the line-item veto at the federal level in 1873. Various state governments already had begun adopting the line item veto after the Civil War.

(*PAZ,* 451)

**Q** **104. What are executive agreements?**

**A** When the president concludes with a foreign government any pact other than a formal treaty, it is called an executive agreement. Unlike treaties, executive agreements do not require congressional approval, giving the president greater flexibility in dealing with foreign governments. Trade agreements, defense pacts, arms control agreements, even agreements annexing territory—executive agreements can accomplish virtually anything a treaty can, except that they cannot supersede U.S. laws when conflicts occur. Since World War II, presidents have relied heavily on executive agreements.

(*PAZ,* 122; 162–3)

(*See 40 What is a treaty?; 41 Who must agree to treaties between the United States and other countries?*)

**105. What are executive orders, and how many have various presidents signed?**

A An executive order is a presidential directive that has the force of law, even though Congress has not approved it. Most executive orders pertain to government officials and agencies, but they also may implement legislative statutes or help enforce the Constitution or treaties. Executive orders sometimes have wide-ranging effects. Beginning with Franklin Roosevelt, for example, presidents have used them to promote the civil rights of minorities and women. President George Washington issued the first eight executive orders. President Franklin Roosevelt issued the most—3,522, an average of almost 286 a year.

(*PAZ,* 96–7, 169–70; *SOW,* 86–7)

Q **106. What is executive privilege?**

A Often a controversial issue, executive privilege is the president's right to withhold sensitive information from Congress. President George Washington refused the House information about the Jay Treaty, a controversial agreement with Britain (1794) that sought to avert a war. Presidents since have rejected congressional inquiries on various grounds, including the need for secrecy. The Eisenhower administration used the term *executive privilege* for the first time, and the Supreme Court first explicitly recognized a constitutional basis for it in the 1974 case *United States v. Nixon.*

(*CAZ,* 135; *PAZ,* 170; *SCAZ,* 158–60; *WHAD,* 594)

(See 534 What did the Court rule in *United States v. Nixon?*)

Q **107. What is a presidential commission?**

A Presidents appoint special commissions to investigate policy questions that are beyond the scope of regular advisers or that pose difficult political problems. The commissions have helped gather information and focus public attention on diverse areas such as defense spending, government waste, and Social Security. Among the noted past commissions are President Franklin Roosevelt's Brownlow Commission, which developed the blueprint for the president's executive office, and the Hoover commissions on government reorganization.

(*PAZ,* 86–7)

(See 202 Who was the first vice president to head a presidential commission?)

**A** As with other top government officials, the president recruits and nominates potential judges and ambassadors. The Senate then approves or rejects the appointees. While the president may participate directly in selecting Supreme Court nominees, the attorney general and the Justice Department generally recruit nominees for federal appeals and district court judgeships. Also, according to an informal rule known as "senatorial courtesy," a potential nominee who will serve a local district may be rejected by a senator from that state, if the senator belongs to the president's party.

(*PAZ*, 12, 98, 105)

(*See 33 Who can appoint and remove officials in the executive branch?*)

**Q** **109. What is patronage?**

**A** Patronage, also called the "spoils system," is the practice of rewarding fellow party members by giving them government jobs. While 90 percent of federal jobs now are classified as civil service positions (hiring based solely on merit), there are still about 5,000 political appointees in the executive branch, including some 200 White House staffers, 14 cabinet department heads, 400 to 500 subcabinet officials, and 150 ambassadors. Until the late nineteenth century, presidents and their subordinates awarded almost all federal jobs based on patronage. But calls for reform, and President James Garfield's assassination by a disgruntled office-seeker in 1881, brought about the Civil Service Reform Act of 1883. The original act set aside about 10 percent of low-level federal jobs for hiring based on merit. Succeeding administrations gradually extended civil service classification to other jobs, eventually excluding most executive branch jobs from patronage.

(*PAZ*, 333–4)

(*See 135 Which presidents were assassinated?; 274 What is pork-barrel politics?*)

**Q** **110. Who have presidents pardoned?**

**A** To help end the 1794 Whiskey Rebellion, a revolt against a whiskey tax, President George Washington granted full pardons to the rebels. After the Civil War, Presidents Abraham Lincoln and Andrew Johnson issued amnesties to former Confederates, thereby restoring their voting and office-holding rights. President Gerald Ford issued perhaps the most controversial pardon to former president Nixon on September 8, 1974, for any Watergate crimes he may have committed. Presidents Ford and Jimmy Carter also offered amnesty to draft evaders and to those who avoided military service by fleeing the country. President George Bush pardoned former defense secretary Caspar Weinberger and five others involved in the Iran-Contra affair, as well as eighteen people sentenced in unrelated cases.

(*PAZ*, 96, 330; *SOW*, 88–9)

(*See 75 What happened in the Iran-Contra affair?; 78 What happened in the Watergate scandal?*)


**Q 111. How many press conferences have various presidents had?**

**A** President Franklin Roosevelt, whose three-plus terms spanned both the depression and World War II, was our most accessible president in terms of media coverage. He held 998 press conferences for an average of 6.9 per month. Total press conferences held by other presidents beginning with Hoover were: Hoover, 268; Truman, 334; Eisenhower, 193; Kennedy, 65; Johnson, 135; Nixon, 39; Ford, 39; Carter, 59; Reagan, 53; Bush, 64; Clinton (as of early 1994), 27.

(*Facts on File 1993*, 1061–2; *Facts on File 1994*, 31–2; *VSAP*, 59)

(*see 153 Who was the first president to hold a press conference?; 154 Who was the first president to have a press secretary?*)


**Q 112. Where can you find presidential papers and speeches?**

**A** Papers of the most recent presidents are easiest to find. The Government Printing Office has published a series called *Public Papers of Presidents of the United States Since Hoover*. In addition, eleven recent presidents have or soon will have special libraries to house their papers. The eleven libraries are:

Hoover—West Branch, Iowa
Franklin Roosevelt—Hyde Park, N.Y.
Truman—Independence, Mo.
Eisenhower—Abilene, Kan.
Kennedy—Dorchester, Mass.
Johnson—Austin, Texas
Nixon—Yorba Linda, Calif.

Ford—Ann Arbor, Mich.

Carter—Atlanta, Ga.

Reagan—Simi Valley, Calif.

Bush—College Station, Texas

Papers and speeches of earlier presidents are reprinted in various collections of official papers, including *A Compilation of the Messages and Papers of the Presidents, 1789–1897,* published by the Government Printing Office.

(*SOW,* 119)

## PRESIDENTIAL DOCTRINES AND PROGRAMS

### Q 113. What is a presidential doctrine?

A A presidential doctrine is an important, far-reaching foreign policy declaration made by, and thereafter closely associated with, a particular president. The declaration does not have the force of law, but the president has considerable executive powers to implement the foreign policy strategy, even if Congress objects. The most famous declaration is the Monroe Doctrine. (Specific doctrines are described in the next questions).

(*PAZ,* 125)

### Q 114. What is the Monroe Doctrine?

A A longstanding U.S. foreign policy principle, the Monroe Doctrine declared U.S. opposition to any outside interference with independent nations in the Americas. Also, while recognizing existing European colonies, it opposed the creation of new ones in the Americas. President James Monroe articulated the doctrine on December 2, 1823, and in 1899 Congress officially endorsed it.

(*PAZ,* 308–9; *WHAD,* 729)

(See 248 Who originated the Monroe Doctrine?)

### Q 115. What is the Roosevelt corollary?

A President Theodore Roosevelt's corollary, popularly called the "big stick," added a new and more determined stricture to the Monroe Doctrine, which had committed the United States to oppose interference with Latin American nations by Europeans and other outside powers. Henceforth, Roosevelt declared in 1904, the United States would intervene directly in any Latin American country to keep the peace or end "chronic wrongdoing." U.S. military forces intervened in Latin American countries several times before the 1930s, when the government adopted a new policy of hemispheric cooperation.

(*RD Encyc. of Amer. Hist.*, 738–9; *WHAD*, 729)

(*See 114 What is the Monroe Doctrine?*)

### Q 116. What is the Truman Doctrine?

**A** The Truman Doctrine established the U.S. policy of "containing" communism early in the Cold War. Confronted by Soviet expansionism in Eastern Europe soon after World War II, President Truman announced the new policy in 1947. He pledged help in preventing communist takeovers and asked for immediate aid to Greece and Turkey, then fighting communist rebels. The United States later organized other programs, such as the Marshall Plan and the North Atlantic Treaty Organization, to support Truman's containment policy.

(*RD Encyc. of Amer. Hist.*, 1140–1; *WHAD*, 1054)

### Q 117. What is the Eisenhower Doctrine?

**A** This foreign policy statement by President Eisenhower committed the United States to preventing communist expansion in the oil-rich Middle East. Following the withdrawal of British and French troops from the Middle East, President Eisenhower in 1957 announced the doctrine to allow direct military intervention in the region, if a Middle Eastern country resisting a communist-inspired revolt requested military assistance. The doctrine soon was put to use. The United States sent Marines to Lebanon the following year, halting an attempted takeover of that country's pro-Western government. The doctrine also became a justification for continued foreign aid to Middle Eastern nations.

(*RD Encyc. of Amer. Hist.*, 377; *WHAD*, 338)

**Q** **118. Did Abraham Lincoln free all the slaves?**

**A** Lincoln's Emancipation Proclamation of January 1, 1863, did not end slavery, as is sometimes thought. Lincoln himself believed only a constitutional amendment could do that, but decided to take action while the Civil War was still being fought. He based the proclamation on his "war power" and so officially freed only the slaves in seceded states. Slaves in border states that had not seceded were unaffected. Lincoln's proclamation had little direct impact on slaves under Confederate control, but it made abolition of slavery a key issue of the war. The Thirteenth Amendment, ratified on December 6, 1865, officially ended slavery.

(*PAZ*, 153–4)

**Q** **119. When were the "First Hundred Days"?**

**A** The "First Hundred Days" refers to an unprecedented period of legislative activity during President Franklin Roosevelt's first three months in office. When Roosevelt entered office on March 4, 1933, the nation faced a banking crisis, severe unemployment, and the general economic collapse accompanying the Great Depression. After ordering banks closed, Roosevelt called an extraordinary session of Congress (March 9–June 15, 1933) and pushed through a host of bills that dealt with the crisis and began his New Deal program. Among them were the Federal Emergency Relief Act, the Civilian Conservation Corps Act, the Glass-Steagall Banking Act, and the Emergency Farm Mortgage Act.

(*CAZ*, 180–1; *PAZ*, 319–20)

(*See 302 How are emergency sessions of Congress called?*)

**Q** **120. What was the New Deal?**

**A** The New Deal was the 1930s program of social and economic reforms initiated by President Franklin Roosevelt in response to the depression. Roosevelt's programs marked a major shift in federal government policy, one that brought direct government involvement in the social and economic welfare of the people, both to attack immediate problems caused by the depression and solve other longstanding social problems. The centerpiece of the New Deal legislation was the Social Security Act of

1935, though Congress passed many other New Deal reforms. The federal government grew rapidly as its role in American life expanded—some sixty new agencies were created—and its regulatory powers increased significantly.

(*PAZ*, 319–21)

**Q** **121. What did the Fair Deal propose?**

**A** President Truman in 1949 sought to extend New Deal reforms with a broad program of domestic reforms he called the Fair Deal, which included federal aid for education and housing, a medical insurance plan, and measures promoting equality for blacks. A reluctant Congress increased minimum wages and Social Security coverage but refused to enact most of Truman's program.

(*RD Encyc. of Amer. Hist.*, 393; *WHAD*, 359)

**Q** **122. What did the New Frontier program try to do?**

**A** President John F. Kennedy's domestic reform program was called the New Frontier and included aid to education, more public housing, Medicare for the aged, an increased minimum wage, and civil rights legislation. Most of Kennedy's programs remained bottled up in Congress during his administration, however. Kennedy's successor, President Johnson, won passage of most of the legislation under his own Great Society program (see next entry).

(*RD Encyc. of Amer. Hist.*, 789; *WHAD*, 766)

**Q** **123. What was the Great Society?**

**A** The Great Society was President Lyndon Johnson's sweeping social reform program, enacted almost in its entirety by Congress during the mid-1960s. Among its many programs were Medicare, Medicaid, the Voting Rights Act, the War on Poverty, the Elementary and Secondary Education Act, the Model Cities Program, and the Community Action Program. Many of Johnson's programs are still in existence and, despite concerns about rising costs, enjoy broad acceptance.

(*PAZ*, 198–9)

(*See 122 What did the New Frontier program try to do?*)

**Q 124. What are the requirements for serving as president and vice president?**

**A** The president must be a native-born citizen of the United States, a resident in the United States for fourteen years, and at least thirty-five years of age. Originally, there were no qualifications for the vice presidency, but the Twelfth Amendment, ratified in 1804, adopted those of the presidency.

(*PAZ, 25, 358; SOW, 57–8*)

(*See 402 Which presidents have been elected without winning the popular vote?*)

**Q 125. How long do the president and vice president serve?**

**A** Both the president and the vice president serve a four-year term of office. By tradition, presidents had never remained in office more than two terms until President Franklin Roosevelt served three full terms and part of a fourth during the 1930s and 1940s. That led to adoption of the Twenty-second Amendment in 1951, limiting presidents to two terms, or to one full term if they already had served more than two years of an unexpired term. The vice president has no such term limit.

(*PAZ, 413, 543–4*)

(*See 29 What do the amendments to the Constitution say, in brief?; 142 Who was the only president to serve more than two terms?; 146 Which president resigned?*)

**Q 126. When is inauguration day?**

**A** The president is inaugurated on January 20, though this was not always so. After our first president's first inauguration on April 30, 1789, the traditional date for presidential inaugurations became March 4th. That lasted until 1937, when the Lame Duck Amendment adjusted the president's term of office, moving the day back to an often chilly January 20.

(*PAZ, 413*)

(*See 37 What is the Lame Duck Amendment?*)

**127. Which president started the tradition of taking the oath of office with one hand on the Bible?**

A George Washington was the first, and since the mid-nineteenth century most presidents have followed suit. The Bible is sometimes opened to a passage selected by the new president.

(*PAZ*, 234–5)

(*See 86 What is the presidential oath of office?*)

Q **128. When did live television coverage of the president's inaugural address begin?**

A Live coverage began with President Harry S. Truman's address in 1949. Every inaugural address since then has been carried live.

(*Guide to Pres.*, 264)

(*See 155 Who was the first president heard on radio? Seen on TV?*)

Q **129. What happens if the president-elect dies or is incapacitated after the electoral college has voted but before inauguration?**

A According to the Twentieth Amendment, if the president-elect dies or is incapacitated after January 6, when Congress has certified the electoral college vote, the vice president-elect becomes president on inauguration day (January 20). However, that leaves out the period between the day in December when the electoral college votes and January 6. The Twentieth Amendment left the matter to Congress, which has never acted. So if during this window of time the president-elect dies, is disabled, withdraws, or is disqualified, there is no set procedure for picking his successor.

(*Guide to Pres.*, 340–1)

(*See 405 How does the electoral college work?*)

Q **130. What happens if the president dies after inauguration?**

A If the president dies, the vice president serves out the remainder of the president's term. The line of succession after the vice president was established in 1947, though it has never been invoked. Successors after the vice president are the Speaker of the

House, president pro tempore of the Senate, secretary of state, secretary of the treasury, secretary of defense, attorney general, and secretary of the interior, followed by the secretaries of agriculture, commerce, labor, health, housing, transportation, energy, education, and veterans affairs—in that order.

(*PAZ,* 123–5, 404)

(*See 203 Who was the first vice president to succeed to the presidency during his term?; 354 Who serves as the president pro tempore of the Senate, and what does the job involve?*)

### Q 131. What happens if the president is incapacitated after inauguration?

A When the president recognizes that he will be temporarily incapacitated because of surgery or medical illness, the vice president becomes acting president. To transfer his powers, the president sends a letter to the Speaker of the House and the president pro tempore of the Senate. Another letter declaring that the disability has ended restores the president to power. Should the president be unable or unwilling to notify Congress, the vice president and a majority of cabinet members can declare the president disabled. The vice president then becomes acting president. Once recovered, say from a serious accident, the president has only to notify Congress by letter to take office again. But if the vice president and a majority of cabinet members contend the president has not recovered—as in the case of mental illness, for example—Congress must decide the matter. A two-thirds vote by both houses of Congress is required to keep the president from returning to power. Two presidents— Garfield and Wilson—were seriously incapacitated before these provisions were enacted in the Twenty-fifth Amendment (1967). Vice President Bush became the first acting president in 1985, when President Reagan underwent cancer surgery.

(*PAZ,* 124–5)

(*See 187 Which first lady had the most influence over national affairs?*)

### Q 132. Which president had successful cancer surgery while in office and managed to keep it a secret?

A President Grover Cleveland, a cigar smoker, had his cancerous upper left jaw removed early in his second term. On taking office in 1893, Cleveland went to great lengths to hide his cancer, in part because an economic crisis loomed and he believed the news might panic the financial market. His advisers arranged the secret operation, which took place aboard a yacht anchored in New York's East River, ostensibly while President Cleveland was on vacation. Amazingly the press never uncovered more than a few sketchy details until long after Cleveland's death from a heart attack in 1908.

(*SOW*, 67)


**Q 133. What happens if the president resigns or is removed from office?**

**A** According to the Twenty-fifth Amendment, the vice president automatically becomes president in either event. The new president then appoints a vice president, subject to confirmation by a majority vote in both houses of Congress.

(*PAZ*, 544)

(*See 143 Who became president without having been elected to that office or to the vice presidency?; 145 Which president was impeached?; 146 Which president resigned?; 203 Who was the first vice president to succeed to the presidency during his term?; 207 How is a vacancy in the vice presidency filled?; 208 When has the country been without a vice president?*)


**Q 134. Which presidents died in office of natural causes?**

**A** (1) William H. Harrison died of pneumonia on April 4, 1841, soon after delivering the longest-ever inaugural address in a driving rain. His one-month presidency is the shortest in U.S. history. (2) President Zachary Taylor died on July 9, 1850, just sixteen months after taking office. He became ill and died after eating heavily during a long, hot Fourth of July ceremony at the Washington Monument. (3) President Warren G. Harding died in San Francisco on August 2, 1923, possibly of a heart attack. The Teapot Dome scandal may have contributed to his death. (4) Weakened by the strain of the wartime presidency, President Franklin Roosevelt collapsed and died of a cerebral hemorrhage on April 12, 1945, while at his Warm Springs, Georgia, vacation home.

(*PAZ*, 113, 203, 205, 374, 412)

(*See 77 What was the Teapot Dome scandal?; 204 Which vice presidents succeeded to the presidency?*)

**Q** **135. Which presidents were assassinated?**

**A** (1) President Abraham Lincoln was shot at Ford's Theater in Washington, D.C., on April 14, 1865, by the actor and Confederate sympathizer John Wilkes Booth. Lincoln died the next day. (2) A disgruntled office-seeker named Charles Guiteau shot President James A. Garfield in Washington on July 2, 1881. Garfield finally succumbed to his wounds on September 19, just months after taking office. (3) President William McKinley was shot in Buffalo, New York, on September 6, 1901, by an anarchist named Leon Czolgosz. McKinley suffered a stomach wound and died on September 14. (4) President John F. Kennedy was killed on November 22, 1963, by Lee Harvey Oswald, who shot at the president's motorcade in Dallas, Texas. All four assassins of presidents were themselves killed or executed.

(*PAZ*, 19–20, 113, 189, 291)

(*See 204 Which vice presidents succeeded to the presidency?*)

**Q** **136. Which presidents survived assassination attempts?**

**A** The first attempt was against President Andrew Jackson on January 30, 1835. He walked away unharmed after a demented house painter named Richard Lawrence drew two pistols and both misfired. On February 15, 1933, in Miami, Florida, President Franklin Roosevelt became the only president-elect ever shot at when a would-be assassin, Joseph Zangara, missed Roosevelt and killed Chicago mayor Anton Cermak. Next, two Puerto Rican nationalists failed in their attempt to shoot President Harry S. Truman on November 1, 1950. Two different women in California tried and failed to shoot President Gerald R. Ford—Lynette (Squeaky) Fromme on September 5, 1975, and Sara Jane Moore on September 22, 1975. Then on March 30, 1981, President Ronald Reagan and three others were wounded in Washington, D.C., by a gunman named John W. Hinckley, Jr.

(*PAZ*, 22, 185, 249, 363; *SOW*, 115–16)

(*See 135 Which presidents were assassinated?*)

## FOR THE RECORD—FIRSTS, ETC.

For more on presidents' backgrounds, personal lives, and careers after the White House, see other sections in this chapter.

**Q** **137. Who was the youngest person to be president?**

**A** Theodore Roosevelt, the youngest president, was just forty-two when he succeeded to the office on September 14, 1901, following President William McKinley's assassination. However, John F. Kennedy became the youngest person ever elected president. He was just four months shy of his forty-fourth birthday when he entered office on January 20, 1961.

(*PAZ*, 26, 263)


**Q** **138. Who was the oldest president?**

**A** President Ronald Reagan was the oldest of any president to date. He took office less than a month before his seventieth birthday and left office just before his seventy-eighth. President William H. Harrison was sixty-eight (he died within a month of delivering his inaugural address in the rain). Presidents Zachary Taylor and James Buchanan were sixty-five on taking office, and President George Bush was sixty-four.

(*PAZ*, 362, 508–9)


**Q** **139. Who was the first president to die in office?**

**A** William H. Harrison took office on March 4, 1841, and died on April 4 of the same year. His inaugural address was the longest ever delivered, and it probably was responsible for his death. Soaked by a driving rainstorm during the speech, he caught a severe cold and on March 27 was confined to bed with pneumonia. President Harrison died eight days later after serving just one month—the shortest term for any president.

(*PAZ*, 205)

(*See 134 Which presidents died in office of natural causes?*)


**Q** **140. Which president served the shortest time in office?**

**A** President William H. Harrison served only one month before dying in office. See the entry above.

(*PAZ*, 205)

(*See 134 Which presidents died in office of natural causes?*)

**Q** **141. Who was the only president to have served nonconsecutive terms?**

**A** Grover Cleveland was the only president who served nonconsecutive terms, 1885 to 1889 and 1893 to 1897. After winning his first term by a slim 60,000-vote margin, Cleveland lost his first reelection bid in 1888 to Benjamin Harrison in another close race. Cleveland actually won 100,000 more votes than Harrison but lost in the electoral college, 233 to 168. Four years later, Cleveland defeated Harrison by a comfortable margin of over 370,000 popular votes and 132 electoral votes.

(*PAZ, 79*)

(*See 402 Which presidents have been elected without winning the popular vote?; 405 How does the electoral college work?*)

**Q** **142. Who was the only president to serve more than two terms?**

**A** President Franklin Roosevelt served three terms and part of a fourth (1933–1937, 1937–1941, 1941–1945, 1945), and was the only president ever to serve more than two terms. Until Roosevelt, presidents traditionally did not seek office after their second term. But because in 1940 the country faced the threat of World War II, Roosevelt decided to break the tradition and run for a third term. Four years later he ran for a fourth term because the war still was not over.

(*PAZ, 372*)

(*See 125 How long do the president and vice president serve?*)

**Q** **143. Who became president without having been elected to that office or to the vice presidency?**

**A** Gerald R. Ford holds that distinction. After Vice President Spiro T. Agnew resigned in 1973 amid allegations of wrongdoing while a Maryland governor, President Richard M. Nixon named Ford vice president, in accordance with the Twenty-fifth Amendment. When Nixon himself resigned in 1974 because of the Watergate scandal, Ford became the president. Ford then named Nelson Rockefeller vice president to fill the resulting vacancy.

(*PAZ, 8, 169; SOW, 67*)

(*See 29 What do the amendments to the Constitution say, in brief?; 78 What happened in the Watergate scandal?*)

**144. When was the first attempt to impeach a president?**

A The House voted down its first presidential impeachment attempt January 10, 1843, quashing an effort to oust President John Tyler. The immediate cause for the impeachment motion was Tyler's veto of a Whig tariff bill, but Tyler and the Whig-dominated Congress had been feuding ever since he had succeeded William H. Harrison as president two years earlier. Tyler, a Whig himself, opposed many programs favored by congressional Whigs. For their part, they regarded Tyler as a mere acting president, while Tyler insisted he had full presidential powers as Harrison's successor.

(*PAZ*, 448; *RD Encyc. of Amer. Hist.*, 1146)

(*See 203 Who was the first vice president to succeed to the presidency during his term?; 266 What is impeachment?*)

Q **145. Which president was impeached?**

A Although Congress seriously considered impeaching Richard M. Nixon, the only president to have been impeached was Andrew Johnson. A southerner and a Democrat, Johnson was often at odds with the heavily Republican Congress once he succeeded to the presidency after Abraham Lincoln's assassination in 1865. On December 6, 1867, Johnson was charged with usurpation of power and corrupt use of power. This first impeachment attempt was overwhelmingly defeated. But Johnson later removed Secretary of War Edwin M. Stanton over the Senate's objections, and the House voted to impeach Johnson on February 24, 1868. On May 26, thirty-five senators voted guilty, but because thirty-six votes were needed to convict him, Johnson was acquitted.

(*PAZ*, 229–31)

(*See 266 What is impeachment?; 267 What is the procedure for impeaching an official?; 269 Who has been impeached by Congress?*)

Q **146. Which president resigned?**

A Richard M. Nixon resigned on August 9, 1974, before the House could vote to impeach him. The House Judiciary Committee had recommended that he be impeached for obstruction of justice, abuse of power, and contempt of Congress for his role in the Watergate scandal. Nixon was succeeded by his vice president, Gerald R. Ford.

(*PAZ*, 325, 367–8; *SCAZ*, 266)

(*See 78 What happened in the Watergate scandal?; 143 Who became president without having been elected to that office or to the vice presidency?*)

**Q 147. Who was the first Democratic president? The others?**

**A** Andrew Jackson became the first Democratic president when he took office in 1829. Since Jackson, thirteen other Democrats have become president: Martin Van Buren, James K. Polk, Franklin Pierce, Andrew Johnson, James Buchanan, Grover Cleveland, Woodrow Wilson, Franklin Roosevelt, Harry S. Truman, John F. Kennedy, Lyndon B. Johnson, Jimmy Carter, and Bill Clinton.

(*PAZ*, 340, 511–14)

(*See 389 When was the Democratic party founded?*)

**Q 148. Who was the first Whig president? The other?**

**A** William H. Harrison became the first Whig party president on March 4, 1841, but he is better known for another first—he was the first president to die in office. The Whig party, a generally conservative coalition that arose in reaction to President Andrew Jackson and his policies, did not fare much better with its second and last president, Zachary Taylor, who also died in office. The Whig party itself splintered and died after 1854.

(*PAZ*, 205; *WHAD*, 1131)

(*See 134 Which presidents died in office of natural causes?*)

**Q 149. Who was the first Republican president? The others?**

**A** The first Republican president was Abraham Lincoln, who took office in 1861 amid the oncoming crisis of the Civil War. Since Lincoln, sixteen Republicans have served as president: Ulysses S. Grant, Rutherford B. Hayes, James A. Garfield, Chester A. Arthur, Benjamin Harrison, William McKinley, Theodore Roosevelt, William H. Taft, Warren G. Harding, Calvin Coolidge, Herbert Hoover, Dwight Eisenhower, Richard M. Nixon, Gerald R. Ford, Ronald Reagan, and George Bush.

(*PAZ*, 512–14; *WHAD*, 897)

(*See 390 When was the Republican party founded?*)

**Q** **150. Who was the first Catholic president?**

**A** President John F. Kennedy in 1961 became the first Catholic to hold office. All other presidents to date have had Protestant backgrounds.

(*PAZ*, 26)

(*See 435 Who was the first Catholic nominated for president by a major party?*)


**Q** **151. Who was the first president to ask Congress to declare war?**

**A** After diplomatic efforts failed to resolve disputes with the British, James Madison became the first president to ask Congress for a declaration of war (June 1, 1812). Both the House (79 to 49) and the Senate (19 to 13) passed the measure, and Madison formally declared war on June 18. That began the War of 1812.

(*PAZ*, 464; *WHAD*, 337)

(*See 62 How many times has the United States declared war?*)


**Q** **152. What was the first presidential appointment ever made?**

**A** The charge d'affaires to France, William Short, was the first. President George Washington appointed him in June 1789.

(*FAP*, 10)

(*See 558 Which president appointed the most justices?*)


**Q** **153. Who was the first president to hold a press conference?**

**A** President Woodrow Wilson held the first press conference on March 15, 1913, less than two weeks after taking office. About 125 reporters attended the news conference in the White House executive office. Wilson also was the first president since John Adams to deliver the State of the Union Address to Congress.

(*FAP*, 175; *PAZ*, 345)

(*See 94 Which presidents have not delivered State of the Union addresses to Congress in person?; 111 How many press conferences have various presidents held?*)

**154. Who was the first president to have a press secretary?**

The first person officially designated as press secretary, George Akerson, served under President Herbert Hoover. But President Woodrow Wilson, who held the first press conferences, had an aide named Joseph P. Tumulty who advised him on the press and coordinated his schedule.

(*PAZ*, 347)

**155. Who was the first president heard on radio? Seen on TV?**

The first president heard by radio listeners was Warren G. Harding when he dedicated the Francis Scott Key Memorial in Baltimore on June 14, 1922. President Franklin Roosevelt became the first president seen on television when NBC broadcast his speech at the opening of the New York World's Fair on April 30, 1939. Some years later on January 19, 1955, President Dwight Eisenhower gave the first televised news conference, though it was filmed before broadcast. John F. Kennedy gave the first live presidential press conference on January 25, 1961.

(*CTC*, 860; *Encyc. of Amer. Facts & Dates*, 461, 586; *FAP*, 207)

(*See 128 When did live television coverage of the president's inaugural address begin?; 153 Who was the first president to hold a press conference?; 300 When did Congress first appear on television?; 415 Has each presidential election since 1960 included televised debates between the candidates?*)

**156. Who was the first president to travel abroad while in office?**

Theodore Roosevelt in 1906 became the first U.S. president to travel abroad. He visited Panama, where in 1903 he had won the United States rights to build the Panama Canal by backing the Panamanian revolt against Colombia. He also was the first president to ride in a car (1902) and the first to submerge in a submarine (1905).

(*SOW*, 105)

(*See 201 Who was the first vice president to make an official trip abroad?*)

**Q 157. Who was the first president to get a pension?**

**A** Harry S. Truman got the first presidential pension beginning in 1958. Until then former presidents got no retirement pay whatsoever, and Truman even paid his own train fare back to Independence, Missouri, when he left office in 1953. The first pension amounted to $25,000 per year, plus $50,000 a year for an office and staff. The presidential pension now is about six times the original sum, and various other benefits—including Secret Service protection and the presidential libraries—run into millions of dollars per year.

(*Guide to Pres.,* 839–40)

(*See 87 What does the president get paid?*)


## PRESIDENTS' BACKGROUNDS

See Presidents' Personal Lives section below for families with more than one president.

**Q 158. Which state has produced the most presidents?**

**A** Eight presidents were natives of Virginia, including four of the country's first five presidents. They were Washington, Jefferson, Madison, Monroe, W. H. Harrison, Tyler, Taylor, and Wilson. Ohio claims seven presidents as native sons—Grant, Hayes, Garfield, Benjamin Harrison, McKinley, Taft, and Harding. Four presidents were native-born New Yorkers—Van Buren, Fillmore, Theodore Roosevelt, and Franklin Roosevelt. Massachusetts had three native sons who became president—John Adams, John Q. Adams, and Kennedy.

(*VSAP,* 257–9)


**Q 159. Which colleges have produced the most presidents?**

**A** Harvard has produced five presidents, more than any other college (John Adams, John Q. Adams, both Roosevelts, and Kennedy). Both Yale and William and Mary claim three presidents (Taft, Bush, and Clinton; Jefferson, Monroe, and Tyler), while Princeton and West Point have two each (Madison and Wilson; Grant and Eisenhower). In all, thirty-two presidents attended college.

(*PAZ,* 26, 507–9)

(*See 575 Which colleges graduated the most justices?*)

**Q** **160. Which presidents never went to college?**

**A** Washington, Jackson, Van Buren, Taylor, Fillmore, Lincoln, Andrew Johnson, Cleveland, and Truman did not attend college.

(*PAZ*, 26, 434, 507–9; *SOW*, 96)


**Q** **161. Which president never attended a school of any type?**

**A** President Andrew Johnson grew up without any formal education. His parents could not read or write, and at age thirteen Johnson was apprenticed to a Raleigh, N.C., tailor. Fellow workers taught him to read and years later he also learned to write. By 1826 the young tailor had opened his own shop in Greenville, Tenn., and two years after that began his political career as a Greenville city council alderman.

(*PAZ*, 253–4)


**Q** **162. Who was the only president to have a Ph.D.?**

**A** President Woodrow Wilson was the only president to earn a doctorate, from Johns Hopkins.

(*PAZ*, 26)


**Q** **163. What experience have presidents had before being elected?**

**A** Twenty-seven presidents served in Congress or its predecessor, the Continental Congress. Nine served in both the House and the Senate—nine in the House alone and six in the Senate alone—but few have gone directly from Congress to the White House. Only James A. Garfield, Warren G. Harding, and John F. Kennedy can claim that distinction. Fourteen vice presidents made the jump to the presidency, either by succeeding to a president's term (nine) or by running after serving out their vice presidential term (five). Eighteen presidents, including Bill Clinton, were state governors; twenty-one gained experience in the state legislature; nine had diplomatic experience; and twelve were generals.

(*CAZ*, 154, 304; *VSAP*, 262)

(*See 143 Who became president without having been elected to that office or to the vice presidency?; 165 Which presidents have been generals?; 167 Which presidents were del-*

*egates to the Continental Congress?; 168 Who never held elective office before reaching the White House?; 169 Who became president after being elected to only one other office—the vice presidency?; 204 Which vice presidents succeeded to the presidency?; 378 Who was the only Speaker to serve as president?)*

**Q 164. What profession is most common for presidents?**

**A** Twenty-five presidents have been admitted to the bar, making law the most common profession. But only three of the last ten presidents have actually practiced law—Richard M. Nixon, Gerald R. Ford, and Bill Clinton. More than half of all presidents have had some farming experience, whether on a family farm, as a farm worker, or as an owner of a farm, ranch, or plantation.

(*PAZ*, 26)

**Q 165. Which presidents have been generals?**

**A** Twelve presidents served as generals before becoming president: George Washington, Andrew Jackson, William H. Harrison, Zachary Taylor, Franklin Pierce, Andrew Johnson, Ulysses S. Grant, Rutherford B. Hayes, James A. Garfield, Chester A. Arthur, Benjamin Harrison, and Dwight Eisenhower. Washington was a three-star general, Grant, a four-star, and Eisenhower, a five-star; each attained the highest possible rank for his time.

(*SOW*, 98)

**Q 166. Which presidents fought in which wars?**

**A** Twenty-six presidents have served in one or more wars. They are:

| | |
|---|---|
| Washington | American Revolution |
| Monroe | American Revolution |
| Jackson | American Revolution, Creek War, War of 1812, Seminole War |
| W. H. Harrison | Northwest Territory wars, Shawnee War, War of 1812 |
| Tyler | War of 1812 |
| Taylor | War of 1812, Seminole War, Black Hawk War, Mexican War |
| Pierce | Mexican War |
| Buchanan | War of 1812 |
| Lincoln | Black Hawk War |

| | |
|---|---|
| A. Johnson | Civil War |
| Grant | Mexican War, Civil War |
| Hayes | Civil War |
| Garfield | Civil War |
| Arthur | Civil War |
| B. Harrison | Civil War |
| McKinley | Civil War |
| T. Roosevelt | Spanish-American War |
| Truman | World War I |
| Eisenhower | World War I, World War II |
| Kennedy | World War II |
| L. Johnson | World War II |
| Nixon | World War II |
| Ford | World War II |
| Carter | Korean War |
| Reagan | World War II |
| Bush | World War II |

(*FAP*, 335–6)

## Q 167. Which presidents were delegates to the Continental Congress?

A George Washington, John Adams, Thomas Jefferson, James Madison, and James Monroe all served as delegates to the Continental Congress. However, only two of them, Washington and Madison, were delegates to the Constitutional Convention.

(*PAZ*, 4, 251, 293, 307, 472; *SOW*, 8)

## Q 168. Who never held elective office before reaching the White House?

A This distinction is shared by Presidents Taylor, Grant, Hoover, and Eisenhower. All except Hoover were war heroes—Taylor had been a key general in the Mexican War, Grant the most celebrated Union general in the Civil War, and Eisenhower the allied supreme commander during World War II. Hoover was not without his own military achievements. During and after World War I, he was widely recognized for his work as head of war relief organizations. He later was appointed to political posts, including secretary of commerce, but never even ran for election prior to his presidential bid.

(*PAZ*, 218, 507–9)

**Q 169. Who became president after being elected to only one other office— the vice presidency?**

**A** Chester A. Arthur became president in 1881, when President James A. Garfield was assassinated. Arthur had been vice president for only about six months. A lawyer and member of the New York Republican party machine, Arthur had held appointive posts, notably the prestigious position of collector of the port of New York, but had never run for election before winning the vice presidency in 1880.

(*PAZ*, 17–18)

**Q 170. Which presidents changed their names?**

**A** Seven presidents changed their names at some point before taking office. Hiram Ulysses Grant changed his name to Ulysses Hiram Grant when he enrolled at West Point, or so he thought. West Point recorded his name as Ulysses S. Grant, and Grant decided to adopt that instead. Calvin Coolidge was born John Calvin Coolidge but dropped his first name when he became an adult. Thomas Woodrow Wilson did likewise, becoming Woodrow Wilson. President Eisenhower also preferred his middle name, switching from David Dwight to Dwight David Eisenhower. Gerald R. Ford changed his name, originally Leslie Lynch King, Jr., when his divorced mother remarried. He took his adoptive father's name to become Gerald R. Ford, Jr. As an adult James Earl Carter, Jr., kept his childhood nickname Jimmy and became the first president to use a nickname in office. At age fifteen, William Jefferson Blythe changed his last name to Clinton, adopting his stepfather's last name.

(*Facts on File 1992*, 520; *PAZ*, 63, 99, 184, 194–5, 488; *SOW*, 106–7)

## AFTER THE WHITE HOUSE

**Q 171. Who is the only president to serve on the Supreme Court after leaving the White House?**

**A** William Howard Taft became the only former president to sit on the high court when President Warren G. Harding, a fellow Republican, appointed him chief justice in 1921. Taft served from 1921 to 1930, retiring just one month before his death.

(*PAZ*, 102; *SCAZ*, 413–14)

**Q** 172. Which president served in the Senate after leaving the White House?

**A** Andrew Johnson was the only former president to serve in the Senate. The Tennessee legislature elected him senator in 1874, but Johnson died of a stroke on July 31, 1875, just five months after being sworn in.

(*PAZ*, 255; *The Senate*, 229)

**Q** 173. Which president served in the House after leaving office?

**A** In 1830, two years after losing his reelection bid, former president John Q. Adams was elected to the House as a representative from Massachusetts. The only president to serve in the House after leaving the White House, Adams continued to represent Massachusetts until his death in 1848.

(*PAZ*, 7)

(*See 176 Who was the only president whose son also became president?*)

**Q** 174. Which former president was elected to the Confederate Congress?

**A** When the Civil War broke out in 1861, President John Tyler, a Virginia native, had already been out of office for over fifteen years. After declaring his allegiance to the South, he was elected to the Confederate Congress in November 1861. Tyler died on January 18, 1862, before taking his seat.

(*PAZ*, 438)

**Q** 175. When were most former presidents alive?

**A** Twice now, five former presidents have all been alive at the same time. Most recently, it was true between January 20, 1993—when President George Bush joined the ranks of four other living former presidents (Ronald Reagan, Jimmy Carter, Gerald R. Ford, and Richard M. Nixon)—and Nixon's death on April 22, 1994. It also was true between March 1861 and January 1862, when Martin Van Buren, John Tyler, Franklin Pierce, Millard Fillmore, and James Buchanan were alive. Tyler died in January 1862, followed by Van Buren some months later.

(*PAZ*, 185, 438, 444)

## PRESIDENTS' PERSONAL LIVES

**Q 176. Who was the only president whose son also became president?**

**A** John Adams, the second president, and John Q. Adams, the sixth, are the only father and son who have both held the office. They each served only one term, John Adams from 1797 to 1801 and his son John Quincy from 1825 to 1829.

(*PAZ*, 3–6, 503)

**Q 177. Which president's grandfather was also president?**

**A** President Benjamin Harrison was the grandson of President William H. Harrison. Benjamin, the twenty-third president, served one term from 1889 to 1893. His grandfather, the ninth president, died in office on April 4, 1841, after serving only one month.

(*PAZ*, 203, 205, 503–5; *SOW*, 95)

(*See 140 Which president served the shortest time in office?*)

**Q 178. Which presidents were distant cousins?**

**A** The twenty-sixth president, Theodore Roosevelt, was a distant cousin—and an uncle by marriage—of the thirty-second president, Franklin Roosevelt. Theodore's brother Elliott was Eleanor Roosevelt's father. The twelfth president, Zachary Taylor, was a second cousin of the fourth, James Madison.

(*SOW*, 95–6)

**Q 179. Who was the only president never to have married?**

**A** President James Buchanan was the first bachelor elected and the only president who never married.

(*PAZ*, 25–6, 35)

**Q 180. Which presidents were bachelors when elected?**

**A** Presidents Thomas Jefferson, Martin Van Buren, Andrew Jackson, and Chester A. Arthur all entered the White House as widowers. President Grover Cleveland married after taking office and President James Buchanan never married.

(*PAZ*, 25–6)

**Q 181. Which presidents got married while in office?**

**A** After the death of his first wife in 1842, President John Tyler married a New York socialite, Julia Gardiner, in New York on June 26, 1844. President Grover Cleveland married his former law partner's daughter in a White House ceremony on June 2, 1886, making him the only president married in the executive mansion. President Woodrow Wilson's first wife died in the White House in 1914. Over a year later, on December 18, 1915, Wilson married Edith Bolling Galt, a widow.

(*PAZ*, 80, 437, 490–1)

(See 187 Which first lady had the most influence over national affairs?)

**Q 182. Who was the first divorced president?**

**A** Ronald Reagan was the first divorced president, though by the time he took office he had been remarried for almost twenty-nine years. Reagan and his first wife, actress Jane Wyman, divorced in 1948 after an eight-year marriage. Four years later, on March 4, 1952, Reagan married Nancy Davis. President Andrew Jackson was the first president married to a divorcee, but she died before his inauguration. The first divorced first lady in the White House was President Warren G. Harding's wife, Florence Kling de Wolfe Harding. She had married Harding in 1891.

(*PAZ*, 26, 182, 202, 362; *SOW*, 108)

**Q** **183. Which president supported an illegitimate child?**

**A** President Grover Cleveland fathered and supported an illegitimate child, a fact that came to light during his 1884 campaign for the presidency. Admitting his paternity after a newspaper broke the story, he instructed his campaign workers to "tell the truth." Cleveland staved off partisan attacks on this and other issues to win the election, but just barely. His margin of victory amounted to only 60,000 votes.

(*PAZ*, 80)

**Q** **184. Which president lived the longest?**

**A** President John Adams lived well into his ninetieth year, dying on July 4, 1826, about four months shy of his ninety-first birthday. President Herbert Hoover missed Adams's mark by just a few months. The second oldest former president, Hoover died on October 20, 1964, two months into his ninetieth year. Four other presidents died in their eighties—Thomas Jefferson (83), James Madison (85), John Q. Adams (80), and Harry S. Truman (88). In September 1994, Ronald Reagan, at 83, was the oldest of our four living former presidents, but only by two years. Gerald Ford was 81.

(*World Almanac 1993*, 471)

(*See 216 Which vice president lived the longest?; 325 Who was the oldest member of Congress?; 552 Who was the oldest justice to serve?*)

**Q** **185. Which presidents died on the Fourth of July?**

**A** Two former presidents, Thomas Jefferson and John Adams, both died on July 4, 1826. It was the fiftieth anniversary of the Declaration of Independence, which both men had worked on and signed. In 1831, just over six years after leaving office, James Monroe became the only other president to die on July 4.

(*PAZ*, 5, 308)

## FIRST LADIES

 **186. Who was the first president's wife to be called "first lady"?**

President Grant's wife, Julia, was the first to be called "first lady." Various earlier attempts at titles for the president's wife, such as "Mrs. President," "presidentress," and "Lady Washington" all had failed to catch on. But Julia Grant and her highly visible successor, Lucy Hayes, helped firmly establish the now traditional title of first lady.

(*SOW,* 108)

**187. Which first lady had the most influence over national affairs?**

Edith Wilson, President Woodrow Wilson's second wife, virtually controlled the government for several months while her husband recovered from a stroke in 1919. During that time she screened his papers and closely guarded access to him. Other first ladies also have been considered powerful public figures, however, with Eleanor Roosevelt and Abigail Adams generally ranked as among the most influential. Today, Hillary Rodham Clinton is recognized as a forceful first lady.

(*PAZ,* 180; *SOW,* 109)

(*See 131 What happens if the president is incapacitated after inauguration?*)

**188. What does the first lady get paid?**

The first lady earns no salary and holds no official position, but she is an important public figure who helps shape public perceptions of the president's administration. She manages the White House domestic staff and is the official hostess for social functions. The first lady oversees administrative and domestic staffs that total less than thirty people.

(*PAZ,* 179–80, *SOW,* 108–9)

(*See 191 How many people are on the first lady's staff now?*)

**189. Which first lady was first to hire her own press agent?**

 In 1844 Julia Tyler, John Tyler's second wife, became the first president's wife to hire a press agent.

(*PAZ*, 179)

(*See 154 Who was the first president to have a press secretary?*)

**Q** **190. Which first lady was first to hire her own staff to answer mail and press questions?**

**A** In 1901 Theodore Roosevelt's wife Edith became the first to hire an aide. Previously, first ladies had relied on the president's staff for answering mail and press questions.

(*PAZ*, 180; *SOW*, 108)

**Q** **191. How many people are on the first lady's staff now?**

Hillary Rodham Clinton's administrative staff numbered thirteen in early 1994.

(*SOW*, 108; *White House, Office of the First Lady*)

(*See 188 What does the first lady get paid?*)

**Q** **192. Which first lady had the most children?**

**A** President William H. Harrison's wife, Anna Tuthill Symmes Harrison, had the most children—six boys and four girls. President John Tyler's first wife, Letitia, and President Rutherford B. Hayes's wife, Lucy, had eight children each. But President Tyler's first and second wives together produced the biggest presidential family. Letitia Tyler gave birth to three boys and five girls, and Julia Tyler, the president's second wife, bore him another five boys and two girls—fifteen children in all.

(*FAP*, 59, 64, 121, 324)

**Q** **193. Did any of the first ladies not have any children?**

**A** Three first ladies never had children. President Andrew Jackson's wife, Rachel Donelson Robards Jackson, had no children by either her earlier marriage or her marriage to Jackson. Both President James K. Polk's wife, Sarah Childress Polk, and President Woodrow Wilson's second wife, Edith Bolling Galt Wilson, also were childless. Three other first ladies had children by earlier husbands but none by their presidential spouses: George Washington's wife, Martha; James Madison's wife, Dolley; and Warren G. Harding's wife, Florence.

(*FAP,* 72, 324)

## VICE PRESIDENTS

Which presidents and vice presidents served when? See 84. What are the requirements for serving as president and vice president? See 124.

**Q** **194. Who originated the term *veep* for vice president?**

**A** Vice President Alben W. Barkley's grandson referred to him as the "veep" because, the *New York Times* noted in 1949, "Mr. Vice President" was too cumbersome. *Veep* caught on and remained in use even after Barkley left office in 1953.

(*Dict. of Amer. Slang,* 564; *PAZ,* 28)

(*See 83 Who thought of the names* president *and* vice president?)

**Q** **195. What does the vice president get paid?**

**A** The vice president earns a salary of $171,500 a year, has an expense account of $10,000 a year, and has at his disposal limousines and *Air Force Two,* the vice presidential plane. The vice president has an official residence (since 1977), the Admiral's House on the U.S. Naval Observatory grounds; and three offices, one in the White House West Wing, one in the Old Executive Office Building, and another on Capitol Hill.

(*Guide to Cong.,* 841–42; *SOW,* 272)

(*See 87 What does the president get paid?*)

**Q** **196. What does the vice president do?**

**A** The vice president replaces the president should the chief executive die, resign, become disabled, or be removed from office (nine vice presidents have succeeded to the presidency). While this is the vice president's most important role, it is far from the only one. Within the executive branch, the vice president serves on the National Security Council, sits in on cabinet meetings, has regular meetings with the president, undertakes diplomatic missions, and promotes the president's policies. The vice president also serves as president of the Senate and casts the deciding vote on a bill in the event of a tie. Though this Senate position is largely ceremonial, the vice president does act as a liaison between the president and Congress, lobbying on behalf of legislation sought by the administration.

(*CAZ*, 405–8; *PAZ*, 451–6)

**Q 197. Which vice presidents have cast the deciding vote in the Senate?**

**A** John Adams, the nation's first vice president, cast twenty-nine tie-breaking votes during his two terms, largely because there were only twenty-two senators at the time. Some years later John Calhoun voted twenty-eight times to break ties, but succeeding vice presidents broke ties much less frequently. By 1993 vice presidents had cast deciding votes a total of only 225 times. The vice presidents and the number of ties they broke are:

| Vice president | Tie-breaking votes cast |
| --- | --- |
| John Adams | 29 |
| Thomas Jefferson | 3 |
| Aaron Burr | 3 |
| George Clinton | 11 |
| Elbridge Gerry | 8 |
| Daniel D. Tompkins | 5 |
| John C. Calhoun | 28 |
| Martin Van Buren | 4 |
| Richard M. Johnson | 14 |
| John Tyler | 0 |
| George M. Dallas | 19 |
| Millard Fillmore | 3 |
| William R. King | 0 |
| John Breckinridge | 10 |
| Hannibal Hamlin | 7 |
| Andrew Johnson | 0 |
| Schuyler Colfax | 13 |
| Henry Wilson | 1 |
| William Wheeler | 5 |
| Chester A. Arthur | 3 |
| Thomas Hendricks | 0 |
| Levi P. Morton | 4 |

| | |
|---|---|
| Adlai Stevenson | 2 |
| Garret A. Hobart | 1 |
| Theodore Roosevelt | 0 |
| Charles Fairbanks | 0 |
| James S. Sherman | 4 |
| Thomas Marshall | 4 |
| Calvin Coolidge | 0 |
| Charles G. Dawes | 2 |
| Charles Curtis | 3 |
| John N. Garner | 3 |
| Henry A. Wallace | 4 |
| Harry S. Truman | 1 |
| Alben W. Barkley | 7 |
| Richard M. Nixon | 8 |
| Lyndon B. Johnson | 0 |
| Hubert H. Humphrey | 4 |
| Spiro T. Agnew | 2 |
| Gerald R. Ford | 0 |
| Nelson Rockefeller | 0 |
| Walter F. Mondale | 1 |
| George Bush | 7 |
| Dan Quayle | 0 |
| Al Gore (through August 1994) | 3 |

(*CAZ*, 473; *The Senate*, 640–6)

**Q 198. How many people work on the vice president's staff?**

**A** The vice president's staff has increased in recent years as the responsibilities of the office have grown. During the Bush administration, for example, the vice president's staff numbered over seventy, and in many ways it mirrored the president's own staff. Vice President Dan Quayle had a national security adviser, a chief of staff, a press secretary, an issues staff, an appointments secretary and scheduling team, and an advance team.

(*Guide to Pres.*, 842)

(*See 89 How many people work in the Executive Office of the President?*)

**Q** **199. Which vice president was the first to serve as acting president?**

**A** Vice President George Bush became the first to serve in this capacity in 1985, when President Ronald Reagan underwent surgery. Bush served only eight hours as acting president in accordance with provisions of the Twenty-fifth Amendment covering temporary incapacitation of the president. When President Reagan was shot in 1981, presidential aides blocked a move to implement the transfer, fearing such a move might cause confusion and make the president appear weak.

(*PAZ*, 455)

(*See 29 What do the amendments to the Constitution say, in brief?; 131 What happens if the president is incapacitated after inauguration?*)

**Q** **200. When did the practice of including the vice president in cabinet meetings become firmly established?**

**A** The vice president regularly attended cabinet meetings during Franklin Roosevelt's presidency and has done so in every administration since then.

(*PAZ*, 453)

**Q** **201. Who was the first vice president to make an official trip abroad?**

**A** John N. Garner, President Franklin Roosevelt's vice president, became the first in 1935. He traveled to the Philippines for the inauguration of its first president under the newly established commonwealth government, and then visited Mexico on a goodwill mission.

(*Guide to Pres.*, 915; *WHAD*, 843)

(*See 156 Who was the first president to travel abroad while in office?*)

**Q** **202. Who was the first vice president to head a presidential commission?**

**A** Vice President Richard M. Nixon became the first in 1953 when President Dwight Eisenhower named him chairman of the new Government Contracts Commission. Eisenhower had formed the commission to monitor and end racial discrimination in federal contracting. Later, Nixon also chaired another presidential commission, the Cabinet Committee on Price Stability for Economic Growth.

(*Guide to Pres.*, 913; *PAZ*, 456)

**Q** **203. Who was the first vice president to succeed to the presidency during his term?**

**A** Vice President John Tyler became the first on April 6, 1841, after President William H. Harrison died just one month into his term. Tyler set the precedent, followed ever since, of the vice president serving out a deceased president's term. Until then it was unclear whether the vice president would become an acting president or serve out the term as president.

(*PAZ*, 436–8)

(See 130 What happens if the president dies after inauguration?; 139 Who was the first president to die in office?)

**Q** **204. Which vice presidents succeeded to the presidency?**

**A** Following are the nine vice presidents who moved into the White House unexpectedly when the president died or resigned:

John Tyler became president on April 6, 1841, following the death of President William H. Harrison two days earlier. Neither party nominated Tyler for a new term in 1844, and he soon after abandoned an independent reelection bid.

Millard Fillmore served just over a year and four months as vice president before President Zachary Taylor died on July 9, 1850. Fillmore was sworn in the following day. Fillmore failed to gain the Whig party nomination in 1852.

Andrew Johnson served just over a month as vice president before President Abraham Lincoln's assassination on April 15, 1865. Johnson was sworn in the same day and served out Lincoln's term.

Chester A. Arthur, vice president from March 4 to September 20, 1881, was sworn in as president after James A. Garfield succumbed to the wound from an assassin's bullet. Arthur served out the remainder of Garfield's term but failed to gain the Republican nomination in 1884.

Just six months after Theodore Roosevelt became vice president, President William McKinley was assassinated. Roosevelt succeeded to the presidency on September 14, 1901, served out McKinley's term, and in 1904 became the first vice president to win a term of his own after succeeding to the presidency. He backed Taft's election in 1908, then failed to win an election bid in 1912.

Vice President Calvin Coolidge was vacationing in Vermont when word of President Warren G. Harding's death on August 2, 1923, reached him. Sworn in August 3, Coolidge served out Harding's term and went on to win a term of his own in 1924. He declined to run again in 1928.

Harry S. Truman had been vice president for less than three months when President Franklin Roosevelt died and he succeeded to the presidency (April 12, 1945). After serving out Roosevelt's term, Truman ran as the underdog in 1948 and won another term in a surprise victory. He declined to run again in 1952.

Vice President Lyndon B. Johnson was riding a car behind the president's when John F. Kennedy was assassinated in Dallas on November 22, 1963. Sworn in that day, Johnson served out Kennedy's term and went on to win one of his own in 1964. By 1968, however, opposition to the Vietnam War and widespread social unrest at home forced him to drop plans for running again.

Appointed to the vice presidency December 6, 1973, because of Spiro T. Agnew's forced resignation, Gerald R. Ford succeeded to the presidency just eight months later when Richard M. Nixon resigned because of the Watergate scandal (August 9, 1974). Ford served out Nixon's term, then lost his bid for a term of his own.

(*PAZ*, 18, 100, 178, 255, 257–8, 376, 436, 437)

(*See 84 Which presidents and vice presidents served when?; 130 What happens if the president dies after inauguration?; 131 What happens if the president is incapacitated after inauguration?; 133 What happens if the president resigns or is removed from office?; 134 Which presidents died in office of natural causes?; 135 Which presidents were assassinated?; 143 Who became president without having been elected to that office or to the vice presidency?; 146 Which president resigned?*)

**Q  205. Which vice presidents resigned from office?**

**A**  Only two vice presidents have ever resigned: John C. Calhoun and Spiro T. Agnew. Calhoun, a strong states' rights advocate, resigned over political differences with President Andrew Jackson. President Richard M. Nixon's first vice president, Agnew resigned October 10, 1973, amid charges of having accepted bribes while serving as the Maryland governor. In a plea bargain, Agnew pleaded no contest to income tax evasion but was not prosecuted further.

(*PAZ*, 8–9, 57, 503)

(See 146 Which president resigned?; 207 How is a vacancy in the vice presidency filled?)


**Q  206. Which vice presidents died in office?**

**A**  Following are the seven vice presidents who died before finishing their terms:

James Madison's first vice president, George Clinton, died at age seventy-two on April 12, 1812.

James Madison's second vice president, the seventy-year-old Elbridge Gerry, also died in office. Gerry passed away on November 23, 1814, after serving less than two years.

Vice President William R. King, sixty-seven, died of tuberculosis on April 18, 1853, after serving under Franklin Pierce for just twenty-five days.

Ulysses S. Grant's second vice president, the sixty-three-year-old Henry Wilson, died of a stroke on November 22, 1875, after about two and one-half years in office.

Eight months after taking office under Grover Cleveland, Vice President Thomas Hendricks died at age sixty-six on November 25, 1885.

President William McKinley's first vice president, Garret A. Hobart, completed almost three years of his term before dying at age fifty-five on November 21, 1899.

James S. Sherman, vice president under William H. Taft, died on October 30, 1912, about four months before finishing his term. Sherman, fifty-seven, is the only vice president, thus far, to die in office in the twentieth century.

(*PAZ*, 81–2, 191–2, 209–10, 217–18, 266–7, 384–5, 487–8, 503–6; *World Almanac 1993*, 472)

(See 208 When has the country been without a vice president?)

## Q 207. How is a vacancy in the vice presidency filled?

**A** The Twenty-fifth Amendment, ratified in 1967, provides for filling vacancies caused by the vice president's succession to the presidency as well as by his resignation, death, or removal from office. When a vacancy occurs, the president selects, and Congress confirms, the new vice president. A majority vote in both houses is required for confirmation. Before 1967 no procedure for naming new vice presidents existed, and, as a result, the office was left vacant sixteen times.

(*PAZ*, 404)

(*See 29 What do the amendments to the Constitution say, in brief?; 129 What happens if the president-elect dies or is incapacitated after the electoral college has voted but before inauguration?; 130 What happens if the president dies after inauguration?; 131 What happens if the president is incapacitated after inauguration?; 208 When has the country been without a vice president?*)

## Q 208. When has the country been without a vice president?

**A** Until ratification of the Twenty-fifth Amendment in 1967, the vice presidency became vacant when the vice president resigned, died, succeeded to the presidency, or was removed from office. Vacancies occurred eighteen times—seven because vice presidents died, two because they resigned, and nine because they succeeded to the presidency. The duration of and reason for each vice presidential vacancy are given below.

| Vacancy | Reason |
|---|---|
| April 12, 1812–March 4, 1813 | George Clinton, James Madison's first vice president, died. |
| November 23, 1814–March 4, 1817 | Elbridge Gerry, Madison's second vice president, died. |
| December 28, 1832–March 4, 1833 | John C. Calhoun, Andrew Jackson's vice president, resigned for political reasons. |
| April 6, 1841–March 4, 1845 | John Tyler, William H. Harrison's vice president, succeeded to the presidency. |
| July 10, 1850–March 24, 1853 | Millard Fillmore, Zachary Taylor's vice president, succeeded to the presidency. |

| | |
|---|---|
| April 18, 1853–March 4, 1857 | William R. King, Franklin Pierce's vice president, died. |
| April 15, 1865–March 4, 1869 | Andrew Johnson, Abraham Lincoln's second vice president, succeeded to the presidency. |
| November 22, 1875–March 4, 1877 | Henry Wilson, Ulysses S. Grant's second vice president, died. |
| September 20, 1881–March 4, 1884 | Chester A. Arthur, James A. Garfield's vice president, succeeded to the presidency. |
| November 25, 1885–March 4, 1889 | Thomas Hendricks, Grover Cleveland's vice president, died. |
| November 21, 1899–March 4, 1901 | Garret A. Hobart, William McKinley's first vice president, died. |
| September 14, 1901–March 4, 1905 | Theodore Roosevelt, McKinley's second vice president, succeeded to the presidency. |
| October 30, 1912–March 4, 1913 | James S. Sherman, William H. Taft's vice president, died. |
| August 3, 1923–March 4, 1925 | Calvin Coolidge, Warren G. Harding's vice president, succeeded to the presidency. |
| April 12, 1945–January 20, 1949 | Harry S. Truman, Franklin Roosevelt's third vice president, succeeded to the presidency. |
| November 22, 1963–January 20, 1965 | Lyndon B. Johnson, John F. Kennedy's vice president, succeeded to the presidency. |
| October 10, 1973–December 6, 1973 | Spiro T. Agnew, Richard M. Nixon's first vice president, resigned; Gerald R. Ford was appointed vice president. |
| August 9, 1974–December 19, 1974 | Gerald R. Ford, Nixon's second vice president, succeeded to the presidency when Nixon resigned; Nelson Rockefeller was appointed vice president. |

(*PAZ*, 503–6)

*(See 84 Which presidents and vice presidents served when?; 130 What happens if the president dies after inauguration?; 134 Which presidents died in office of natural causes?; 135 Which presidents were assassinated?; 143 Who became president without having been elected to that office or to the vice presidency?; 146 Which president resigned?)*

**Q 209. Who was the youngest vice president elected?**

**A** Vice President John Breckinridge, who served under President James Buchanan, was the youngest. He was just thirty-six when elected in 1856.

(*PAZ*, 30)

*(See 137 Who was the youngest person to be president?)*

**Q 210. Who was the oldest vice president elected?**

**A** Harry S. Truman's vice president, Alben W. Barkley, was the oldest. A thirty-six-year veteran of Congress, he was seventy-one when he took office in 1949.

(*PAZ*, 28)

*(See 138 Who was the oldest president?; 221 Which vice president served longest in Congress?)*

**Q 211. Which vice president served the longest?**

**A** Four vice presidents share this distinction, each having served eight years. They were: Daniel D. Tompkins, under President James Monroe (1817–1825); Thomas Marshall, under President Woodrow Wilson (1913–1921); Richard M. Nixon, under President Dwight Eisenhower (1953–1961); and George Bush, under President Ronald Reagan (1981–1989). John Adams served two terms under President George Washington, but his term of service was just shy of eight years, beginning on April 30, 1789, and ending on March 4, 1797. Another vice president who served a little less than eight years was John N. Garner. Garner, who twice was Franklin Roosevelt's vice president, served from March 4, 1933, to January 20, 1941.

(*PAZ*, 503–6)

*(See 84 Which presidents and vice presidents served when?; 126 When is inauguration day?)*

**Q 212. Which vice president served the shortest term?**

**A** President Franklin Pierce's vice president, William R. King, served the shortest term—just twenty-five days. King, who had traveled to Cuba in hopes of curing his tuberculosis, was sworn in there on March 24, 1853. He died in Alabama less than a month later, on April 18. Vice President John Tyler served only slightly longer— thirty-three days, from March 4 to April 6, 1841. Vice President Andrew Johnson served just forty-two days. Other vice presidents who served only a few months or less were Chester A. Arthur, Thomas Hendricks, Theodore Roosevelt, Harry S. Truman, and Gerald R. Ford.

(*PAZ*, 503–6; *SOW*, 123)

(*See 84 Which presidents and vice presidents served when?; 204 Which vice presidents succeeded to the presidency?*)

**Q 213. Which vice presidents served under more than one president?**

**A** Former New York Governor George Clinton served as vice president in two administrations, those of Thomas Jefferson (1805–1809) and James Madison (1809–1812). Clinton died in 1812 before completing his second term, becoming the first vice president to die in office. John C. Calhoun, the noted South Carolina Congressman and states' rights advocate, also was vice president during two administrations, serving under Presidents John Q. Adams (1825–1829) and Andrew Jackson (1829–1832). Calhoun became the first vice president to resign the office when he stepped down just two months before his term expired.

(*SCAZ*, 56; *PAZ*, 56–7, 83)

(*See 205 Which vice presidents resigned from office?; 211 Which vice president served the longest?*)

**Q 214. Which vice president killed a man while in office?**

**A** Thomas Jefferson's vice president, Aaron Burr, shot and killed political rival Alexander Hamilton in a duel at Weehawken, New Jersey, on July 11, 1804. His term as vice president nearly over, Burr had entered the New York gubernatorial race in 1804 but had lost to a candidate backed by Hamilton. Burr challenged Hamilton to the duel over negative remarks made during the campaign; the contest over, Burr fled back to Washington, D.C. Resuming his duties as vice president, Burr simply ignored

New Jersey and New York arrest warrants—criminals could not then be extradited from the District of Columbia.

(*PAZ*, 47–8)

### Q 215. Which vice president was tried for treason?

A Shortly before leaving office in 1805, Vice President Aaron Burr began plotting a wild scheme that called for inciting a revolt in the western United States and for the military conquest of Mexico. His goal was to create an empire of his own with New Orleans as its capital. Captured after assembling some sixty to eighty men, he was tried for treason in 1807 with Chief Justice John Marshall presiding. Burr won an acquittal because he had not yet committed an act of treason.

(*RD Encyc. of Amer. Hist.,* 162–3; *PAZ*, 48)

### Q 216. Which vice president lived the longest?

A Franklin Roosevelt's first vice president, John N. Garner, was two weeks shy of his ninety-ninth birthday when he died on November 7, 1967. Garner lived longer than any other vice president or president, but he was not alone in reaching his nineties. Former Vice President Levi Morton died at ninety-six.

(*PAZ*, 190; *World Almanac 1993*, 471–2)

(*See 184 Which president lived the longest?; 325 Who was the oldest member of Congress?* )

### Q 217. Which state has produced the most vice presidents?

A New York was the birthplace of eight vice presidents, more than any other state. They were: George Clinton, Daniel D. Tompkins, Martin Van Buren, Millard Fillmore, Schuyler Colfax, William Wheeler, Theodore Roosevelt, and James S. Sherman.

(*FAP,* 415)

(*See 158 Which state has produced the most presidents?*)

**Q** **218. Which vice president held no other elective office?**

**A** The only elective office Henry A. Wallace, President Franklin Roosevelt's second vice president, ever won was the vice presidency in 1940. Before that, Wallace had served as Roosevelt's secretary of agriculture from 1933 to 1940. Lasting only one term as vice president, he later made an unsuccessful third-party bid for the presidency and retired from politics.

(*PAZ*, 462)

**Q** **219. Which vice presidents have also been senators?**

**A** Twenty-two vice presidents have also been senators. They are listed below.

| Vice President | Years in Senate | Years as vice president |
|---|---|---|
| Aaron Burr | 1791–1797 | 1801–1805 |
| John C. Calhoun | 1832–1843, 1845–1850 | 1825–1832 |
| Martin Van Buren | 1821–1828 | 1833–1837 |
| Richard M. Johnson | 1819–1829 | 1837–1841 |
| John Tyler | 1827–1836 | 1841 |
| George M. Dallas | 1831–1833 | 1845–1849 |
| William R. King | 1819–1844, 1848–1852 | 1853 |
| John Breckinridge | 1861 | 1857–1861 |
| Hannibal Hamlin | 1848–1857, 1857–1861, 1869–1881 | 1861–1865 |
| Andrew Johnson | 1857–1862 | 1875 1865 |
| Henry Wilson | 1855–1859, 1859–1873 | 1873–1875 |
| Thomas Hendricks | 1863–1869 | 1885 |
| Charles Fairbanks | 1897–1905 | 1905–1909 |
| Charles Curtis | 1907–1913, 1915–1929 | 1929–1933 |
| Harry S. Truman | 1935–1945 | 1945 |
| Alben W. Barkley | 1927–1949, 1955–1956 | 1949–1953 |
| Richard M. Nixon | 1950–1953 | 1953–1961 |
| Lyndon B. Johnson | 1949–1961 | 1961–1963 |
| Hubert H. Humphrey | 1949–1964, 1971–1978 | 1965–1969 |

| Vice President | Years in Senate | Years as vice president |
|---|---|---|
| Walter F. Mondale | 1964–1976 | 1977–1981 |
| Dan Quayle | 1981–1989 | 1989–1993 |
| Al Gore | 1985–1993 | 1993– |

(*The Senate*, 230)

(See 163 What experience have presidents had before being elected?; 172 Which president served in the Senate after leaving the White House?)

**Q 220. Which vice presidents served in the House?**

**A** Twenty-four vice presidents were former House members. They are listed below.

| Vice President | Years in House | Years as vice president |
|---|---|---|
| Elbridge Gerry | 1789–1793 | 1813–1814 |
| John C. Calhoun | 1811–1817 | 1825–1832 |
| Richard M. Johnson | 1807–1819, 1829–1837 | 1837–1841 |
| John Tyler | 1817–1821 | 1841 |
| William R. King | 1811–1816 | 1853 |
| Millard Fillmore | 1833–1835, 1837–1843 | 1849–1850 |
| John Breckinridge | 1851–1855 | 1857–1861 |
| Hannibal Hamlin | 1843–1847 | 1861–1865 |
| Andrew Johnson | 1843–1853 | 1865 |
| Schuyler Colfax | 1855–1869 | 1869–1873 |
| William Wheeler | 1861–1863, 1869–1877 | 1877–1881 |
| Thomas Hendricks | 1851–1855 | 1885 |
| Levi P. Morton | 1879–1881 | 1889–1893 |
| Adlai Stevenson | 1875–1877, 1879–1881 | 1893–1897 |
| James S. Sherman | 1887–1891, 1893–1909 | 1909–1912 |
| Charles Curtis | 1893–1907 | 1929–1933 |
| John N. Garner | 1903–1933 | 1933–1941 |
| Alben W. Barkley | 1913–1927 | 1949–1953 |
| Richard M. Nixon | 1947–1950 | 1953–1961 |
| Lyndon B. Johnson | 1937–1949 | 1961–1963 |
| Gerald R. Ford | 1949–1973 | 1973–1974 |
| George Bush | 1967–1971 | 1981–1989 |

| Dan Quayle | 1977–1981 | 1989–1993 |
| Al Gore | 1977–1985 | 1993– |

(*FAP*, 423–4; *PAZ*, 503–6)

*(See 163 What experience have presidents had before being elected?; 173 Which president served in the House after leaving office?)*

**Q 221. Which vice president served longest in Congress?**

**A** Before becoming vice president under Harry S. Truman, Alben W. Barkley amassed thirty-six consecutive years of experience in Congress, more than any other vice president. Barkley served in the House from 1913 to 1927, and then in the Senate from 1927 to 1949. In 1955 he returned to the Senate for another year before dying of a stroke during a speaking engagement.

(*PAZ*, 27–8)

*(See 163 What experience have presidents had before being elected?; 172 Which president served in the Senate after leaving the White House?; 173 Which president served in the House after leaving office?; 210 Who was the oldest vice president elected?)*

**Q 222. Which vice presidents served in the Continental Congress?**

**A** Four vice presidents served in the Continental Congress (John Adams, Thomas Jefferson, George Clinton, and Elbridge Gerry), but only Gerry served in both the Continental Congress and the U.S. Congress.

(*FAP*, 423)

*(See 163 What experience have presidents had before being elected?; 221 Which vice president served longest in Congress?)*

## CABINET

**Q 223. What is the cabinet?**

**A** The cabinet is an advisory group headed by the president and consisting of the vice president, the fourteen executive department heads, officials holding cabinet rank, and any others the president may invite. The cabinet has been part of every administration, but each president decides what its role will be. And though some presidents have promised to make the cabinet a decision-making body, it usually has functioned only as an advisory board. Members' diverse responsibilities and competing interests have made full cabinet meetings unwieldy; presidents have addressed this problem by turning to a smaller group of close advisors such as senior White House aides or members of their ``inner cabinet''—the secretaries of state, defense, and treasury, and the attorney general. But individual cabinet members do meet with the president privately to offer advice on policy matters relating directly to their own departments.

(*PAZ*, 51–6)

**Q 224. When were the departments represented in the cabinet created?**

**A** Congress created the first three departments—State, War, and Treasury—along with the post of attorney general in 1789. The other eleven cabinet departments were formed as follows:

| | |
|---|---|
| Interior | Established as a cabinet department in 1849. |
| Justice | Organized as a cabinet department in 1870, under the attorney general's control. |
| Agriculture | Created in 1862 and given cabinet status 1889. |
| Labor | Created as a bureau in and given cabinet status as part of the Commerce and Labor Department in 1903. Made a separate cabinet department in 1913. |
| Commerce | Established as part of the Commerce and Labor Department in 1903. Made a separate cabinet department in 1913. |
| Health and Human Services | Begun as the Federal Security Agency in 1939 and made the cabinet department of Health, Education, and Welfare in 1953. The current name was adopted in 1979 after the creation of a separate Education Department. |
| Housing and Urban Development | Organized as a cabinet department in 1965. |
| Transportation | Formed as a cabinet department in 1966. |
| Energy | Organized in 1977, in response to the energy crisis. |

| Education | Created as an agency in 1867, then made part of the Department of Health, Education, and Welfare in 1953. Became a separate cabinet department in 1979. |
| Veterans Affairs | Begun as the Veterans' Bureau in 1921, then reorganized as a cabinet department in 1988. |

(*PAZ*, 9, 85–6, 134, 159, 208, 223, 242–3, 260, 271, 399, 427, 429, 446–7)

**Q 225. What does the Agriculture Department do?**

**A** Agriculture assists farmers by conducting extensive research in areas such as animal diseases and crop production as well as by granting farmers subsidies, credit, and rural development loans. The department also establishes quality standards for foods and oversees inspection of processing plants. It supports conservation programs, manages the national forests, and administers the food stamp, school lunch, and food for the needy programs.

(*PAZ*, 9–10)

**Q 226. What does the Commerce Department do?**

**A** Commerce promotes economic development, tourism, international trade, and dissemination of technological advances in business and industry. The department also studies the earth's physical environment, oversees weather forecasting, grants patents, and registers trademarks.

(*PAZ*, 85–6)

**Q 227. What does the Defense Department do?**

**A** Defense is responsible for guarding the national security. The largest cabinet department, it is composed of the army, the navy, and the air force, as well as many subordinate agencies and multiservice commands.

(*PAZ*, 115–17)

**228. What does the Education Department do?**

**A** Education administers the bulk of federal assistance to education, largely through grants to states. The department also monitors compliance with civil rights laws and funds research and demonstration projects.

(*PAZ*, 134–5)

**Q 229. What does the Energy Department do?**

**A** Energy administers federal energy programs, promotes energy conservation and new energy technology, and is responsible for a nuclear weapons program.

(*PAZ*, 158–9)

**Q 230. What does the Health and Human Services Department do?**

**A** Health and Human Services oversees many social programs, including Medicare and assistance to needy families. The department also is responsible for medical research and for food and drug inspection.

(*PAZ*, 208–9)

**Q 231. What does the Housing and Urban Development Department do?**

**A** Housing and Urban Development is concerned with the nation's housing needs. Federal Housing Administration mortgage assistance is among the department's many programs. Others include an association to assure an adequate supply of mortgage credit and programs to promote fair housing, assist with community and neighborhood development, and protect home buyers.

(*PAZ*, 223)

**Q 232. What does the Interior Department do?**

**A** Interior manages over 500 million acres of federal land and oversees the conservation and development of natural resources such as minerals, water, and fish and wildlife (but not national forests). The department also administers programs for native

Americans and manages hydroelectric power systems, irrigation projects in the West, and national scenic and historic areas.

(*PAZ*, 242–4)

**Q 233. What does the Justice Department do?**

**A** Justice, headed by the attorney general, acts as the nation's chief legal counsel and law enforcement officer. Through its subordinate agencies, the department investigates federal crimes, prosecutes offenders, and imprisons those who are found guilty. It also is responsible for maintaining domestic security, overseeing legal and illegal aliens, and policing narcotics trafficking. The department advises the president and others in the government on legal matters, and its attorneys represent the United States in all cases against the government that come before the Supreme Court.

(*PAZ*, 260–1)

**Q 234. What does the Labor Department do?**

**A** Labor is concerned with issues and programs affecting workers, including occupational health and safety, job training, minority employment, minimum wages, workers' compensation, unemployment insurance, and collective bargaining.

(*PAZ*, 271–2)

**Q 235. What does the State Department do?**

**A** State coordinates and provides overall direction for U.S. relations with foreign countries. The department serves as the president's primary means of negotiating with foreign leaders and provides information, analysis, and advice on foreign relations.

(*PAZ*, 399–400)

**Q 236. What does the Transportation Department do?**

**A** Transportation coordinates national transportation policy and includes nine operating administrations: the Federal Highway, Federal Railroad, Federal Aviation, National Highway Traffic Safety, Urban Mass Transportation, and Maritime Administrations as well as the U.S. Coast Guard, the Saint Lawrence Seaway Development Corporation, and the Research and Special Programs Administration.

(*PAZ*, 426–7)

## Q 237. What does the Treasury Department do?

A Treasury manages the federal government's monetary resources, operates U.S. mints, regulates U.S. banks, collects taxes and customs duties, enforces tax and tariff laws, determines international economic policy, and oversees the Secret Service, which protects the president and investigates counterfeiting cases.

(*PAZ*, 429–30)

## Q 238. What does the Veterans Affairs Department do?

A Veterans Affairs is responsible for programs that benefit veterans and their families, including medical care (veterans' hospitals, nursing homes, and other facilities), home loan assistance (VA loans), disability compensation and rehabilitation, pensions, and education. The department also operates the national cemeteries.

(*PAZ*, 445–6)

## Q 239. What does the attorney general do?

A The attorney general is the nation's top legal officer, its chief law enforcement officer, and the head of the Justice Department. Within the Justice Department, the attorney general oversees the various divisions, including the antitrust, civil, criminal, and civil rights divisions. He or she also oversees the Federal Bureau of Investigation, which is the principal investigative arm of the department, and the solicitor general, who represents the United States before the Supreme Court. Department officials in turn monitor the activities of U.S. attorneys in the federal district courts and handle cases before the courts of appeals. The attorney general routinely helps the president screen possible judicial nominees for federal courts.

(*SCAZ*, 27–8)

(*See 602 What are the solicitor general's responsibilities?*)

**Q 240. Who were the first female, black, and Hispanic members of the cabinet?**

**A** President Franklin Roosevelt's labor secretary, Frances Perkins, became the first woman to hold a cabinet-level post in 1933. The first black cabinet member was Robert C. Weaver, President Lyndon B. Johnson's secretary of housing and urban development from 1966 to 1968. The first black woman to serve was Patricia Roberts Harris—President Jimmy Carter's health, education, and welfare secretary between 1977 and 1979. Education Secretary Lauro S. Cavazos, the first Hispanic cabinet member, served from 1988 to 1990 under Presidents Ronald Reagan and George Bush.

(*SOW*, 72–5)

(*See 328 Who were the first black, Hispanic, native American, female, Asian, Indian, and Hawaiian representatives and senators?; 562 Who was the first woman justice?; 564 Who was the first black justice?*)

**Q 241. Who served longest in the cabinet?**

**A** Agriculture Secretary James Wilson served continuously for almost sixteen years, more than any other cabinet member. Appointed by William McKinley in 1897, Wilson remained agriculture secretary through the administrations of Theodore Roosevelt and William H. Taft. He left office just one day shy of his sixteenth year of service.

(*FAP*, 403; *PAZ*, 525)

**Q 242. Who held the most cabinet posts?**

**A** The record belongs to Elliot L. Richardson, who held four cabinet posts under two presidents. He was Richard M. Nixon's health, education, and welfare secretary from 1970 to 1973, his defense secretary in 1973, and his attorney general in 1973. Richardson then served as President Gerald R. Ford's commerce secretary from 1976 to 1977.

(*FAP*, 403; *SOW*, 72)

**Q 243. Who served in the cabinet of the most presidents?**

**A** Henry L. Stimson did, having served under five presidents, four as war secretary and one as secretary of state. Stimson was war secretary from 1911 to 1913 under both William H. Taft and Woodrow Wilson, and later became Herbert Hoover's secretary of state from 1929 to 1933. During World War II Stimson returned to the cabinet as war secretary, serving from 1940 to 1945 under both Franklin Roosevelt and Harry S. Truman.

(*SOW,* 72)

**Q** **244. Which presidents once served in the cabinet?**

**A** Nine presidents served as a cabinet secretary before becoming the chief executive. They are listed below.

| President | Cabinet office | Years of service |
| --- | --- | --- |
| Thomas Jefferson | secretary of state | 1790–1793 |
| James Madison | secretary of state | 1801–1809 |
| James Monroe | secretary of state | 1811–1814, 1815–1817 |
| | secretary of war | 1814–1815 |
| John Q. Adams | secretary of state | 1817–1825 |
| Martin Van Buren | secretary of state | 1829–1831 |
| James Buchanan | secretary of state | 1845–1849 |
| Ulysses S. Grant | secretary of war | 1867–1868 |
| William H. Taft | secretary of war | 1904–1908 |
| Herbert Hoover | secretary of commerce | 1921–1928 |

(*FAP,* 333–4; *Guide to Pres.,* 1457; *PAZ,* 519–21, 525, 527)

(*163 What experience have presidents had before being elected?*)

**Q** **245. Who failed to be confirmed by the Senate for a cabinet post?**

**A** Only nine cabinet nominees have been rejected by the Senate, but others facing near certain defeat have withdrawn before a vote could be taken. Two nominees, Caleb Cushing and Charles B. Warren, lost more than one Senate vote. The rejected nominees are:

| | |
| --- | --- |
| 1834 | Roger B. Taney, for treasury secretary by Andrew Jackson |
| 1843 | Caleb Cushing, for treasury secretary by John Tyler (rejected three times) |

| 1844 | David Henshaw, for navy secretary by Tyler |
| 1844 | James M. Porter, for war secretary by Tyler |
| 1844 | James S. Green, for treasury secretary by Tyler |
| 1868 | Henry Stanbery, for attorney general by Andrew Johnson |
| 1925 | Charles B. Warren, for attorney general by Calvin Coolidge (rejected twice) |
| 1959 | Lewis L. Strauss, for commerce secretary by Dwight Eisenhower |
| 1989 | John Tower, for defense secretary by George Bush |

(*CAZ,* 16; *VSAP,* 280)

(*See 33 Who can appoint and remove officials in the executive branch?*)


**Q 246. When was the post office founded?**

**A** In July 1775, soon after the Revolution had begun, the Continental Congress established a colonial postal service to replace the British-run system. Benjamin Franklin, who had been postmaster general under the British, became the colonies' first postmaster general. Later, the Framers of the Constitution also recognized the need for a reliable postal system and mandated the creation of a federal post office in Article I, Section 8. In 1789 President George Washington appointed Samuel Osgood the first postmaster general under the Constitution. The postmaster at that time was a member of the president's cabinet.

(*Dict. of Amer. Hist.,* vol 5, 370–1)


**Q 247. When did the post office become a government-run corporation?**

**A** The federal Post Office Department, headed by a member of the president's cabinet, was converted to a government corporation on July 1, 1971. The change, backed by President Richard M. Nixon and enacted by Congress in 1970, culminated reform efforts to end massive government subsidies for the post office and to stop the hiring of postal workers based on political patronage. The new corporation, called the U.S. Postal Service, functions as an independent agency under the direction of a board of governors, who are appointed by the president. Hiring is based strictly on merit.

(*Dict. of Amer. Hist.,* vol 5, 374; *PAZ,* 194)

**Q** **248. Who originated the Monroe Doctrine?**

**A** President James Monroe's secretary of state, John Q. Adams, first proposed that the United States make an independent announcement of its opposition to new European colonies in Latin America. Monroe took the advice and turned down a British offer to make a joint U.S.-British declaration against further colonization. Then on December 2, 1823, Monroe outlined for the first time what became known as the Monroe Doctrine.

(*PAZ*, 308–9)

*(See 113 What is a presidential doctrine?; 114 What is the Monroe Doctrine?)*

# III

# CONGRESS

## IN GENERAL

**Q 249. What does Congress do?**

**A** Congress is the legislative branch. It makes the laws needed to run the federal government, determines which government agencies and programs will be created, and approves all funds spent by the government. While Congress has specific powers, such as the right to pass measures to collect taxes, raise armies, declare war, regulate commerce, and provide for the general welfare, it also can act more generally by passing any law necessary to execute the powers granted to it by the Constitution. As a legislative body, Congress cannot implement legislation; it can only enact it. The responsibility for implementation is left to the executive branch, which collects taxes, for example, and organizes and administers its many agencies. But Congress does retain oversight power and may investigate how the executive branch has administered the programs or laws Congress has approved.

(*CAZ*, 499–501; *RD Encyc. of Amer. Hist.*, 272–3; *WHAD*, 261–2)

(*See 35 What is the oversight power?; 93 What does the president do?; 466 What does the chief justice do?*)

**Q 250. What is a Congress?**

**A** Each two-year term of the U.S. Congress is called a Congress. Congresses are numbered consecutively from the 1st (1789–1791) to the current 103rd (1993–1995). A Congress always begins on January 3 of odd-numbered years and has two regular sessions, one each year beginning in January. All representatives, who serve just two-year terms, are sworn in as the first session opens. Only about a third of all senators (a Senate class) are sworn in at this time, as they serve staggered six-year terms. A session of Congress may continue for the entire year, and bills under consideration remain alive from one session to the next. Bills that have not been approved by the close of the Congress die automatically. Until ratification of the Twentieth Amendment in 1933, sessions of Congress began in December.

(*CAZ*, 392)

(*See 37 What is the Lame Duck Amendment?; 353 What are Senate classes?*)

Q **251. How many House seats did each state have on entering the Union?**

A With ten seats, Virginia claimed more than any of the other original thirteen states in 1789. Pennsylvania and Massachusetts each had eight. As of 1990, California had the most with 52, followed by New York with 31, and Texas with 30. The table below shows how seats have been apportioned over the years.

| STATE | YEAR OF STATEHOOD | NUMBER OF HOUSE SEATS | | | | |
|---|---|---|---|---|---|---|
| | | Year of statehood | 1850 | 1900 | 1950 | 1990 |
| Alabama | 1819 | 1 | 7 | 9 | 9 | 7 |
| Alaska | 1959 | 1 | — | — | — | 1 |
| Arizona | 1912 | 1 | — | — | 2 | 6 |
| Arkansas | 1836 | 1 | 2 | 7 | 6 | 4 |
| California | 1850 | 2 | 2 | 8 | 30 | 52 |
| Colorado | 1876 | 1 | — | 3 | 4 | 6 |
| Connecticut | 1789 | 5 | 4 | 5 | 6 | 6 |
| Delaware | 1789 | 1 | 1 | 1 | 1 | 1 |
| Florida | 1845 | 1 | 1 | 3 | 8 | 23 |
| Georgia | 1789 | 3 | 8 | 11 | 10 | 11 |
| Hawaii | 1959 | 1 | — | — | — | 2 |
| Idaho | 1890 | 1 | — | 1 | 2 | 2 |
| Illinois | 1818 | 1 | 9 | 25 | 25 | 20 |
| Indiana | 1816 | 1 | 11 | 13 | 11 | 10 |
| Iowa | 1846 | 2 | 2 | 11 | 8 | 5 |
| Kansas | 1861 | 1 | — | 8 | 6 | 4 |
| Kentucky | 1792 | 2 | 10 | 11 | 8 | 6 |
| Louisiana | 1812 | 1 | 4 | 7 | 8 | 7 |
| Maine | 1820 | 7 | 6 | 4 | 3 | 2 |
| Maryland | 1789 | 6 | 6 | 6 | 7 | 8 |
| Massachusetts | 1789 | 8 | 11 | 14 | 14 | 10 |

| STATE | YEAR OF STATEHOOD | NUMBER OF HOUSE SEATS | | | | |
|---|---|---|---|---|---|---|
| | | Year of statehood | 1850 | 1900 | 1950 | 1990 |
| Michigan | 1837 | 1 | 4 | 12 | 18 | 16 |
| Minnesota | 1858 | 2 | — | 9 | 9 | 8 |
| Mississippi | 1817 | 1 | 5 | 8 | 6 | 5 |
| Missouri | 1821 | 1 | 7 | 16 | 11 | 9 |
| Montana | 1889 | 1 | — | 1 | 2 | 1 |
| Nebraska | 1867 | 1 | — | 6 | 4 | 3 |
| Nevada | 1864 | 1 | — | 1 | 1 | 2 |
| New Hampshire | 1789 | 3 | 3 | 2 | 2 | 2 |
| New Jersey | 1789 | 4 | 5 | 10 | 14 | 13 |
| New Mexico | 1912 | 1 | — | — | 2 | 3 |
| New York | 1789 | 6 | 33 | 37 | 43 | 31 |
| North Carolina | 1789 | 5 | 8 | 10 | 12 | 12 |
| North Dakota | 1889 | 1 | — | 2 | 2 | 1 |
| Ohio | 1803 | 1 | 21 | 21 | 23 | 19 |
| Oklahoma | 1907 | 5 | — | — | 6 | 6 |
| Oregon | 1859 | 1 | — | 2 | 4 | 5 |
| Pennsylvania | 1789 | 8 | 25 | 32 | 30 | 21 |
| Rhode Island | 1789 | 1 | 2 | 2 | 2 | 2 |
| South Carolina | 1789 | 5 | 6 | 7 | 6 | 6 |
| South Dakota | 1889 | 2 | — | 2 | 2 | 1 |
| Tennessee | 1796 | 1 | 10 | 10 | 9 | 9 |
| Texas | 1845 | 2 | 2 | 16 | 22 | 30 |
| Utah | 1896 | 1 | — | 1 | 2 | 3 |
| Vermont | 1790 | 2 | 3 | 2 | 1 | 1 |
| Virginia | 1789 | 10 | 13 | 10 | 10 | 11 |
| Washington | 1889 | 1 | — | 3 | 7 | 9 |
| West Virginia | 1863 | 3 | — | 5 | 6 | 3 |
| Wisconsin | 1848 | 2 | 3 | 11 | 10 | 9 |
| Wyoming | 1890 | 1 | — | 1 | 1 | 1 |

(*GUSE*, 688; *Hist. Atlas*, 6–7; *VSAP*, 199–200)

**Q  252. Why do states sometimes gain or lose seats in Congress?**

**A**  Every ten years, following the national census, the 435 seats in the House of Representatives are reapportioned among the states according to the latest population figures. States with large population gains since the previous census get more seats; those with losses, or gains below the national average, get fewer seats. For example, following the 1990 census, California gained 7 seats and New York lost 3, reflecting an ongoing population shift to the Sun Belt states. Every state has at least 1 representative, and in the early 1990s California had the most, 52. Senate seats are fixed at two for each state by the Constitution.

(*CAZ*, 320–5, 379; *World Almanac 1994*, 620–1)

**Q  253. What happens when new districts must be drawn in a state?**

**A**  Redistricting is done by the state's legislature, which is required to increase or decrease the number of congressional districts when the census shows the state's population has changed. New districts must be drawn so that all have populations as nearly equal as possible. Redistricting that intentionally dilutes minorities is illegal, and districts also must be contiguous, with no isolated pockets. States with histories of past discrimination must submit redistricting plans to the Justice Department for review. (See also the next question.)

(*CAZ*, 322–5)

**Q  254. What are majority-minority districts?**

**A**  These districts are an outgrowth of efforts to ensure increased representation of blacks and other minority groups in Congress. During the redistricting that followed the 1990 census, some states—mostly in the South—tried to create districts where blacks and other minorities would be in the majority and so have a good chance of electing a minority member of Congress. The effort did result in more minority members being elected to Congress in 1992, but some especially odd-shaped majority-minority districts also drew court challenges against what was seen as racial gerrymandering. The Supreme Court's 1993 ruling on a North Carolina district in *Shaw v. Reno* held that districts created with race as the sole common interest could be found unconstitutional, and the case was returned to lower courts. By early 1994 challenges to majority-minority districts were also working their way through the courts in Florida, Georgia, Louisiana, and Texas.

(*CQ Weekly Report,* Feb. 19, 1994, 384–5)

**Q  255. What is a gerrymander?**

**A**  A voting district shaped to benefit a particular politician, party, or group of voters is called a gerrymander. The name comes from the 1812 state legislative district in Massachusetts that was designed to contain most of the state's Federalists, thus leaving the Antifederalists in the majority in all other districts. The Federalist district looked like a salamander, and was named a "GerryMander" after Governor Elbridge Gerry, who headed the Massachusetts Antifederalists. Gerrymandering recently became an issue when odd-shaped majority-minority districts were drawn by some states to increase minority representation in Congress. (See also the previous question.)

(*Amer. Cong. Dict.,* 122–3; *CAZ,* 160–1)

**Q  256. How much does a member of Congress get paid?**

**A**  Both senators and representatives earned salaries of $133,600 in 1993 and now are entitled to automatic cost-of-living increases each year. They also enjoy various perks, including the franking privilege, a travel allowance, free office space and a staff allowance ("clerk hire"), a generous pension plan, paid health insurance, and free parking. In 1991 the Senate joined the House in banning outside income from speeches and articles in exchange for the automatic cost-of-living increases.

(*CAZ,* 293; *SOW,* 155)

(*See 87 What does the president get paid?; 275 How did the frank get started, and can members of Congress frank all their mail?; 467 How much does a justice get paid?*)

**Q  257. What is the oath of office for a member of Congress?**

**A**  The oath for senators and representatives is the same. It reads: "I, (name), do solemnly swear (or affirm) that I will support and defend the Constitution of the United States against all enemies, foreign and domestic; that I will bear true faith and allegiance to the same; that I take this obligation freely, without any mental reservation or purpose of evasion, and that I will well and faithfully discharge the duties of the office on which I am about to enter. So help me God."

(*CAZ*, 278)

(*See 86 What is the presidential oath of office?; 543 What is the Court's oath of office?*)

## Q 258. What does the presiding officer do in the Senate? The House?

A In both houses the presiding officer—always a majority party member—oversees the floor debate. Members may speak only if recognized by the presiding officer, who, in consultation with the parliamentarian, also decides points of order. When the House is in regular session, the presiding officer is the Speaker. When the House meets as the Committee of the Whole, the Speaker appoints a majority party member as presiding officer. In the Senate the vice president is the official presiding officer, but he rarely oversees floor debate. The president pro tempore may preside in the absence of the vice president but usually does not. As a rule, freshman members take turns presiding.

(*CAZ*, 306)

(*See 196 What does the vice president do?; 292 What do the House and Senate parliamentarians do?; 295 What is a point of order?; 354 Who serves as the president pro tempore of the Senate, and what does the job involve?; 355 Who was the first woman to preside over the Senate?; 373 What does the Speaker do?; 383 What is the Committee of the Whole?*)

## Q 259. How many women have served in Congress?

A As of 1993, 159 women had served in Congress—138 in the House, 18 in the Senate, and 3 in both the House and the Senate. The first woman representative was Jeannette Rankin, a Montana Republican who served from 1917 to 1919 and from 1941 to 1943. Rebecca L. Felton served briefly as the first woman senator. Appointed to fill a vacancy in 1922, she gave up her seat after only one day so that the duly elected replacement could be sworn in. Hattie W. Caraway became the first woman senator to serve a full term. An Arkansas Democrat, she remained in office from 1931 to 1945.

(*CAZ*, 457–8)

(*See 328 Who were the first black, Hispanic, native American, female, Asian, Indian, and Hawaiian representatives and senators?; 329 Which female member of Congress served the longest?; 330 Who were the first women to chair committees in the House and*

**Q 260. Which blacks have served in Congress?**

**A** Eighty-seven blacks have been members of Congress—83 in the House and 4 in the Senate. Thirty-seven were House members and 1 held a Senate seat in 1993. Black members are listed below.

*Senate*

| | |
|---|---|
| 1870–71 | Hiram R. Revels, R-Miss. |
| 1875–81 | Blanche K. Bruce, R-Miss. |
| 1967–79 | Edward W. Brooke, R-Mass. |
| 1993– | Carol Moseley-Braun, D-Ill. |

*House*

| | |
|---|---|
| 1870–1879 | Joseph H. Rainey, R-S.C. |
| 1870–1871 | Jefferson F. Long, R-Ga. |
| 1871–1873 | Robert C. De Large, R-S.C. |
| 1871–1874 | Robert B. Elliott, R-S.C. |
| 1871–1873 | Benjamin S. Turner, R-Ala. |
| 1871–1876 | Josiah T. Walls, R-Fla. |
| 1873–1875; 1877–1879 | Richard H. Cain, R-S.C. |
| 1873–1877; 1882–1883 | John R. Lynch, R-Miss. |
| 1873–1875 | Alonzo J. Ransier, R-S.C. |
| 1873–1875 | James T. Rapier, R-Ala. |
| 1875–1877 | Jeremiah Haralson, R-Ala. |
| 1875–1877 | John A. Hyman, R-N.C. |
| 1875–1877 | Charles E. Nash, R-La. |
| 1875–1879; 1882–1883; 1884–1887 | Robert Smalls, R-S.C. |
| 1883–1887 | James E. O'Hara, R-S.C. |

*House*

| | |
|---|---|
| 1889–1893 | Henry P. Cheatham, R-N.C. |
| 1880–1891 | John M. Langston, R-Va. |
| 1890–1891 | Thomas E. Miller, R-S.C. |
| 1893–1895; 1896–1897 | George W. Murray, R-S.C. |
| 1897–1901 | George H. White, R-N.C. |
| 1929–1935 | Oscar De Priest, R-Ill. |
| 1935–1943 | Arthur W. Mitchell, D-Ill. |
| 1943–1970 | William L. Dawson, D-Ill. |
| 1945–1967; 1969–1971 | Adam Clayton Powell, Jr., D-N.Y. |
| 1955–1980 | Charles C. Diggs, Jr., D-Mich. |
| 1958–1979 | Robert N. C. Nix, D-Pa. |
| 1963–1991 | Augustus F. Hawkins, D-Calif. |
| 1965– | John Conyers, Jr., D-Mich. |
| 1969–1983 | Shirley Chisholm, D-N.Y. |
| 1969– | William L. Clay, D-Mo. |
| 1969– | Louis Stokes, D-Ohio |
| 1970–1972 | George W. Collins, D-Ill. |
| 1971– | Ronald V. Dellums, D-Calif. |
| 1971–1978 | Ralph H. Metcalfe, D-Ill. |
| 1971–1987 | Parren J. Mitchell, D-Md. |
| 1971– | Charles B. Rangel, D-N.Y. |
| 1973–1979 | Yvonne B. Burke, D-Calif. |
| 1973– | Cardiss Collins, D-Ill. |
| 1973–1979 | Barbara C. Jordan, D-Texas |
| 1973–1977 | Andrew Young, D-Ga. |
| 1975– | Harold E. Ford, D-Tenn. |
| 1979– | Julian C. Dixon, D-Calif. |
| 1979–1991 | William H. Gray III, D-Pa. |
| 1979–1989 | George T. Leland, D-Texas |
| 1979–1981 | Bennett McVey Stewart, D-Ill. |
| 1981–1991 | George W. Crockett, Jr., D-Mich. |
| 1981–1993 | Mervin M. Dymally, D-Calif. |
| 1981–1993 | Gus Savage, D-Ill. |
| 1981–1983 | Harold Washington, D-Ill. |

| 1983–1985 | Katie Hall, D-Ind. |
| 1983–1993 | Charles A. Hayes, D-Ill. |
| 1983– | Major R. Owens, D-N.Y. |
| 1983– | Edolphus Towns, D-N.Y. |
| 1983– | Alan Wheat, D-Mo. |
| 1986–1987 | Alton R. Waldon, Jr., D-N.Y. |
| 1987–1993 | Mike Espy, D-Miss. |
| 1987– | Floyd H. Flake, D-N.Y. |
| 1987– | John Lewis, D-Ga. |
| 1987– | Kweisi Mfume, D-Md. |
| 1989– | Donald M. Payne, D-N.J. |
| 1990– | Craig Washington, D-Texas |
| 1991– | Lucien E. Blackwell, D-Pa. |
| 1991– | Barbara-Rose Collins, D-Mich. |
| 1991– | Gary Franks, R-Conn. |
| 1991– | William J. Jefferson, D-La. |
| 1991– | Maxine Waters, D-Calif. |
| 1992– | Eva Clayton, D-N.C. |
| 1993– | Sanford Bishop, D-Ga. |
| 1993– | Corrine Brown, D-Fla. |
| 1993– | James E. Clyburn, D-S.C. |
| 1993– | Cleo Fields, D-La. |
| 1993– | Alcee L. Hastings, D-Fla. |
| 1993– | Earl F. Hilliard, D-Ala. |
| 1993– | Eddie Bernice Johnson, D-Texas |
| 1993– | Cynthia McKinney, D-Ga. |
| 1993– | Carrie Meek, D-Fla. |
| 1993– | Mel Reynolds, D-Ill. |
| 1993– | Bobby L. Rush, D-Ill. |
| 1993– | Robert C. Scott, D-Va. |
| 1993– | Bennie Thompson, D-Miss. |
| 1993– | Walter R. Tucker, D-Calif. |
| 1993– | Melvin Watt, D-N.C. |
| 1993– | Albert R. Wynn, D-Md. |

(*CAZ*, 459–60)

**261. Which Hispanics have served in Congress?**

A As of 1993, 31 Hispanics had been members of Congress—29 in the House only, 1 in the Senate only, and 1 in both the House and the Senate (Dennis Chavez, D-N.M., served in both houses). Hispanic members are listed below.

*Senate*

| 1935–1962 | Dennis Chavez, D-N.M. |
| 1964–1977 | Joseph Montoya, D-N.M. |

*House*

| 1877–1878;<br>1879–1883 | Romualdo Pacheco, R-Calif. |
| 1913–1927 | Ladislas Lazaro, D-La. |
| 1915–1917;<br>1919–1921 | Benigno Hernandez, R-N.M. |
| 1921–1923 | Nestor Montoya, R-N.M. |
| 1931–1935 | Dennis Chavez, D-N.M. |
| 1931–1941 | Joachim Fernandez, D-La. |
| 1943–1956 | Antonia Fernandez, D-N.M. |
| 1961– | Henry B. Gonzalez, D-Tex. |
| 1963–1993 | Edward R. Roybal, D-Calif. |
| 1965– | E. "Kika" de la Garza, D-Tex |
| 1969–1989 | Manuel Lujan, Jr., R-N.M. |
| 1971–1977 | Herman Badillo, D-N.Y. |
| 1978–1990 | Robert Garcia, D-N.Y. |
| 1979–1989 | Tony Coelho, D-Calif. |
| 1982– | Matthew G. Martinez, D-Calif. |
| 1983– | Solomon P. Ortiz, D-Tex. |
| 1983– | William B. Richardson, D-N.M. |
| 1983– | Esteban E. Torres, D-Calif. |
| 1985–1993 | Albert G. Bustamante, D-Tex |
| 1989– | Ileana Ros-Lehtinen, R-Fla. |
| 1990– | José E. Serrano, D-N.Y. |

| 1991– | Ed Pastor, D-Ariz. |
| 1993– | Xavier Becerra, D-Calif. |
| 1993– | Henry Bonilla, R-Tex. |
| 1993– | Lincoln Diaz-Balart, R-Fla. |
| 1993– | Luis V. Gutierrez, D-Ill. |
| 1993– | Robert Menendez, D-N.J. |
| 1993– | Lucille Roybal-Allard, D-Calif. |
| 1993– | Frank Tejeda, D-Tex. |
| 1993– | Nydia M. Velázquez, D-N.Y. |

(*CAZ*, 461)

(*See 334 Which Hispanic member of Congress has served the longest?*)

## Q 262. Which members of Congress have been expelled?

A Fifteen senators and four representatives have been expelled, all but two during the Civil War when southern states seceded. Expulsion, the removal of a representative or senator from office, is the harshest punishment Congress can impose on a member. Since the Civil War cases, the Senate has begun expulsion proceedings ten times and the House, fourteen. But only one representative has actually been expelled in that time, Pennsylvania Democrat Michael J. "Ozzie" Myers for involvement in the Abscam scandal. Eight accused representatives escaped with censure, and several members resigned to avoid expulsion. Expelled members are listed below.

*Senate*

1797   William Blount (Ind-Tenn.), for anti-Spanish conspiracy.

1861   James M. Mason (D-Va.), Robert M.T. Hunter (D-Va.), Thomas L. Clingman (D-N.C.), Thomas Bragg (D-N.C.), James Chestnut Jr. (States Rights-S.C.), Alfred O.P. Nicholson (D-Tenn.), William K. Sebastian (D-Ark.), Charles B. Mitchel (D-Ark.), John Hemphill (State Rights D-Texas), Louis T. Wigfall (D-Texas), and John C. Breckinridge (D-Ky.), all for supporting rebellion.

1862   Trusten Polk (D-Mo.), Jesse D. Bright (D-Ind.), and Waldo P. Johnson (D-Mo.), all for supporting rebellion.

*House*

1861    John B. Clark (D-Mo.), Henry C. Burnett (D-Ky.), and John W. Reid (D-Mo.), all for supporting rebellion.

1980    Michael J. "Ozzie" Myers (D-Pa.), for corruption.

(*CAZ,* 103–5, 462; *The Senate,* 669–72)

*(See 69 What was Abscam?)*

**Q** **263. Which members of Congress have been censured or reprimanded?**

**A** Ten senators and twenty-two representatives have been censured for various offenses, and two representatives have escaped censure with reprimands. Censure is a formal condemnation of a member's actions, read aloud in the chamber with the accused standing before the assembled legislators. The House uses the reprimand as a milder form of censure: the accused is not required to stand before the House members while the condemnation is read. In the Senate there is little difference between the terms *censured, condemned,* and *denounced.* Unless otherwise specified, the following members were censured:

*Senate*

1811    Timothy Pickering (Fed-Mass.), for breach of confidence

1844    Benjamin Tappan (D-Ohio), for breach of confidence

1902    John McLaurin (D-S.C.), for assault

1902    Benjamin R. Tillman (D-S.C.), for assault

1929    Hiram Bingham (R-Conn.), for bringing the Senate into disrepute (condemned)

1954    Joseph R. McCarthy (R-Wis.), for obstruction of the legislative process and other offenses (condemned)

1967    Thomas J. Dodd (D-Conn.), for financial misconduct

1979    Herman E. Talmadge (D-Ga.), for financial misconduct (denounced)

1990    Dave Durenberger (R-Minn.), for financial misconduct (denounced)

1991    Alan Cranston (D-Calif.), for improper conduct (reprimanded)

*House*

1832    William Stanbery (JD-Ohio), insulting the Speaker

1842    Joshua R. Giddings (Whig-Ohio), for writing an offensive paper

1856    Laurence M. Keitt (D-S.C.), for complicity in an assault on a senator

| 1864 | Alexander Long (D-Ohio), for a treasonable utterance |
|------|-----------------------------------------------------|
| 1864 | Benjamin G. Harris (D-Md.), for a treasonable utterance |
| 1866 | John W. Chanler (D-N.Y.), for insulting the House |
| 1866 | Lovell H. Rousseau (R-Ky.), for assaulting a representative |
| 1867 | John W. Hunter (Ind-N.Y.), for insulting a representative |
| 1868 | Fernando Wood (D-N.Y.), for an offensive utterance |
| 1868 | E. D. Holbrook (territ. del., D-Idaho), for an offensive utterance |
| 1870 | Benjamin F. Whittemore (R-S.C.), for corruption |
| 1870 | Roderick R. Butler (R-Tenn.), for corruption |
| 1870 | John T. Deweese (D-N.C.), for corruption |
| 1873 | Oakes Ames (R-Mass.), for corruption |
| 1873 | James Brooks (D-N.Y.), for corruption |
| 1875 | John Y. Brown (D-Ky.), for insulting a representative |
| 1890 | William D. Bynum (D-Ind.), for an offensive utterance |
| 1921 | Thomas L. Blanton (D-Texas), for abuse of leave to print |
| 1978 | Edward R. Roybal (D-Calif.), for lying to a House committee (reprimanded) |
| 1979 | Charles C. Diggs, Jr. (D-Mich.), for misusing clerk-hire funds |
| 1980 | Charles H. Wilson (D-Calif.), for financial misconduct |
| 1983 | Gerry E. Studds (D-Mass.), for sexual misconduct |
| 1983 | Daniel B. Crane (R-Ill.), for sexual misconduct |
| 1990 | Barney Frank (D-Mass.), for discrediting the House (reprimanded) |

(*CAZ*, 105–7, 464–5; *SOW*, 146–9)

## Q 264. What is exclusion?

A The House and Senate may prevent newly elected members from being seated if they do not meet the constitutional requirements for membership. Called exclusion, this disciplinary procedure once was used more widely to keep out members-elect charged with past misconduct. But in 1967 the flamboyant Rep. Adam Clayton Powell, Jr., challenged his exclusion. The Supreme Court's 1969 ruling in *Powell v. McCormack* limited exclusion to cases in which new members do not meet the constitutional requirements for age, citizenship, or residence in the proper state or district.

(*CAZ*, 108)

(*See 348 What are the requirements for being a senator?; 366 What are the requirements for being a representative?*)

**Q** **265. What is congressional immunity?**

**A** In theory, congressional immunity shields members of Congress from civil lawsuits and criminal charges relating to their official duties. In practice, congressional immunity is less clear-cut, and court cases have limited its scope, though not always consistently. The "speech and debate" clause in the Constitution appears to protect members from arrest while in the Capitol or while handling legislative duties. But in 1979 the Supreme Court ruled that legislators could be sued for libelous statements made in news releases or newsletters they sent out. The Court added that legislators could not be sued for statements made on the House or Senate floor. Congressional ethics committees monitor the behavior of legislators and may discipline them for improper conduct.

(*CAZ*, 103, 186–7)

**Q** **266. What is impeachment?**

**A** Impeachment is the bringing of charges to remove a high public official from office, but it does not necessarily mean the official will be removed. The impeachment process begins with the House of Representatives, which has the sole authority to bring impeachment charges. Only a simple majority is needed to approve the articles of impeachment. The Senate then tries the accused official, with a two-thirds majority needed to convict.

(*SOW*, 146)

*(See 145 Which president was impeached?; 269 Who has been impeached by Congress?)*

**Q** **267. What is the procedure for impeaching an official?**

**A** The House Judiciary Committee begins the impeachment proceedings by investigating the charges brought against an accused official. If the evidence warrants, the committee draws up articles of impeachment for consideration by the full House. Only a simple majority is required to approve the impeachment resolution, which when passed impeaches (accuses) the official. The Senate still must hold a trial before the official can be removed from office, however. The House selects several members to present the case, and senators take a special oath promising impartiality for the proceeding. The chief justice of the Supreme Court presides over the Senate if the president is being tried. The trial itself resembles a criminal hearing, with both the defendant and his or her accusers presenting witnesses and evidence. Afterward the Senate votes on each article of impeachment, and if any one receives a two-thirds vote, the defendant is convicted. (See also the next question.)

(*CAZ*, 188)

(*See 266 What is impeachment?*)

**Q 268. Can an official who has been impeached and convicted ever hold public office again?**

**A** The Constitution specifies that convicted officials may be removed from office and disqualified from holding further public office, but in the past the Senate has always considered disqualification separately. Only seven impeachment trials have resulted in convictions and removal from office. In three of those cases, the Senate voted separately on disqualification and approved it twice. Recently the separate vote proved crucial to Florida judge Alcee L. Hastings, who had been impeached and removed from office in 1989 for perjury and bribery. Hastings, acquitted in criminal court before his impeachment, won election to the House as a Democrat in 1992. He took his seat in 1993 because the Senate did not vote to disqualify him.

(*CAZ*, 189–90)

(*See Article I, Section 3, of the Constitution in the appendix.*)

**Q 269. Who has been impeached by Congress?**

**A** Though the House has started impeachment proceedings more than sixty times, it actually has impeached just sixteen federal officials—one president, one cabinet official, one senator, one Supreme Court justice, and twelve other federal judges. Seven federal judges were ultimately convicted and removed from office, but other officials resigned rather than face impeachment, among them President Richard M. Nixon. The sixteen impeached officials and the results of their trials are listed below.

| | |
|---|---|
| 1798–1799 | Sen. William Blount—charges dismissed after his expulsion |
| 1804 | Judge John Pickering (district court)—removed from office |
| 1805 | Supreme Court Justice Samuel Chase—acquitted |
| 1830–1831 | Judge James Peck (district court)—acquitted |

| 1862 | Judge West Humphreys (district court)—removed from office |
| 1868 | President Andrew Johnson—acquitted |
| 1873 | Judge Mark Delahay (district court)—resigned before his trial |
| 1876 | Secretary of War William Belknap—acquitted after his resignation |
| 1905 | Judge Charles Swayne—acquitted |
| 1912–1913 | Judge Robert Archbald (commerce court)—removed from office |
| 1926 | Judge George English (district court)—resigned, charges dismissed |
| 1933 | Judge Harold Louderback (district court)—acquitted |
| 1936 | Judge Halsted Ritter (district court)—removed from office |
| 1986 | Judge Harry Claiborne (district court)—removed from office. |
| 1989 | Judge Alcee L. Hastings (district court)—removed from office |
| 1989 | Judge Walter Nixon, Jr. (district court)—removed from office |

(*CAZ*, 187–90; *The Senate*, 731–3)

(*See 145 Which president was impeached?; 146 Which president resigned?; 266 What is impeachment?; 569 Who was the only justice to be impeached?*)

**Q** **270. How much of the annual budget goes to the legislative branch?**

**A** The budget for salaries to members of Congress, their staffs, and administrative and support personnel, as well as other operating expenses for the legislative branch, amounted to $2.9 billion for fiscal 1995. That amounted to less than two-thousandths of one percent of the total budget. Expenses for the legislature were expected to rise to $3.4 billion by fiscal 1999, according to 1994 estimates.

(*Budget of the U.S. Govt., Analyt. Perspectives*, 252)

(*See 52 How was federal money allocated in a recent budget?*)

**Q** **271. How many people work for Congress?**

**A** Almost 39,000 staffers and other support personnel worked for the legislative branch in November 1993. Among them were staff assistants for individual members of both houses, House and Senate committee staffers, employees of support agencies (General Accounting Office, Congressional Research Service, and others), and other support personnel, including the Capitol police and maintenance workers. About 12,000 worked as members' personal staff assistants, while the largest support agency, the

General Accounting Office, employed just over 5,000. House members are allowed apersonal staff of up to 22 people, while senators generally employ between 30 and 40.

(*CAZ*, 363–6; *Fed. Civ. Workforce Stats.*, 10; *VSC* 126–7)

(*See 11 How many people work for the federal government?; 60 What does the General Accounting Office do?*)

## Q 272. What is a shadow senator or representative?

A The practice of sending non-voting "shadow" representatives and senators to Congress dates from the early nineteenth century, when six territories preparing for admission as states sent shadow senators to Washington. Since 1990 the District of Columbia has had two shadow senators and one shadow representative, elected for the express purpose of lobbying Congress for District statehood.

(*CAZ*, 99)

(*See 6 Why is the District of Columbia not a state?*)

## Q 273. What do lobbyists do?

A As representatives of special interest groups, lobbyists work to pass laws favoring their clients and to defeat or alter bills that might harm them. Lobbying is not illegal, and groups such as the American Medical Association and the American Association of Retired Persons actively lobby Congress. Even presidents lobby Congress on behalf of their legislation. The First Amendment sanctions the right to petition Congress for "redress of grievances," and lobbyists can help the legislative process by providing members of Congress with data and accurate assessments of a bill's impact. Lobbyists also make campaign contributions—in part, to gain access to members—and over the years have resorted to other, less salutary means to win influence, such as special favors and lavish entertainment. Cases of outright bribery have been relatively rare.

(*CAZ*, 245–8; *SOW*, 255–60)

(*See 69 What was Abscam?*)

## Q 274. What is pork-barrel politics?

A First used in the early twentieth century, the term *pork-barrel politics* refers to those federal projects that benefit a particular lawmaker's district or state and are won by political clout rather than an objective assessment of need. Such projects often involve large sums of money and traditionally have included roads, bridges, and dams, but recently university research grants, defense contracts, and environmental cleanup projects also have been pork-barrel favorites. Several presidents have proposed a line-item veto to eliminate the pork-barrel projects usually tacked onto appropriations bills.

(*CAZ*, 299–300)

(*See 102 What is the line-item veto?*)

**Q 275. How did the frank get started, and can members frank all their mail?**

**A** Members of Congress can send their mail without a stamp—only their signature, or "frank," need appear on the envelope. Franking dates back to seventeenth-century Britain, where members of Parliament won the privilege to help them keep constituents fully informed. In 1775 the first Continental Congress adopted franking for the same reason, and it has been a congressional privilege ever since. Members of Congress, members-elect, the vice president, and certain House and Senate officers had almost unrestricted use of the frank until stricter controls were imposed in 1973. Today, only newsletters, government publications, responses to constituents' queries, and other materials connected with a legislator's official duties can be franked.

(*CAZ*, 155–6)

## MAKING LAWS AND DEBATING

**Q 276. How does a bill become law?**

**A** Most laws begin as similar proposals in both the House and Senate. In both chambers, once a bill is introduced, it is assigned to the appropriate committee (depending on the subject matter) and then often (especially in the House) to a subcommittee. The subcommittee reviews the bill, may hold hearings and amend the bill, and finally may recommend approval of the new version by the full committee. If it concurs, the full committee sends (reports) the bill, with any additional amendments it votes, to the floor for debate and a final vote. In the House, the bill first must pass through the Rules Committee before it goes to the floor. The House and Senate must approve the bill in identical form before sending it to the president, so any differences must be worked out in a conference committee. With the differences resolved, the president can then sign the bill, veto it, or pocket veto it. Once signed (or if the veto is overridden), the bill becomes a law. If the president does not sign or veto the bill within ten days while Congress is in session, the bill automatically becomes law. The enacted bill also may be called an act or, more formally, an act of Congress.

(*CAZ*, 233; *SOW*, 133)

(*See 95 What is a veto?; 96 What is a pocket veto?; 277 Can a bill be amended?; 309 What types of committees are there?; 311 What is a conference committee?; 312 What committees are there now in Congress?; 384 What does the House Rules Committee do?*)

### Q 277. Can a bill be amended?

A Bills can be amended at each stage of the legislative process. Amendments may be offered during the initial review of a new bill by a subcommittee ("marking up"), during review by the full committee, during floor action, or during conference, to resolve differences between House and Senate versions of the bill. A "substitute" amendment may be offered during floor debate to alter an earlier amendment. A provision on which House and Senate conferees cannot reach a compromise is called an "amendment in disagreement" and is sent back to the full chambers to be resolved. A conference compromise that violates the rules of one or both chambers is called an "amendment in technical disagreement." After accepting a partial conference report, each chamber votes separately on these two types of amendments. The bill will fail if agreement is not reached.

(*See 317 What is a mark-up session?*)

### Q 278. What is a legislative veto?

A Legislative vetoes—most of which have been declared unconstitutional—allowed Congress to reject programs and regulations recommended by the president or by executive departments and agencies. Written into some two hundred bills by the early 1980s, the vetoes variously gave one or both houses, and sometimes even a committee, the right to block a program or regulation, usually by acting within thirty to sixty days. The president generally had no right to approve or veto Congress's action once the initial bill was signed into law. Presidents since Herbert Hoover opposed legislative vetoes, and in 1983 the Supreme Court ruled unconstitutional all such vetoes that did not reach the president's desk for approval or veto. Some legislation has been rewritten to provide for presidential action, but in many cases Congress continues to exercise a legislative veto informally.

(*CAZ*, 240–1; *PAZ*, 277–8)

(*See 35 What is the oversight power?; 95 What is a veto?; 511 What did the Court rule in* Immigration and Naturalization Service v. Chadha?)

**Q 279. Can a law be overturned?**

**A** Congress can repeal the law, the Supreme Court can rule it unconstitutional, or a constitutional amendment can invalidate it. Congress rarely reverses itself, but there have been a few cases. For example, Congress in 1989 repealed a landmark expansion of the Medicare program, enacted amid great fanfare the previous year, after senior citizens angrily protested being forced to pay the entire costs of the new benefits. In addition to repealing a law outright, Congress can pass legislation that drastically revises and, in effect, supercedes an earlier law. The Supreme Court, exercising its power of judicial review, has struck down over 125 acts of Congress. That the process of amending the Constitution is a difficult one limits it as a means for overturning laws, but it has permitted passage of a small number of amendments. In 1933 the Twenty-first Amendment, for example, repealed Prohibition, which also had been enacted by constitutional amendment (the Eighteenth, in 1919).

(*Guide to Cong.*, 579; *SCAZ*, 433)

(*See 29 What do the amendments to the Constitution say, in brief?; 463 How many acts of Congress have been declared unconstitutional?; 485 What is judicial review?; 490 What is a test case?*)

**Q 280. What is the difference between a public and a private bill?**

**A** The subject of the bill determines whether it is classified as public or private. Public bills usually deal with matters affecting the general public or the government. Private bills usually deal with legislative relief for individuals, such as claims against the government and immigration cases. Both public and private bills become law when approved by Congress and signed by the president or enacted over his veto.

(*CAZ*, 46, 228)

**Q** **281. What is the difference between an authorization bill and an appropriations bill?**

**A** Authorization bills create new programs or continue existing ones for a specified period. These bills also may establish program policies and procedures or set a cap on program spending, but authorization bills never actually provide the money. That is done by an appropriations bill, which releases funds to operate a program through the current fiscal year. Though an authorization bill should be passed before money is appropriated, Congress often waives this rule.

(*CAZ*, 17, 24; *SOW*, 144)

(*See 47 How is the budget prepared?*)

**Q** **282. How does a joint resolution differ from a bill?**

**A** Joint resolutions are used for purposes other than general legislation and most often deal with such things as correcting errors in existing law, making a continuing appropriation, and establishing a permanent joint committee. Congress also uses joint resolutions for proposed constitutional amendments. Like bills, joint resolutions become law when enacted. The House and Senate consider and pass both bills and joint resolutions in the same manner, and except for proposed amendments, joint resolutions also must be signed by the president to become law. Amendments go directly to the states for ratification without the president's signature.

(*Amer. Cong. Dict.*, 139; *CAZ*, 288)

(*See 26 How can the Constitution be amended?*)

**Q** **283. What are resolutions and concurrent resolutions?**

**A** Resolutions and concurrent resolutions are internal measures that do not require the president's signature and do not become law. Resolutions are passed by only one house and usually deal with its routine "housekeeping" matters, such as revising standing rules. Concurrent resolutions, on the other hand, must be passed by both chambers and may deal either with routine internal matters or with wider issues. For example, Congress uses concurrent resolutions to fix the time of adjournment, to formalize "sense of Congress" resolutions on domestic and foreign issues, and to set annual spending goals.

(*Amer. Cong. Dict.*, 60; *CAZ*, 228)

**Q  284. What are continuing resolutions? How often are they used?**

**A** Continuing resolutions are interim funding bills. Congress uses them to keep government agencies operating when regular appropriations bills have not been enacted before October 1, the first day of the government's fiscal year. Congress has resorted to at least one continuing resolution every year from 1954 to 1993 (except 1988). Most have covered a few days or weeks, but for a time in the 1980s, Congress passed continuing resolutions lasting the entire fiscal year. Because of their urgency, continuing resolutions have become frequent targets for rider amendments.

(*CAZ*, 92–3)

(*See 47 How is the budget prepared?; 48 Why does the government's fiscal year begin in October?; 287 What is a rider?*)

**Q  285. Where can you find copies of laws? Of bills, with legislative histories?**

**A** The *United States Code* is a compilation of federal laws arranged by subject. Published every six years, it presents each law's most current version. *United States Code Congressional and Administrative News*, a monthly publication, provides the text of new laws as they are passed, along with amendments and changes to existing laws listed in the *United States Code*. Copies of slip laws with references to their legislative history—committee reports on the bill, proposed amendments, and other relevant documents—can be found in *United States Statutes at Large*, published by the Office of the Federal Register.

(*Legis. Drafter's DR*, 332–42, 392–4)

**Q  286. What is a clean bill?**

**A** A bill extensively amended in committee is usually reorganized into a new bill, called a clean bill. All changes, deletions, and additions, along with whatever is left of the original bill, are included in the new bill, which is renumbered and reintroduced into the chamber. This saves time during floor action—rather than having to vote on the original bill and on each change made to it, the House or Senate votes only once to approve the entire clean bill (if no further amendments are added).

(*Amer. Cong. Dict.*, 44; *CAZ*, 229)

(*See 317 What is a mark-up session?*)

**Q 287. What is a rider?**

**A** Amendments unrelated to the subject matter of a bill are called riders. They are considered fair play in the Senate, and, despite rules against them, they sometimes appear in House bills as well. Riders may be used as "sweeteners" to win approval of a bill, or they may be designed to arouse enough opposition to make sure it fails. Controversial legislation and provisions favoring special interest groups also may become riders. Urgent legislation, such as an emergency funding bill for the federal government, often attracts riders because it must be passed quickly. Tax and trade legislation also are frequent targets.

(*CAZ*, 334–5)

**Q 288. What is a Christmas tree bill?**

**A** Louisiana Democrat Russell B. Long claimed he originated this type of bill in 1966. As Senate Finance Committee chairman, he helped adorn a trade bill with unrelated special interest amendments (riders), which were likened to ornaments on a Christmas tree. His bill aided, among others, presidential candidates, hearse owners, and scotch whisky importers. Such bills, often enacted as Congress prepared to adjourn for the winter holidays, became less common in the 1980s. Legislators have since tacked special interest amendments onto emergency funding bills and other legislation likely to win approval.

(*CAZ*, 67–8)

(*See 287 What is a rider?*)

**Q 289. What does a floor manager do?**

**A** In the House and Senate, the floor manager guides a bill through the floor debate to a final vote. The chair of the committee or subcommittee handling the bill usually becomes the floor manager and operates from a designated aisle seat in the House or Senate. The committee's ranking minority party member often leads opposition to the bill. No matter what their personal views may be, floor managers must present their committees' bills in the best possible light and strive for passage without major changes.

(*CAZ*, 146)

**290. What are fast-track procedures?**

Changes in Senate or House rules to speed up the legislative process are called fast-track procedures. The Senate uses "unanimous consent agreements" to make such changes. The House speeds passage of legislation by suspending rules, adopting rules for special procedures, and other means.

*(Amer. Cong. Dict., 107)*

*(See 297 What is unanimous consent?)*

**291. What is a motion to table?**

When approved by a simple majority vote, this parliamentary device halts further action on amendments and bills. Among the most widely used parliamentary procedures, the motion to table is not debatable and often provides a way for legislators to avoid voting against a controversial bill; they vote to table it instead. Both the Senate and House use a parliamentary device called "tabling the motion to reconsider," which formally ends floor action on a bill or amendment. The Senate uses tabling motions to halt debate as well. When the House sits as the Committee of the Whole, it cannot use tabling motions.

*(CAZ, 326–7, 388)*

*(See 383 What is the Committee of the Whole?)*

**292. What do the House and Senate parliamentarians do?**

Considered two of the most powerful employees of Congress, parliamentarians advise the presiding officers of the House and Senate about parliamentary rules and precedents. They also advise individual members of Congress on procedures for routing legislation and decide which committees have jurisdiction over bills. In addition, parliamentarians compile precedents established in each chamber.

*(CAZ, 285)*

**293. What do the House and Senate sergeants-at-arms do?**

As the House and Senate police officers, the sergeants-at-arms enforce the rules and maintain order within their respective chambers. In addition, they are responsible for maintaining security within the Capitol and associated buildings and for supervising the Capitol police force. On rare occasions the sergeants-at-arms also have rounded up members for floor votes, physically bringing to the floor any member refusing to attend. The House sergeant-at-arms has charge of the mace (see the next question). The Senate has no comparable symbol of the sergeant-at-arms's authority.

(*CAZ*, 258–9, 355–6)

### Q 294. Has the House mace ever been used?

A The sergeant-at-arms has purposefully removed the mace—a forty-six-inch-long staff topped by a silver globe and an eagle with outstretched wings—from its pedestal to restore order on several occasions. Sometimes the Speaker has ordered the sergeant-at-arms to parade it up and down the aisles to quiet boisterous members. At other times, again on the Speaker's orders, the sergeant-at-arms has "presented" the mace directly before an unruly member. A traditional symbol of legislative authority, the mace was adopted by the House at its first session in 1789. It rests on a tall pedestal alongside the Speaker's desk when the House is in regular session, and on a lower pedestal when the House sits as the Committee of the Whole.

(*CAZ*, 258–9)

*(See 383 What is the Committee of the Whole?)*

### Q 295. What is a point of order?

A A House or Senate member may object if he or she believes rules governing the chamber's conduct of business are being violated. Called "raising a point of order," such an objection usually halts all parliamentary proceedings until the chair rules on the objection. The chair generally allows debate on the point before sustaining or overruling it, and the chair's decision may be reversed by the chamber's membership. Only a recorded vote cannot be stopped by raising a point of order.

(*CAZ*, 296)

### Q 296. What is a quorum?

A To transact business, both the House and Senate require a minimum number of members to be present, what is called a "quorum." Provided there are no vacant seats, a quorum in the Senate is 51 and in the House, 218—in each house a majority of the total membership. When the House sits as the Committee of the Whole, which it does to consider bills for amendment, the quorum is just 100 members. No matter how few members are present, a quorum is always assumed until a member asks for a quorum call. Then, during the roll call, members quickly stream into the chamber to make up the quorum.

(*CAZ*, 317)

(*See 383 What is the Committee of the Whole?*)

## Q 297. What is unanimous consent?

A Both chambers use unanimous consent to expedite floor action, especially on non-controversial bills. A unanimous consent request can be blocked by a single objection, but an objection is rarely raised in the case of routine matters. The House puts non-controversial bills on its Consent Calendar, passing them by unanimous consent when no one objects. For major legislation, the Senate often uses a "unanimous consent agreement" to limit debate, restrict amendments, and schedule votes.

(*CAZ*, 397)

(*See 307 What kinds of votes are there?; 386 What is the Consent Calendar?*)

## Q 298. Does the *Congressional Record* report what happens on the floors of the Senate and House?

A The *Record* publishes each chamber's debates, but members can edit their remarks before publication, correcting grammar and even deleting something. Members also can insert newspaper articles and speeches, but the *Record* will indicate material never really delivered on the floor. The *Record* also includes many of the members' votes and some scheduling information for future committee meetings and future debates.

(*CAZ*, 84–5, 136)

## Q 299. Who was the last president to attend Congress during a floor debate?

A President George Washington in 1789 was the first, and last, to do so. After the Senate balked at Washington's presence during debate on an Indian treaty he had presented personally, he made it a practice to stay away from the Capitol. In his place he sent cabinet members—Secretary of State Thomas Jefferson and Treasury Secretary Alexander Hamilton—to confer with legislators.

(*PAZ*, 87)

(*See 41 Who must agree to treaties between the United States and other countries?*)

**Q** **300. When did Congress first appear on television?**

**A** The first television coverage of the House chamber came in January 1947, when the House let cameras record the opening session of the 80th Congress. House leaders promptly barred any further television coverage of the chamber and committee activities, however. In following years, Senate committees made ample use of television, allowing coverage of the highly publicized Kefauver crime hearings (1950–1951), the sensational Army-McCarthy hearings (1954), and years later, the Senate Watergate hearings (1973), probably the most sensational to date. But fear of television coverage in Congress prevented regular broadcasts of floor debate in both chambers for decades. The House finally approved "gavel-to-gavel" coverage of its proceedings in 1979, and the Senate followed suit in 1986.

(*CAZ*, 390; *Guide to Congress*, 165, 357, 377)

(*See 128 When did live television coverage of the president's inaugural address begin?; 155 Who was the first president heard on radio? Seen on TV?; 410 When was the first political convention televised?; 415 Has each presidential election since 1960 included televised debates between the candidates?*)

## SESSIONS AND VOTES

**Q** **301. How does Congress adjourn?**

**A** Daily sessions of the House almost always end with adjournment, but for procedural reasons the Senate is more likely to recess. That continues the Senate's legislative day, which can go on for weeks until the chamber finally adjourns. Congress may adjourn briefly in mid-session for a holiday or vacation; this is called "adjournment to a day certain." To end a session of Congress, the House and Senate adjourn *sine die*, which is Latin for "without a day." Congress then meets next year on the day fixed for starting a new session, January 3.

(*CAZ*, 4–5)

**Q** **302. How are emergency sessions of Congress called?**

**A** The president, by proclamation, may convene an extraordinary (or special) session if the need arises after Congress has adjourned. Presidents have done so only five times since 1933, the last being in 1994, when President Bill Clinton recalled Congress to enact trade legislation. Congress also uses a device known as a "call back." During the Eightieth Congress (1947–1948), when there was no vice president, Congress adjusted its adjournment procedure to allow for a possible call back. It empowered the president pro tempore, Senate majority leader, House Speaker, and House majority leader to recall Congress should something happen to the president. Congress again activated the call-back option from 1973 to 1975 during the Watergate crisis, and in 1983, 1985, 1989, and 1990.

(*The Senate*, 449–51, 454–6)

(*See 78 What happened in the Watergate scandal?*)

**Q** **303. When has Congress been called into emergency session and why?**

**A** Presidents have called twenty-seven emergency sessions of Congress. Each of them is given below.

| Congress, session | Called by (president) | Reason | Date convened– date adjourned |
|---|---|---|---|
| 5th, 1st | Adams | Break in relations with France | May 15–July 10, 1797 |
| 8th, 1st | Jefferson | Spain ceded Louisiana to France | Oct. 17, 1803–Mar. 27, 1804 |
| 10th, 1st | Jefferson | Problem with U.S.-British relations | Oct. 26, 1807–Apr. 25, 1808 |
| 12th, 1st | Madison | Problem with U.S.-British relations | Nov. 4, 1811–July 6, 1812 |
| 13th, 3rd | Madison | War with Britain | Sept. 19, 1814–Mar. 3, 1815 |
| 25th, 1st | Van Buren | Specie payment suspension | Sept. 4–Oct. 16, 1837 |
| 27th, 1st | Tyler | Nation's poor financial condition | May 31–Sept. 13, 1841 |

| | | | |
|---|---|---|---|
| 34th, 2nd | Pierce | Army appropriations | Aug. 21–30, 1856 |
| 37th, 1st | Lincoln | Civil War begun | July 4–Aug. 6, 1861 |
| 45th, 1st | Hayes | Army appropriations | Oct. 15–Dec. 3, 1877 |
| 46th, 1st | Hayes | Appropriations | Mar. 18–July 1, 1879 |
| 53rd, 1st | Cleveland | Repeal Silver Purchase | Aug. 7–Nov. 3, 1893 |
| 55th, 1st | McKinley | Dingley Tariff | Mar. 15–July 24, 1897 |
| 58th, 1st | Roosevelt | Cuban trade treaty | Nov. 9–Dec. 7, 1903 |
| 61st, 1st | Taft | Payne-Aldrich Tariff | Mar. 15–Aug. 5, 1909 |
| 62nd, 1st | Taft | Canadian trade | Apr. 4–Aug. 22, 1911 |
| 63rd, 1st | Wilson | Federal Reserve Act | Apr. 7–Dec. 1, 1913 |
| 65th, 1st | Wilson | World War I | Apr. 2–Oct. 6, 1917 |
| 66th, 1st | Wilson | Rising cost of living | May 19–Nov. 19, 1919 |
| 67th, 1st | Harding | Emergency tariff | Apr. 11–Nov. 23, 1921 |
| 67th, 3rd | Harding | Independent Merchant Marine | Nov. 20–Dec. 4, 1922 |
| 71st, 1st | Hoover | Smoot-Hawley Tariff | Apr. 15–Nov. 22, 1929 |
| 73rd, 1st | Roosevelt | New Deal legislation | Mar. 9–June 15, 1933 |
| 75th, 2nd | Roosevelt | Wages and Hours Act | Nov. 15–Dec. 21, 1937 |
| 76th, 2nd | Roosevelt | Neutrality legislation | Sept. 21–Nov. 3, 1939 |
| 80th, 1st | Truman | Domestic issues | Nov. 17–Dec. 19, 1947 |
| 80th, 2nd | Truman | Domestic issues | July 26–Aug. 7, 1948 |
| 103rd, 3rd | Clinton | Trade treaty | Nov., 1994 |

(*CAZ*, 478–86; *The Senate*, 454–6)

**Q 304. What is an executive session?**

**A** Congressional committees, and sometimes the full House or Senate, may hold an executive session, which only members and necessary staff attend. A House committee may call an executive session when certain witnesses testify or when Defense Department officials present classified information, for example. The public and press are excluded, but other members of Congress may be invited.

(*CAZ*, 135)

**Q** 305. What are the differences between a joint session and a joint meeting?

**A** Joint sessions and joint meetings of Congress differ in two important ways: why and how they are called. Joint sessions are held to hear the president's State of the Union address and, once every four years, to count electoral votes. Joint meetings are held when foreign leaders address Congress (the first to do so was the Marquis de Lafayette, in 1824). To call a joint session, both chambers must adopt a concurrent resolution; calling a joint meeting is easier—a recess allowing the two bodies to meet is declared in a unanimous consent agreement. Joint sessions and meetings are always held in the House chamber because it has a larger seating capacity than the Senate chamber.

(*CAZ*, 206)

*(See 283 What are resolutions and concurrent resolutions?)*


**Q** 306. Where can you find members' voting records?

**A** The *Congressional Quarterly Almanac* lists the recorded votes of all representatives and senators on key legislation during the session covered.

(*CQ Almanac*)


**Q** 307. What kinds of votes are there?

**A** The Senate regularly votes in two ways: by voice vote and by roll-call vote. In a voice vote, the presiding officer calls first for yeas and then for nays, with senators shouting their responses. The presiding officer determines the outcome. A roll-call vote, used for important questions, involves reading senators' names one-by-one and recording their spoken votes. House members may vote in four different ways: by voice vote and roll-call vote (procedures identical to those followed in the Senate), by "standing vote," and by "recorded vote." The quickest of the four is the voice vote. In a standing vote, or "division," members voting in favor stand and are counted, followed by those voting against. For important questions the House usually turns to a recorded vote. The

House has an electronic voting system that automatically records the votes and displays them on a giant electronic board behind the Speaker's desk. Both the House and Senate also use informal votes. If no one objects, a matter is passed by "unanimous consent."

(*CAZ*, 412–13)

*(See 297 What is unanimous consent?)*

### Q 308. What is logrolling?

A Logrolling is a common practice in both houses of Congress. A member seeking votes for a bill will promise to support another member's future legislation—in return for a vote now. Logrolling is most common when legislation benefits a particular district, but a classic example of it occurred between Democratic factions in 1964. Southern Democrats voted for a permanent food-stamp program (sought by northern Democrats), and in return northern Democrats voted for cotton and wheat price supports (sought by southern Democrats).

(*CAZ*, 253)

## COMMITTEES AND CAUCUSES

### Q 309. What types of committees are there?

A Congress has five types of committees. House and Senate *standing committees* are permanent committees that handle most of the legislative business. Each has a broad area of legislative responsibility—for example, veterans' affairs or appropriations—and the membership size varies. The Appropriations Committees in the House and Senate are the largest standing committees (sixty and twenty-nine members, respectively). Most standing committees also have *subcommittees*, which in some cases, especially in the House, handle much of the actual legislative work. The House and Senate also form *select* or *special committees* to investigate specific problems, such as drug abuse, aging, and hunger. These committees usually are temporary and generally cannot report legislation, though they may issue recommendations. (The House and Senate Select Intelligence Committees are exceptions, however.) *Joint committees* usually are permanent and include members of both houses (chairmanships generally alternate-between the House and Senate every two years). Issues handled by joint committees include taxation, the economy, the government printing office, and the Library of Congress. *Conference committees* are a special kind of joint congressional committee.

(*CAZ*, 78–9)

(*See 311 What is a conference committee?*)

## Q 310. What do committee staffers do?

A Committee staffers play an important role in the legislative process. They arrange hearings, negotiate agreements, draft compromises, write reports, and provide technical expertise on specific topics. As many as thirty professional and clerical staffers work for most House committees, while Senate committees may employ forty or more. Though staff organization varies from committee to committee, most committees have a staff director, a legislative counsel, a chief clerk, legislative aides, researchers, investigators, and secretaries.

(*CAZ*, 366)

(*See 271 How many people work for Congress?*)

## Q 311. What is a conference committee?

A Before the president can sign a bill, both houses must pass the legislation in identical form. When they do not, a temporary House-Senate conference committee may resolve the differences between the two bills. Although conferences are convened on a relatively small number of measures, these bills generally include the most important legislation before Congress. Conference committees vary in size from fewer than 10 to over 250 conferees, who are also called managers. Conferees often rewrite bills, even though they are not supposed to add new material or alter passages that do not conflict. A majority of conferees in both the House and Senate delegations must separately approve compromise provisions. Next, the full Senate and House must approve the conference report and resolve any remaining differences before the compromise bill can be sent to the president.

(*CAZ*, 82)

(*See 276 How does a bill become law?*)

**Q 312. What committees are there now in Congress?**

**A** HOUSE COMMITTEES

*Standing*

Agriculture
Appropriations
Armed Services
Banking, Finance, and Urban Affairs
Budget
District of Columbia
Education and Labor
Energy and Commerce
Foreign Affairs
Government Operations
House Administration
Judiciary
Merchant Marine and Fisheries
Natural Resources
Post Office and Civil Service
Public Works and Transportation
Rules
Science, Space, and Technology
Small Business
Standards of Official Conduct
Veterans' Affairs
Ways and Means

*Select*

Intelligence

SENATE COMMITTEES

*Standing*

Agriculture, Nutrition, and
   Forestry
Appropriations
Armed Services
Banking, Housing, and Urban Affairs
Budget
Commerce, Science, and Transportation
Energy and Natural Resources
Environment and Public Works
Finance
Foreign Relations
Government Affairs
Judiciary
Labor and Human Resources
Rules and Administration
Small Business
Veterans' Affairs

*Select or special*

Aging
Ethics
Indian Affairs
Intelligence

*Joint*

Economic
Library
Printing
Taxation

*(CAZ, 77)*

*(See 383 What is the Committee of the Whole?; 384 What does the House Rules Committee do?; 385 What is the role of the House Ways and Means Committee?)*

## Q 313. How are committee chairs chosen?

A Committee chairs are selected by the majority party caucus in each chamber. At the beginning of each new Congress, the Democratic or Republican caucus, whichever has the majority, votes for the various committee heads. Causus members usually select their party's most senior member on the committee, but this is not always the case. While committee membership is traditionally bipartisan, it is always weighted in the majority party's favor. The parties assign members to committees at the beginning of the new Congress.

*(CAZ, 76–81; Guide to Cong., 451)*

*(See 318 What are caucuses?)*

## Q 314. How can members lose their committee chairmanships?

A Since 1980 loss of a House chairmanship has been automatic for a member who is censured, indicted, or convicted of a felony with a sentence of two years or more. The House majority-party caucus also may oust committee chairs for other, nondisciplinary reasons, such as ineffective leadership. The Senate does not have a system for removing committee chairmen when an indictment has been made or when disciplinary action is necessary.

*(CAZ, 107–8, 352–3)*

*(See 263 Which members of Congress have been censured or reprimanded?)*

## Q 315. What is the seniority system?

A Seniority is the system by which both parties once automatically awarded positions of authority to senators and representatives who had served the longest. Congress recognizes two types of seniority—length of service in Congress and time served on a particular committee. The first is the less important of the two and may result in some special privileges. The second, however, once dictated who got the coveted committee chairmanships. This system concentrated power in the hands of the most experienced members, but in the House especially, younger members criticized it as too rigid and as unfairly weighted in favor of a few older members. In the 1970s reformers pushed through measures that reduced the importance of seniority. Seniority remains the biggest factor in the decision to name a committee chair, but now members can oust chairs who become autocratic or otherwise cease to be effective leaders.

(*CAZ,* 351–3)

*(See 313 How are committee chairs chosen?)*

**Q 316. What is the "College of Cardinals"?**

**A** The name refers to the appropriations subcommittee chairs, reflecting their considerable influence over appropriations bills. In this same vein, the appropriations committee chairs are sometimes called "popes."

(*Amer. Cong. Dict.,* 49)

**Q 317. What is a mark-up session?**

**A** Marking up is the process of proposing and voting on amendments to a particular bill. Bills being considered by either house usually are reviewed first by a subcommittee, which may hold one or more mark-up sessions before passing the bill, with proposed amendments, to the full committee. The full committee then may hold additional mark-up sessions to consider both the subcommittee amendments and others it wants added. If the full committee approves the bill, it sends (reports) the measure to its chamber. A measure with extensive changes may be reported as a clean bill or with a single "amendment in the nature of a substitute," which is an amendment that replaces the entire text of a bill. Still other amendments may be added to the bill during floor debate.

(*Amer. Cong. Dict.,* 7, 159; *CAZ,* 10–11)

*(See 276 How does a bill become law?; 277 Can a bill be amended?; 286 What is a clean bill?)*

**Q 318. What are caucuses?**

**A** Two basic types of caucuses are held in Congress: party caucuses and special caucuses. Party caucuses are the formal organizations of Democratic and Republican members within each chamber. They include the Democratic and Republican Senate Conferences, the House Republican Conference, and the House Democratic Caucus. At the beginning of a new Congress, party caucuses vote on House and Senate party leadership, committee chairmanships, and other posts. They also meet to discuss legislative policy and other party concerns. Special caucuses, on the other hand, tend to be organized around common interests or concerns, such as the Conservative Democratic Forum, the Congressional Caucus on Women's Issues, and the Congressional Black Caucus. Many special caucuses function almost as internal interest groups, lobbying committees and individuals to advance a particular cause.

(*CAZ*, 61–6)

## MEMBERS' ARRIVALS AND DEPARTURES

**Q 319. What are the rates of incumbents winning reelection?**

**A** In recent years nearly all House members running for reelection have won new terms. Senators have fared less well, but nevertheless have enjoyed a high reelection rate. During the 1980s House members had a reelection rate of 90 percent or better; in 1988 that rate peaked at over 98 percent. Competition increased in 1992, however, when only about 88 percent of House incumbents ran and won—the lowest rate since 1974. Senate reelection rates varied more widely than House rates during the 1980s, though they also remained high. Only 55 percent of senators seeking reelection were returned to office in 1980, the lowest percentage since 1946, but for most other years in the 1980s, reelection rates stayed in the 80 to 90 percent range. Like that in the House, the Senate reelection rate dipped in 1992, falling to 82 percent.

(*VSC*, 45, 58–9)

(*See 326 Who served the longest time in Congress?*)

**Q 320. Which states have passed term limitation legislation?**

**A** As of 1993, fifteen states have voted to impose limits on the number of terms their members of Congress may serve. Four have imposed overall limits, but most have restricted consecutive terms instead—a representative might be allowed to serve only six years during an eight-year period, for example. Only North Dakota has imposed limits on members of Congress but not on state legislators. (Oklahoma has state term limits but none for members of Congress.) Legal challenges to term limits have been raised, and the Supreme Court was expected to rule on Arkansas's term limit in 1995. If the Court strikes down term limits, a constitutional amendment imposing them is still possible, however. The states with congressional term limits are:

Arizona
Arkansas
California
Colorado
Florida
Michigan
Missouri
Montana

Nebraska
North Dakota
Ohio
Oregon
South Dakota
Washington
Wyoming

(*CQ Weekly Report,* Jun. 25, 1994, 1679; *VSAP,* 46)

## Q 321. What have retirement rates been for members?

A Following the House banking scandal, sixty-five representatives retired (or sought other offices) rather than run for reelection in 1992, the most ever in recent years. Normally, anywhere from about twenty-five to thirty-five representatives decide against running for reelection—about 6 to 8 percent of the 435 members. Among senators, retirements are fewer because the number of seats up for reelection is much smaller. Usually, from four to six senators decide against running when the time comes, but in 1978 ten retired, the most since 1946. In 1994 eight opted for retirement.

(*CQ Weekly Report,* Jun. 18, 1994, 1648; *VSC,* 60)

(*See 71 What was the banking scandal in the House about?*)

## Q 322. Who served first in the Senate and then in the House?

A Fifty-four senators later became representatives, though it is much more common for House members to move on to the Senate. Some of the fifty-four served as cabinet officers or state governors before entering the House, and a few went from the House to the Senate and back again. John Q. Adams had already been both a senator and a president by the time he reached the House. Former senators who became representatives are listed on the following page.

| Senate Term | | House Term |
|---|---|---|
| 1789–1793 | Paine Wingate (Anti-Admin.-N.H.) | 1793–1795 |
| 1790–1793 | Joseph Stanton, Jr. (Anti-Admin.-R.I.) | 1801–1807 |
| 1793–1794 | Albert Gallatin (Anti-Admin.-Pa.) | 1801–1814 |
| 1796–1799 | Richard Stockton (Fed.-N.J.) | 1813–1815 |
| 1796–1799 | Theodore Sedgwick (Fed.-Mass.) | 1789–1796; 1799–1801 |
| 1798–1799 | Franklin Davenport (Fed.-N.J.) | 1799–1801 |
| 1798–1801 | Charles Pinckney (Dem.-Repub.-S.C.) | 1819–1821 |
| 1799–1801 | James Schureman (Fed.-N.J.) | 1789–1791; 1797–1799; 1813–1815 |
| 1800–1803 | Jonathan Mason (Fed.-Mass.) | 1817–1820 |
| 1801–1806 | Robert Wright (Dem.-Repub.-Md.) | 1810–1817; 1821–1823 |
| 1803–1808 | John Q. Adams (Fed.-Mass.) | 1831–1848 |
| 1803–1809; 1809–1817 | John Condit (Dem.-Repub.-N.J.) | 1799–1803; 1819 |
| 1803–1811 | Timothy Pickering (Fed.-Mass.) | 1813–1817 |
| 1803–1815; 1822–1833 | Samuel Smith (Dem.-Repub.-Md.) | 1793–1803; 1816–1822 |
| 1804–1809 | Samuel L. Mitchill (Dem.-Repub.-N.Y.) | 1801–1804; 1810–1813 |
| 1806–1807; 1810–1811; 1831–1842; 1849–1852 | Henry Clay (Whig-Ky.) | 1811–1814; 1815–1821; 1823–1825 |
| 1806–1813 | Philip Reed (Dem.-Repub.-Md.) | 1817–1819; 1822–1823 |
| 1807–1813 | John Pope (Dem.-Repub.-Ky.) | 1837–1843 |

| | | |
|---|---|---|
| 1813–1819 | Jeremiah Morrow (Dem.-Repub.-Ohio) | 1803–1813; 1840–1843 |
| 1817–1819; 1835–1841; 1842–1848; 1855–1861 | John J. Crittenden (Whig-Ky.) | 1861–1863 |
| 1818–1819; 1829–1834 | John Forsyth (Dem.-Repub.-Ga.) | 1813–1818; 1823–1827 |
| 1818–1824; 1844–1849 | Henry Johnson (Dem.-Repub.-La.) | 1834–1839 |
| 1821–1851 | Thomas Hart Benton (D-Mo.) | 1853–1855 |
| 1823–1829 | John Branch (Jacksonian-N.C.) | 1831–1833 |
| 1826–1831; 1837 | John McKinley (Jacksonian-Ala.) | 1833–1835 |
| 1827–1833 | Samuel A. Foot (Anti-Jacksonian-Conn.) | 1819–1821; 1823–1825; 1833–1834 |
| 1831–1834 | William Wilkins (Jacksonian-Pa.) | 1843–1844 |
| 1837–1839 | Lucius Lyon (Jacksonian-Mich.) | 1843–1845 |
| 1839–1845 | Albert S. White (Whig-Ind.) | 1837–1839; 1861–1863 |
| 1842–1843 | Charles M. Conrad (Whig-La.) | 1849–1850; 1859–1861 |
| 1845–1850 | Thomas Corwin (Whig-Ohio) | 1831–1840; 1859–1861 |
| 1851 | Robert Rantoul, Jr. (D-Mass.) | 1851–1852 |
| 1851–1852 | John J. McRae (D-Miss.) | 1858–1861 |
| 1859–1865 | Morton S. Wilkinson (R-Minn.) | 1869–1871 |
| 1861–1867 | James W. Nesmith (D-Ore.) | 1873–1875 |
| 1865–1867 | Luke P. Poland (R-Vt.) | 1867–1875; 1883–1885 |

| Senate Term | | House Term |
|---|---|---|
| 1868–1872;<br>1877–1883 | William P. Kellogg (R-La.) | 1883–1885 |
| 1871–1877 | Thomas M. Norwood (D-Ga.) | 1885–1889 |
| 1875–1881 | William W. Eaton (D-Conn.) | 1883–1885 |
| 1879–1891 | Henry W. Blair (R-N.H.) | 1875–1879;<br>1893–1895 |
| 1880 | Luke Pryor (D-Ala.) | 1883–1885 |
| 1886–1887 | Washington C. Whitthorne (D-Tenn.) | 1871–1873;<br>1887–1891 |
| 1897–1903 | William E. Mason (R-Ill.) | 1887–1891;<br>1917–1921 |
| 1900–1901 | Charles A. Towne (D-Minn.) | 1895–1897;<br>1905–1907 |
| 1909–1915;<br>1928–1929 | Theodore E. Burton (R-Ohio) | 1889–1891;<br>1895–1909;<br>1921–1928 |
| 1915–1927 | James W. Wadsworth, Jr. (R-N.Y.) | 1933–1951 |
| 1923–1925 | Magnus Johnson (Farmer-Labor-Minn.) | 1933–1935 |
| 1923–1929;<br>1931–1941;<br>1949–1958 | Matthew M. Neely (D-W. Va.) | 1913–1921;<br>1945–1947 |
| 1930–1932 | Cameron A. Morrison (D-N.C.) | 1943–1945 |
| 1936–1951 | Claude D. Pepper (D-Fla.) | 1963–1989 |
| 1940–1942 | Berkeley L. Bunker (D-Nev.) | 1945–1947 |
| 1945–1946 | Hugh B. Mitchell (D-Wash.) | 1949–1953 |
| 1949–1950 | Garrett Lee Withers (D-Ky.) | 1952–1953 |
| 1953–1954 | Alton A. Lennon (D-N.C.) | 1957–1973 |

(*The Senate,* 210–12; *Guide to Cong.,* 4–B to 171–B)

**323. Which members have died in the Capitol?**

Two members of Congress have died while performing their duties in the Capitol Building. John Q. Adams, a representative from Massachusetts and a former U.S. president, collapsed February 21, 1848, while working at his desk on the House floor. Moved to the Speaker's room, he died there two days later. Another representative, Tennessee Democrat Edward Eslick, collapsed and died while giving a speech on the House floor June 14, 1932. Sen. Estes Kefauver, also a Tennessee Democrat, suffered a heart attack August 8, 1963, while speaking before the Senate. Despite the pain, he finished the speech and drove to the hospital, where he died soon after.

(*SOW,* 175)

(*See 173 Which president served in the House after leaving office?*)

## FOR THE RECORD—FIRSTS, ETC.

See also House and Senate sections below.

**324. Who was the youngest member of Congress?**

The youngest senator was in fact too young to be a senator. In 1818, when Tennessee Republican John H. Eaton was sworn in, he was only twenty-eight years, four months, and twenty-nine days old—over a year and seven months short of the required thirty-year minimum for senators. The youngest representative was William Charles Cole Claiborne, a Tennessee Republican who entered office in 1797. At that time Clairborne was only twenty-two years old, three years under the required minimum of twenty-five.

(*SOW,* 127–8)

(*See 137 Who was the youngest person to be president?; 209 Who was the youngest vice president elected?; 551 Who was the youngest justice to serve on the Court?*)

**325. Who was the oldest member of Congress?**

Sen. Theodore F. Green (D-R.I.) won this distinction in 1961, when he retired at age ninety-three. He lived five more years.

*(SOW,* 157)

*(See 138 Who was the oldest president?; 210 Who was the oldest vice president elected?; 552 Who was the oldest justice to serve?)*

### Q 326. Who served the longest time in Congress?

**A** When Carl T. Hayden quit his job as a county sheriff to become Arizona's first representative in 1912, he had no idea his congressional career would last nearly fifty-seven years. When he finally retired in 1969 at age ninety-one, after fifteen years as a representative and almost forty-two as a senator, Hayden had amassed more years in Congress than any other member. A fellow Democrat, Rep. Jamie L. Whitten of Mississippi, ranks second with over fifty-three years in the House. A member since November 1941, he announced in 1994 that he would retire at the end of the 103rd Congress because of poor health.

*(CAZ,* 264; *SOW,* 157; *The Senate,* 201)

*(See 142 Who was the only president to serve more than two terms?; 329 Which female member of Congress served the longest?; 331 Which black member served the longest?; 351 Which member has served longest in the Senate?; 368 Which member has served longest in the House?; 553 Which justice has served longest on the Court?)*

### Q 327. Who missed the fewest votes?

**A** Kentucky Democrat William H. Natcher, a House member since 1953, had the longest string of consecutive votes in Congress—18,401. Natcher had not missed a vote in forty years before ill health finally kept him from voting on March 3, 1994. Doctors had wheeled Natcher into the House chamber on a hospital gurney for his last four votes, and just weeks later he died of heart failure at age eighty-four. Wisconsin Democrat William Proxmire holds the record for the Senate. When he retired in 1988, he had not missed a roll-call vote in twenty-two years.

*(SOW,* 138; *Washington Post,* Mar. 4, 1994, A7)

**Q 328. Who were the first black, Hispanic, native American, female, Asian, Indian, and Hawaiian representatives and senators?**

**A** The first members of minority groups to sit in the House and Senate are listed below.

| Group | First representative | First senator |
|---|---|---|
| Blacks | Joseph Rainey, 1870–1879 | Hiram R. Revels, 1870–1871 |
| Hispanics | Romualdo Pacheco, 1877–1878; 1879–1883 | Dennis Chavez, 1935–1962 |
| Native Americans | Charles Curtis, 1893–1907 | Charles Curtis, 1907–1913; 1915–1929 |
| Females | Jeannette Rankin, 1917–1919; 1941–1943 | Rebecca L. Felton, 1922 |
| Chinese | — | Hiram L. Fong, 1959–1977 |
| Japanese | Daniel K. Inouye, 1959–1963 | Daniel K. Inouye, 1963– |
| Indians | Daliph Singh Saund, 1957–1963 | — |
| Black females | Shirley Chisholm, 1969–1983 | Carol Moseley-Braun, 1993– |
| Hawaiians | Daniel Akaka, 1977–1990 | Daniel Akaka, 1990– |
| Hispanic females | Ileana Ros-Lehtinen, 1989– | — |
| Koreans | Jay C. Kim, 1993– | — |

(*CAZ*, 457–61; *Guide to Cong.*, 4–B; *SOW*, 161–5)

(*See 394 When were blacks allowed to vote in national elections?; 395 When were women allowed to vote in national elections?; 562 Who was the first woman justice?; 564 Who was the first black justice?*)

**Q 329. Which female member of Congress served the longest?**

**A** Rep. Edith Nourse Rogers, a Massachusetts Republican, holds the women's record for congressional service—thirty-five consecutive years from 1925 to 1960. The longest-serving female senator is Margaret Chase Smith, a Maine Republican who held office for twenty-four consecutive years between 1949 and 1973.

(*SOW*, 163)

(*See 259 How many women have served in Congress?; 326 Who served the longest time in Congress?*)

**Q** **330. Who were the first women to chair committees in the House and Senate?**

**A** New York Republican Mae Ellen Nolan was the first woman to lead a House committee. She chaired the Committee on Expenditures in the Post Office Department from 1923 to 1925. Arkansas Democrat Hattie W. Caraway, the first elected female senator, also was the first woman to chair a Senate committee—the Committee on Enrolled Bills in 1943.

(*SOW*, 163–5)

(*See 259 How many women have served in Congress?; 328 Who were the first black, Hispanic, native American, female, Asian, Indian, and Hawaiian representatives and senators?*)

**Q** **331. Which black member served the longest?**

**A** Rep. John Conyers, Jr., a Michigan Democrat, has served twenty-nine consecutive years in the House, longer than any other black member of Congress. First elected in 1965, he was reelected to the 103rd Congress. Illinois Democrat William L. Dawson came in a close second, having served twenty-seven consecutive years in the House between 1943 and 1970. Sen. Edward Brooke, a Massachusetts Republican, had the longest tenure in the Senate—twelve years, from 1967 to 1979.

(*CAZ*, 459)

(*See 260 Which blacks have served in Congress?; 334 Which Hispanic member of Congress has served the longest?*)

**Q** **332. How many black members have been Republicans?**

**A** Of the eighty-seven black members of Congress, three senators and twenty-two representatives have been Republicans. Only three black Republicans have served in the House since 1900, the most recent being Gary Franks of Connecticut, a representative since 1991. The only black Republican senator in this century was Edward Brooke, who served from 1967 to 1979.

(*CAZ*, 459–60)

**A** Twenty-eight states have never done so. Among southern states, only three—Arkansas, Kentucky, and West Virginia—have not elected a black to Congress, and four New England states have not elected any blacks—Maine, New Hampshire, Rhode Island, and Vermont. Some of the twenty-eight states listed below, it should be noted, have relatively small black populations.

| | |
|---|---|
| Alaska | Nevada |
| Arizona | New Hampshire |
| Arkansas | New Mexico |
| Colorado | North Dakota |
| Delaware | Oklahoma |
| Hawaii | Oregon |
| Idaho | Rhode Island |
| Iowa | South Dakota |
| Kansas | Utah |
| Kentucky | Vermont |
| Maine | Washington |
| Minnesota | West Virginia |
| Montana | Wisconsin |
| Nebraska | Wyoming |

(*CAZ*, 459–60)

**Q** 334. Which Hispanic member of Congress has served the longest?

**A** Rep. Henry B. Gonzalez, a Texas Democrat, holds the record with thirty-three consecutive years. Gonzalez entered the House in 1961 and is still in office. Dennis Chavez, a Democrat from New Mexico, served a total of thirty-one years in Congress, four as a representative (1931–1935) and twenty-seven (1935–1962) as a senator. California Democrat Edward R. Roybal served thirty consecutive years in the House (1963–1993).

(*CAZ*, 461)

*(See 261 Which Hispanics have served in Congress?)*

**Q** **335. Who were the first Catholics in the House and Senate? The first Jews?**

**A** The first Catholics served in the First Congress (1789–1791)—two in the House and one in the Senate. The two representatives were Daniel Carroll of Maryland and Thomas Fitzsimons of Pennsylvania. Carroll's cousin, Marylander Charles Carroll, served as the first Catholic senator from 1789 to 1792. The first Jewish representative, Israel Jacobs, served in the Second Congress (1791–1793). A Louisiana Whig named Judah P. Benjamin, who served from 1853 to 1861, was the first Jewish senator.

(*SOW,* 160–1)

(*See 150 Who was the first Catholic president?; 565 Who was the first Catholic justice?; 566 Has there ever been more than one Catholic on the Court at once?; 567 Who was the first Jewish justice?; 568 Has there ever been more than one Jewish justice at a time?*)

**Q** **336. What session was the longest?**

**A** The longest was the third session of the Seventy-sixth Congress, which lasted from January 3, 1940, to January 3, 1941 (366 days), during the early stages of World War II. The Seventy-seventh's first session ran nearly as long, from January 3, 1941, to January 2, 1942, or 365 days.

(*CAZ,* 478–86)

**Q** **337. What was the shortest session?**

**A** The shortest session was a mere three days, a lame duck session called to vote on the General Agreement on Tariffs and Trade. It was the third session of the 103rd Congress, lasting from November 29 to December 1, 1994. Another short session— this one ten days—was the second of the 34th Congress, beginning August 21, 1856, and ending August 30, 1856.

(*CAZ* 478–86; *The Senate,* 455)

(*See 302 How are emergency sessions of Congress called?*)

**Q** **338. When was the last lame duck session of Congress?**

**A** Before adoption of the Lame Duck Amendment in 1933, such sessions occurred frequently. But between 1933 and 1994, Congress held only seven lame duck sessions, the last of which came in November 1994. Among the more important of these seven were the 1954 session (Senate only) that saw Sen. Joseph R. McCarthy censured for his anti-communist investigations, the 1974 session that approved the appointment of Nelson A. Rockefeller as vice president, and the 1994 session on the international trade agreement.

(*CAZ,* 219–220)

(*See 37 What is the Lame Duck Amendment?; 143 Who became president without having been elected to that office or to the vice presidency?*)

**Q 339. Have two foreign leaders ever addressed a joint meeting of Congress together?**

**A** The first time two foreign leaders appeared before both houses of Congress was July 26, 1994, when Israeli Prime Minister Yitzhak Rabin and Jordan's King Hussein both spoke about peace in the Middle East. The day before, the two signed the Washington Declaration at the White House, which ended the long-standing state of belligerency between Israel and Jordan but which was not a formal peace treaty. A formal treaty ending the hostilities was signed in a ceremony along the Israeli-Jordanian border on October 26, 1994.

(*CQ Weekly Report,* Jul. 30, 1994, 2156)

**Q 340. Which Congress enacted the most public laws?**

**A** Between 1955 and 1957, the Eighty-fourth Congress enacted a record 1,028 public laws as well as 893 private laws. The total of 1,921 laws was just short of the Eighty-first Congress's overall legislative record—2,024 bills enacted between 1949 and 1951 (921 public and 1,103 private). Enacted laws represent only a small fraction of those introduced, however. The Ninetieth Congress set that record with 26,460 bills introduced, of which 1,002 became law. Since the 1980s only about 10,000 bills have been introduced in each Congress, in part because more cosponsors are now allowed on identical bills.

(*SOW,* 135–6; *VSAP,* 218)

(*See 280 What is the difference between a public and a private bill?*)

**Q 341. What percent of members have been lawyers?**

**A** Interestingly, the number of representatives who previously worked in law has declined steadily since the beginning of the 1970s. About 56 percent of representatives during the 1950s and 1960s were lawyers, but that figure dropped to about 42 percent by 1993. In the 103rd Congress, House Democrats who are lawyers outnumber House Republicans who are lawyers by a margin of two to one. Among senators, the number of lawyers has remained fairly steady since the 1950s, usually ranging from 60 to 65 percent. As in the House, Democratic lawyers outnumber Republican lawyers in the Senate, but by a smaller margin.

(*VSC*, 22–3, 24–5, 28–33)

(*See 164 What profession is most common for presidents?; 577 Who was the last justice not to have a law degree?*)

**Q 342. What percent of members have worked in medicine?**

**A** Usually, only about 1 percent of House members have worked in the medical profession before entering Congress. Since 1953 no more than six medical professionals have served in the House at one time. (Exactly six served in 1993.) The Senate generally has a slightly higher percentage of former medical workers within its ranks—anywhere from 1 to 4 percent—but the actual number is lower than that in the House (usually just one senator). Since 1789 thirty-three senators have been practicing physicians before taking office.

(*The Senate*, 291–2; *VSC*, 22–3, 28–9)

(*See 164 What profession is most common for presidents?*)

**Q 343. Which members of Congress have married other members?**

**A** In 1976 House Democrats Martha Keys of Kansas and Andrew Jacobs of Indiana became the first sitting members of Congress to marry. Thirteen years later, House Republican Olympia J. Snowe of Maine married a former House member, John R. McKernan, Jr., then governor of Maine. More recently, New York Republican Reps.

Bill Paxon and Susan Molinari got married in 1994.

(*SOW,* 166–7)

(*See 181 Which presidents got married while in office?*)

## Q 344. Which members have fought each other in duels?

A The only fatal duel between members of Congress occurred February 24, 1838, on the Maryland Pike outside Washington. Rep. William Graves of Kentucky shot and killed Rep. Jonathan Cilley of Maine over remarks Cilley had made. A remark by Rep. Barent Gardenier of New York sparked another—nonfatal—duel between members of Congress in March 1808. Rep. George W. Campbell, angered by Gardenier's assertion that the House was under French influence, wounded him at Bladensburg, Maryland. Gardenier recovered but left the House in 1811. Sen. David Broderick of California also died in a duel, though his opponent was not a member of Congress. Reacting to Broderick's charges of corruption, former California Supreme Court chief justice David Terry mortally wounded him on September 12, 1859.

(*SOW,* 171–4)

(*See 214 Which vice president killed a man while in office?; 594 Has any justice been assassinated?*)

## Q 345. Have any members assaulted one another in Congress?

A Rep. Matthew Lyon was censured in 1798 for spitting tobacco juice in the face of Rep. Roger Griswold. Griswold, who had accused Lyon of cowardice during the American Revolution, later attacked him with a hickory walking stick. By far the most serious assault occurred May 1856, during the often fiery debates over slavery. Rep. Preston S. Brooks of South Carolina, a states' rights supporter, walked onto the Senate floor and bludgeoned Charles Sumner, the Massachusetts antislavery senator, with a cane. Senator Sumner, who had criticized Brooks's uncle two days before, spent three years recovering from the resulting head injuries.

(*CAZ,* 383; *SOW,* 171–2)

(*See 263 Which members of Congress have been censured or reprimanded?*)

**Q** **346. What are the special duties of the Senate?**

**A** While the Senate shares legislative powers with the House, the Framers of the Constitution also assigned it other special duties as part of the system of checks and balances. For example, the Senate shares certain executive powers with the president—confirmation of appointments, including both executive branch officials and judicial branch nominees, and ratification of treaties. In addition the Senate shares impeachment power with the House—first the House brings charges against an accused official, then the Senate conducts the trial for removal from office. Following presidential elections, both the Senate and the House count the electoral votes. If the vice presidential candidate fails to win an electoral majority, the Senate decides the winner; the House chooses the president if no candidate wins an electoral majority in that race.

(*CAZ*, 343–4, 376)

(*See 31 What is separation of powers?; 32 What are checks and balances?; 245 Who failed to be confirmed by the Senate for a cabinet post?; 404 Which vice presidential elections did Congress decide?*)

**Q** **347. Has the Senate ever originated a tax bill?**

**A** Yes, in 1982 the Senate did so by taking advantage of its power to amend revenue bills passed by the House. The House normally originates all revenue (tax) bills, as required by the Constitution, though in the past the Senate has regularly added numerous amendments to them. In this case the Senate went even further, adding the largest peacetime tax increase in U.S. history to what was otherwise a minor tax bill already passed by the House. The bill then went straight to a House-Senate conference committee.

(*CAZ*, 342)

(*See 365 What are the special duties of the House?*)

**Q** **348. What are the requirements for being a senator?**

**A** The only constitutional requirements are that senators must be residents of the state they represent, must have been citizens for at least nine years, and must be at least thirty years old. Three senators have been sworn in despite their being under the minimum required age: Armistead Mason of Virginia, age twenty-eight and five months on being sworn in (1816); John H. Eaton of Tennessee, age twenty-eight and four months (1818); and Henry Clay of Kentucky, age twenty-nine and eight months (1806). Sen. Rush D. Holt of Virginia was twenty-nine when he was elected in November 1934; he met the age requirement by not taking his seat until after his thirtieth birthday in June 1935.

(*CAZ,* 350; *SOW,* 127)

(*See 124 What are the requirements for serving as president and vice president?; 324 Who was the youngest member of Congress?; 366 What are the requirements for being a representative?; 541 What are the requirements for becoming a justice?*)


**Q** **349. When were senators first elected by popular vote?**

**A** Direct election of Senators went into effect on May 31, 1913, following ratification of the Seventeenth Amendment. The Framers of the Constitution originally believed Senators should represent the states' interests and should be selected by state legislatures. (Directly elected House members represented the people.) But the choosing of senators regularly locked state legislatures in pitched political battles, encouraged corruption, and eventually was criticized as undemocratic. Congress finally voted for the Seventeenth Amendment in 1912.

(*CAZ,* 99–101)

(*See 16 What was the "Great Compromise" made by the Framers of the Constitution?; 29 What do the amendments to the Constitution say, in brief?*)


**Q** **350. How long does a senator serve?**

**A** Senators serve a six-year term, which generally is considered an advantage over the two-year term served by House members, who must run for reelection much more frequently. While senators once could expect to act as statesmen during the first half of their term and to engage in campaign politics during the second half, today they must be concerned with reelection the moment they take office.

(*CAZ,* 349)

(*See 367 How long does a House member serve?*)

**Q** **351. Which member has served longest in the Senate?**

**A** Sen. Carl Hayden, an Arizona Democrat and holder of the congressional career service record (almost fifty-seven years in both the House and the Senate), was elected to seven consecutive Senate terms. Serving from 1927 to 1969, he spent forty-one years and ten months in office, more than any other senator to date. Sen. John C. Stennis, a Mississippi Democrat, finished his long senatorial career in 1989 with forty-one years and two months of service, just eight months short of Hayden's record.

(*CAZ*, 264; *The Senate*, 201)

(*See 141 Who was the only president to have served nonconsecutive terms?; 326 Who served the longest time in Congress?; 368 Which member has served longest in the House?; 553 Which justice served longest on the Court?*)

**Q** **352. Which senator served the shortest time?**

**A** Sen. Rebecca Felton of Georgia holds several records, including the one for the shortest Senate service—one day. The first woman senator, she was appointed to fill a temporary vacancy and was sworn in November 21, 1922. In addition to being the first woman senator, the eighty-seven-year-old Democrat was also the oldest new senator. Felton served only until November 22, when the Democrat elected to the seat arrived.

(*SOW*, 164)

(*See 325 Who was the oldest member of Congress?; 326 Who served the longest time in Congress?; 328 Who were the first black, Hispanic, native American, female, Asian, Indian, and Hawaiian representatives and senators?*)

**Q** **353. What are Senate classes?**

**A** Senators are divided into three groups, or classes, according to the year in which they were elected. The Constitution staggered the terms of the first senators so that about a third of the Senate would be up for reelection every two years. So when the Senate convened in 1789, the first class was to serve only two years, from 1789 to 1791; the second class four years, from 1789 to 1793; and the third class the full six-year term, from 1789 to 1795. Thereafter, senators in each of the three classes served full six-year terms. The first class was up for reelection again in 1994, the second will run in 1996, and the third will run in 1998.

(*People Speak*, 263)

**Q** **354. Who serves as the president pro tempore of the Senate, and what does the job involve?**

**A** The majority party's senior senator almost always becomes the president pro tempore. In this capacity, he presides when the Senate president—the vice president of the United States—is away. Largely a ceremonial position, it confers less influence than that of the party floor leader, though the senator who serves as president pro tempore may be quite powerful in his own right. Usually other majority party members handle the day-to-day routine of actually presiding over the Senate. But the president pro tempore is third in the line of presidential succession, after the vice president and the House Speaker.

(*CAZ*, 303–4)

(*See 130 What happens if the president dies after inauguration?; 131 What happens if the president is incapacitated after inauguration?; 196 What does the vice president do?; 356 Who serves as the Senate majority and minority leaders?*)

**Q** **355. Who was the first woman to preside over the Senate?**

**A** Arkansas Democrat Hattie W. Caraway, the first woman elected a senator, became the Senate's first woman presiding officer in 1943. By then she already had served twelve years in the Senate and would continue in office until 1945. She also became the first woman to chair a Senate committee, the Committee on Enrolled Bills.

(*CAZ*, 457; *SOW*, 164)

(*See 259 How many women have served in Congress?; 330 Who were the first women to chair committees in the House and Senate?*)

**Q** **356. Who serves as the Senate majority and minority leaders?**

**A** Majority and minority leaders, usually senior senators from their respective parties, are elected by party members as each Congress begins. They also are called majority and minority floor leaders. Unlike the House Speaker, the Senate majority leader is not part of the Senate's institutional structure, but wields considerable power nevertheless, especially through his control of the Senate's legislative agenda. The majority leader can schedule floor action and votes to suit his party's interests. The minority leader plays an important role as well by making the minority party's positions known, by marshalling support for or opposition to legislation, and by consulting with the majority leader on the legislative schedule.

*(CAZ, 222–4, 238–9)*

*(See 373 What does the Speaker do?)*

 **357. Has any Senate majority leader ever resigned?**

No, but in 1989, at the beginning of the 101st Congress, West Virginia Democrat Robert C. Byrd became the first to step down. He voluntarily relinquished the post to become president pro tempore and Appropriations Committee chairman. Maine Democrat George Mitchell succeeded him. Byrd had been the Democratic majority leader from 1977 to 1981 and from 1987 to 1989. Between 1981 and 1987, he had served as the Democratic minority leader.

*(CAZ, 44–5; SOW, 132)*

*(See 377 Has any Speaker ever resigned?)*

**358. What do the Senate whips do, and how are they chosen?**

Majority and minority whips are elected by their respective parties and rank immediately below floor leaders. Like floor leaders, whips are not part of the Senate's formal institutional structure, but they play an important role in the legislative process. Whips try to keep fellow senators from breaking ranks with the party's legislative agenda, inform members about impending floor action, poll members before floor votes, and even round up party members for tight votes. The term *whip*, first used in Congress in 1897, was borrowed from British Parliament, which in turn had adopted it from *whipper-in*, a fox-hunting term for the person who keeps the hounds in a pack.

*(CAZ, 222–3)*

*(See 380 What do the House whips do?)*

**359. What does the secretary of the Senate do?**

The secretary is the Senate's chief administrator and as such maintains records, compiles reports, pays Senate employees, and distributes office supplies and equipment to members of the Senate. Unlike the whips, floor leaders, and other leaders in the Senate, the secretary is not himself a senator. He is chosen by the majority party and usually remains in office until that party loses control of the Senate. The secretary's House counterpart is the clerk of the House.

*(CAZ, 341)*

*(See 381 What does the clerk of the House do?)*

### 360. What is a filibuster, and how can one be ended?

A Senate tradition, the filibuster involves prolonged debate and other delaying tactics aimed at blocking passage of legislation favored by a majority of senators. Tactics may involve holding the floor—and thereby halting all other legislative action—by reading long speeches, or forcing repeated roll calls to cause the delay. In the past, filibusters have stalled legislation on slavery, civil rights, and, more recently, campaign finance law. While the Senate prides itself on allowing unlimited debate, it moved to control stalling tactics in 1917 when it adopted the first cloture rule. The rule, which limited debate on a pending proposal, called for a two-thirds vote of the full Senate to invoke cloture, but by 1975 that requirement had been reduced to just sixty votes, making it much easier to stop filibusters. The filibuster has no counterpart in the House, where rules impose time limits on debate.

*(CAZ, 137–40)*

### 361. When was the longest filibuster, and what was it about?

A Though filibusters can go on for days at a time, the longest single speech ever delivered in the Senate was part of a 1957 filibuster against a civil rights bill. Sen. Strom Thurmond of South Carolina spoke for a record twenty-four hours and eighteen minutes.

*(CAZ, 138; SOW, 134–5)*

### 362. Which senators have represented more than one state?

A As of 1993, just two senators had switched from one state to another while in the senate. The first, Sen. James Shields, served as a senator from Illinois between 1849 and 1855, from Minnesota between 1858 and 1859, and from Missouri between January and March, 1879. Sen. Waitman T. Willey was a senator from Virginia between 1861 and 1863, and from West Virginia between 1863 and 1871. Twenty-one members (listed below) sat as House members from one state and as senators from another. Seven others served variously as territorial or Continental Congress delegates before becoming senators from a different state.

| Member of Congress | State represented in House | State represented in Senate |
|---|---|---|
| John Brown | Virginia (1789–1792) | Kentucky (1792–1805) |
| Robert G. Harper | South Carolina (1795–1801) | Maryland (1816) |
| Edward Livingston | New York (1795–1801) Louisiana (1823–1829) | Louisiana (1829–1831) |
| William C. Claiborne | Tennessee (1797–1801) | Louisiana (1817) |
| David Holmes | Virginia (1797–1809) | Mississippi (1820–1825) |
| John Chandler | Massachusetts (1805–1809) | Maine (1820–1829) |
| William R. King | North Carolina (1811–1816) | Alabama (1819–1844, 1848–1852) |
| Israel Pickens | North Carolina (1811–1817) | Alabama (1826) |
| Daniel Webster | New Hampshire (1813–1817), Massachusetts (1823–1827) | Massachusetts (1827–1841, 1845–1850) |
| Albion K. Parris | Massachusetts (1815–1818) | Maine (1827–1828) |
| John Holmes | Massachusetts (1817–1820) | Maine (1820–1827, 1829–1833) |
| Samuel Houston | Tennessee (1823–1827) | Texas (1846–1859) |
| Jesse Speight | North Carolina (1829–1837) | Mississippi (1845–1847) |
| John B. Weller | Ohio (1839–1845) | California (1852–1857) |
| William M. Gwin | Mississippi (1841–1843) | California (1850–1855; 1857–1861) |
| Alexander Ramsey | Pennsylvania (1843–1847) | Minnesota (1863–1875) |
| Edward D. Baker | Illinois (1845–1846, 1849–1851) | Oregon (1860–1861) |
| James H. Lane | Indiana (1853–1855) | Kansas (1861–1866) |
| Charles H. Van Wyck | New York (1859–1863, 1867–1869, 1870–1871) | Nebraska (1881–1887) |

| | | |
|---|---|---|
| Charles A. Towne | Minnesota (1895–1897), New York (1905–1907) | Minnesota (1900–1901) |
| James H. Lewis | Washington (1897–1899) | Illinois (1913–1919, 1931–1939) |

(*The Senate,* 224–8)

**Q 363. Which sitting senators have been indicted?**

**A** As of mid-1994, a total of nine senators had been indicted while serving in Congress. They are listed below.

| *Year of indictment* | *Senator* | *Reason for indictment* |
|---|---|---|
| 1806 | John Smith (D-Ohio) | Conspiring with Aaron Burr to commit treason. Found not guilty. |
| 1903 | Charles Dietrich (R-Neb.) | Bribery. Found not guilty. |
| 1904 | Joseph Burton (R-Kan.) | Receiving illegal compensation. Convicted. Resigned from the Senate. |
| 1905 | John Mitchell (R-Ore.) | Receiving kickbacks. Convicted. |
| 1919 | Truman Newberry (R-Mich.) | Illegal campaign activities. Conviction reversed by the Supreme Court. |
| 1924 | Burton Wheeler (D-Mont.) | For activities related to the Teapot Dome scandal. Acquitted. |
| 1974 | Edward Gurney (R-Fla.) | Bribery and lying to a grand jury. Acquitted after resigning his seat. |
| 1980 | Harrison Williams, Jr. (D-N.J.) | Bribery and conspiracy. Convicted. |
| 1993 | Dave Durenberger (R-Minn.) | Filing false expense claims. First indictment dismissed; reindicted on same charges in 1994. |

(*Guide to Cong.,* 786–809; *Washington Post,* Apr. 6, 1993, A19)

(*See 69 What was Abscam?*)

**Q** **364. What state has had a female senator and a female governor at the same time?**

**A** Kansas had a woman governor, Democrat Joan Finney, and a woman senator, Republican Nancy Kassebaum, from 1991 to the end of Finney's term in 1995. Finney decided against running for reelection in 1994.

(*CQ Weekly Report,* Feb. 19, 1994, 396; *SOW,* 23)

(*See 328 Who were the first black, Hispanic, native American, female, Asian, Indian, and Hawaiian representatives and senators?*)

## THE HOUSE OF REPRESENTATIVES

**Q** **365. What are the special duties of the House?**

**A** The Constitution gives it three special duties. The House (1) originates all revenue-raising bills, (2) initiates impeachment proceedings against federal officials, and (3) chooses the president if no candidate wins a majority in the electoral college.

(*CAZ,* 180–1)

(*See 44 Where does the government get the money it needs to operate?; 267 What is the procedure for impeaching an official?; 269 Who has been impeached by Congress?; 347 Has the Senate ever originated a tax bill?; 403 Which presidential elections were decided by Congress?; 405 How does the electoral college work?*)

**Q** **366. What are the requirements for being a representative?**

**A** Representatives must be at least twenty-five years old, must be residents of the state they represent, and must have been U.S. citizens for at least seven years. Most representatives live in the districts that elect them, but that is not required.

(*CAZ,* 182; *SOW,* 127)

(*See 124 What are the requirements for serving as president and vice president?; 256 How much does a member of Congress get paid?; 257 What is the oath of office for a member of Congress?; 348 What are the requirements for being a senator?; 541 What are the requirements for becoming a justice?*)

**Q** **367. How long does a House member serve?**

**A** Representatives serve two-year terms, so that all House members are elected (or reelected) before a new Congress starts. Because they face reelection within a relatively short period of time, representatives must pay especially close attention to their constituents' political concerns.

(*CAZ,* 177, 349)

(*See 350 How long does a senator serve?*)


**Q** **368. Which member has served longest in the House?**

**A** Mississippi Democrat Jamie L. Whitten, a representative since 1941, has served the longest—fifty-two years as of January 1994. Georgia Democrat Carl Vinson held the record previously, with just over fifty years of service (from 1914 to 1965).

(*CAZ,* 264; *SOW,* 157)

(*See 142 Who was the only president to serve more than two terms?; 326 Who served the longest time in Congress?; 351 Which member has served longest in the Senate?; 553 Which justice served longest on the Court?*)


**Q** **369. Can you be represented by more than one member of the House?**

**A** At one time some states had multimember districts, making it possible to have more than one representative. In the early 1800s, for example, New York had five such districts, while a few other states elected their representatives on an at large basis. The number of representatives allotted to states remained the same whether they had single or multimember districts, but voters in multimember districts elected two or more representatives instead of just one. Congress banned multimember districts in 1842, however, and since then no district has had more than one representative in the House. In the mid-1990s the concept was being debated again as a means to enhance the voting power of blacks and other minorities.

(*SOW,* 126–7)

**Q 370. How many people does a representative serve?**

**A** Each House member serves about 588,000 people. The number can be somewhat larger or smaller depending on a state's population and the number of representatives it has been alloted.

(*SOW,* 126)

(*See 251 How many seats did each state have on entering the Union?*)

**Q 371. Which are the richest and poorest congressional districts?**

**A** The 1990 census showed that Maryland's Eighth Congressional District was the country's richest. The Eighth District had a median family income of $64,199, almost twice that of the national median family income of $35,225. New Jersey's Eleventh and Twelfth, New York's Third, and California's Tenth rounded out the country's five wealthiest districts. The poorest district was New York's Sixteenth, which had a median family income of $16,683. The four other poorest districts (in ascending order) were Kentucky's Fifth, Louisiana's Fourth, Mississippi's Second, and Texas's Fifteenth.

(*CD 1990s,* xvi)

**Q 372. How long has the House had 435 members?**

**A** The number of House seats has been fixed since 1911, except for a temporary increase to 437 caused by the admission of Alaska and Hawaii as states in 1959. The House returned to 435 members in 1963, following reapportionment. The original House had just sixty-five members in 1789, but population increases and the admission of new states quickly raised that number. During the early 1900s, the House threatened to become so large as to impair the legislative process, and in 1911 legislators imposed the 435-member limit. Since then, seats have been allocated to states by a complex system of reapportionment after each census.

(*CAZ,* 321)

(*252 Why do states sometimes gain or lose seats in Congress?; 253 What happens when new districts must be drawn in a state?; 255 What is a gerrymander?*)

**Q 373. What does the Speaker do?**

**A** The Speaker is the presiding officer of the House, as well as spokesman and leader of the House majority party. The Constitution does not spell out the duties of the office, but they have evolved to include certain formal powers. For example, the Speaker refers bills to committees and schedules floor action, thereby controlling the flow of legislation. During floor debate, the Speaker recognizes members wishing to speak and, with advice from the House parliamentarian, decides points of order. Speakers rarely vote except to break a tie. The Speaker's other duties include appointing members of conference committees and special committees, and naming the chair of the Committee of the Whole. The Speaker also seeks to maintain party discipline and to implement the party's legislative agenda. The Speaker follows the vice president in the line of presidential succession. The Speaker has no counterpart in the Senate.

(*CAZ*, 358–9)

(See 133 *What happens if the president resigns or is removed from office?*; 258 *What does the presiding officer do in the Senate? The House?*; 309 *What types of committees are there?*; 311 *What is a conference committee?*; 354 *Who serves as the president pro tempore of the Senate, and what does the job involve?*; 383 *What is the Committee of the Whole?*)

**Q 374. Who has served as Speaker?**

**A** The first influential Speaker was Henry Clay. Among this century's strongest House Speakers were Republican Joseph G. Cannon and Democrat Sam Rayburn. Thomas S. Foley (D-Wash.) became the first Speaker voted out of office in over one hundred years, when he lost his reelection bid in 1994. Following is a list of Speakers of the House.

| Congress (years) | Speaker |
| --- | --- |
| 1st (1789–1791) | Frederick A.C. Muhlenberg, Pa. |
| 2nd (1791–1793) | Jonathan Trumbull, F-Conn. |
| 3rd (1793–1795) | Muhlenberg |
| 4th (1795–1797) | Jonathan Dayton, F-N.J. |
| 5th (1797–1799) | Dayton |
| 6th (1799–1801) | Theodore Sedgwick, F-Mass. |
| 7th–9th (1801–1807) | Nathaniel Macon, D-N.C. |
| 10th–11th (1807–1811) | Joseph B. Varnum, Mass. |
| 12th–13th (1811–1814) | Henry Clay, R-Ky. |

| Congress (years) | Speaker |
|---|---|
| 13th (1814–1815) | Langdon Cheves, D-S.C. |
| 14th–16th (1815–1820) | Clay |
| 16th (1820–1821) | John W. Taylor, D-N.Y. |
| 17th (1821–1823) | Philip P. Barbour, D-Va. |
| 18th (1823–1825) | Clay |
| 19th (1825–1827) | Taylor |
| 20th–23rd (1827–1834) | Andrew Stevenson, D-Va. |
| 23rd (1834–1835) | John Bell, W-Tenn. |
| 24th–25th (1835–1839) | James K. Polk, D-Tenn. |
| 26th (1839–1841) | Robert M. T. Hunter, D-Va. |
| 27th (1841–1843) | John White, W-Ky. |
| 28th (1843–1845) | John W. Jones, D-Va. |
| 29th (1845–1847) | John W. Davis, D-Ind. |
| 30th (1847–1849) | Robert C. Winthrop, W-Mass. |
| 31st (1849–1851) | Howell Cobb, D-Ga. |
| 32nd–33rd (1851–1855) | Linn Boyd, D-Ky. |
| 34th (1855–1857) | Nathaniel P. Banks, R-Mass. |
| 35th (1857–1859) | James L. Orr, D-S.C. |
| 36th (1859–1861) | William Pennington, R-N.J. |
| 37th (1861–1863) | Galusha A. Grow, R-Pa. |
| 38th–40th (1863–1868) | Schuyler Colfax, R-Ind. |
| 40th (1868–1869) | Theodore M. Pomeroy, R-N.Y. |
| 41st–43rd (1869–1875) | James G. Blaine, R-Maine |
| 44th (1875–1876) | Michael C. Kerr, D-Ind. |
| 44th–46th (1876–1881) | Samuel J. Randall, D-Pa. |
| 47th (1881–1883) | Joseph W. Keifer, R-Ohio |
| 48th–50th (1883–1889) | John G. Carlisle, D-Ky. |
| 51st (1889–1891) | Thomas Brackett Reed, R-Maine |
| 52nd–53rd (1891–1895) | Charles F. Crisp, D-Ga. |
| 54th–55th (1895–1899) | Reed |
| 56th–57th (1899–1903) | David B. Henderson, R-Iowa |
| 58th–61st (1903–1911) | Joseph G. Cannon, R-Ill. |
| 62nd–65th (1911–1919) | James B. "Champ" Clark, D-Mo. |
| 66th–68th (1919–1925) | Frederick H. Gillett, R-Mass. |
| 69th–71st (1925–1931) | Nicholas Longworth, R-Ohio |
| 72nd (1931–1933) | John N. Garner, D-Texas |

| 73rd (1933–1934) | Henry T. Rainey, D-Ill. |
| 74th (1935–1936) | Joseph W. Byrns, D-Tenn. |
| 74th–76th (1936–1940) | William B. Bankhead, D-Ala. |
| 76th–79th (1940–1947) | Sam Rayburn, D-Texas |
| 80th (1947–1949) | Joseph W. Martin, Jr., R-Mass. |
| 81st–82nd (1949–1953) | Rayburn |
| 83rd (1953–1955) | Martin |
| 84th–87th (1955–1961) | Rayburn |
| 87th–91st (1962–1971) | John W. McCormack, D-Mass. |
| 92nd–94th (1971–1977) | Carl Albert, D-Okla. |
| 95th–99th (1977–1987) | Thomas P. O'Neill, Jr., D-Mass. |
| 100th–101st (1987–1989) | Jim Wright, D-Texas |
| 101st–103rd (1989–1995) | Thomas S. Foley, D-Wash. |

(*CAZ*, 358–9, 445–6)

## Q 375. Who had the longest term as Speaker?

A Democrat Sam Rayburn of Texas served as Speaker 1940–1947, 1949–1953, and 1955–1961, for a total of seventeen years (he was minority leader 1947–1949 and 1953–1955). No other Speaker has served longer than ten years in all. Among the other long-serving Speakers were Henry Clay, 1811–1814, 1815–1820, 1823–1825; Thomas P. O'Neill, Jr., 1977–1987; John W. McCormack, 1962–1971; Joseph G. Cannon, 1903–1911; and James B. "Champ" Clark, 1911–1919.

(*CAZ*, 54, 68, 258, 279–80, 319–20, 358–62, 446)

(*See 326 Who served the longest time in Congress?*)

## Q 376. Who had the least seniority in the House when elected Speaker?

A The House chose Henry Clay of Kentucky for the job the day he took office in 1811, making him the least-senior Speaker. Clay had already filled two unexpired terms in the Senate before being elected to the House. His skill as a debater and formidable presiding officer helped him become the first Speaker ever to exert real influence over the House. Clay served as Speaker the entire time he was a representative from 1811 to 1825. He resigned his seat twice, in 1814 and 1820, but both times was renamed Speaker upon his return. William Pennington of New Jersey also was elected Speaker in his first term, but—unlike Clay—not because of his experience elsewhere in government. Pennington was a political unknown who was chosen as a compromise candidate for Speaker. He served only one term, from December 5, 1859 (he won the speakership on the forty-fourth ballot, on February 1, 1860), to March 3, 1861.

(*CAZ*, 68; *PAZ*, 78–9)

### Q 377. Has any Speaker been forced to resign?

A Texas Democrat Jim Wright was the only Speaker forced to resign in mid-term. In 1988, the House ethics committee began investigating alleged improprieties in Wright's personal finances. Eventually the committee charged him with accepting improper gifts, using book royalties to sidestep income limits, and violating other House rules. Wright resigned from Congress in 1989, before the disciplinary hearing convened.

(*CAZ*, 173, 367)

### Q 378. Who was the only Speaker to serve as president?

A The only Speaker to do so was James K. Polk. A Democrat, Polk served as House Speaker from 1835 to 1839, when he became governor of Tennessee. In 1844 a deadlocked Democratic Party convention nominated Polk as its presidential candidate, and he went on to defeat his Whig opponent, Henry Clay. Polk served as president from 1845 to 1849 and declined to run for a second term.

(*PAZ*, 343–4)

(See 163 What experience have presidents had before being elected?; 173 Which president served in the House after leaving office?)

### Q 379. What do the House majority and minority leaders do?

A The House majority leader acts as the Speaker's chief lieutenant. Elected with other party leaders at the start of each Congress, the majority leader handles legislation on the House floor and oversees debate, amendments, and voting. The minority leader is the minority party's chief spokesperson and serves as its top House official. The minority leader has no direct control over scheduling of legislation but may influence it to advance the minority party's interests. Majority and minority leaders also are called majority and minority floor leaders.

(CAZ, 222)

(See 356 Who serves as the Senate majority and minority leaders?)

## Q 380. What do the House whips do?

**A** House majority and minority whips rank next after the majority and minority leaders in their party hierarchies and are elected by party caucuses. Whips try to convince fellow party members to support the party's legislative agenda, poll them before floor votes, keep them informed about upcoming floor action, and make sure they are present for tight votes. Both majority and minority whips have numerous assistants, sometimes numbering over one hundred each and including chief deputy whips, deputy whips, floor whips, assistant deputy whips, and zone or regional whips (representing an area of the country). Congress first adopted the term "whip" in 1897. It came from British Parliament, which had earlier adopted it from *whipper-in*, a foxhunting term for the person who keeps the hounds in a pack.

(CAZ, 222–3)

(See 358 What do the Senate whips do, and how are they chosen?)

## Q 381. What does the clerk of the House do?

**A** As the chief administrative officer of the House, the clerk reports debates and keeps the official House *Journal*, certifies passage of bills, records and prints bills and reports, attests and fixes the House seal to subpoenas, pays the salaries of House employees, and distributes office supplies to members. Chosen by the majority party, the clerk, who is not himself a member of the House, usually remains in office as long as the party maintains a majority. The secretary of the Senate is the clerk's counterpart.

(CAZ, 68)

(See 359 What does the secretary of the Senate do?)

## Q 382. What do delegates to the House do?

**A** The four delegates provide limited representation for the District of Columbia, the Virgin Islands, Guam, and American Samoa. Puerto Rico is represented by its resident commissioner, who has the same powers as a delegate. These five can make speeches and vote in committees—like the 435 regular House members—but until recently they could not join in floor votes. A 1993 rule change extended their privileges to voting on amendments when the House sits as the Committee of the Whole, as long as their combined votes do not affect the outcome.

(*CAZ*, 98–9)

*(See 272 What is a shadow senator or representative?)*

### Q 383. What is the Committee of the Whole?

A The House uses this parliamentary device to hasten floor action on bills. While the Committee of the Whole includes all House members, the quorum needed to transact business is only 100—less than half the 218 required for a regular House session. Members not attending are thus free to conduct other business. A rule limiting debate on amendments, though often ignored, helps speed up the legislative process. The Committee of the Whole considers bills after House committees have completed their work, and can attach any amendments it sees fit. But only the House in regular session can actually pass or reject legislation. There is no counterpart of the Committee of the Whole in the Senate.

(*CAZ*, 76)

### Q 384. What does the House Rules Committee do?

A Often described as the House traffic cop, this committee decides which bills reach the floor, which amendments are considered, and the order in which amendments are debated. Its opposition can effectively kill either the bill or proposed amendments to it, even though another committee has approved them. Because the committee exercises so much control over the legislative process, the majority party ensures its membership is heavily weighted in the party's favor. The House Speaker names the majority party members who sit on the committee and thereby keeps tight control over the committee's activities.

(*CAZ*, 336)

### Q 385. What is the role of the House Ways and Means Committee?

A Ways and Means is in charge of approving House bills that raise revenue for running the government. It also handles legislation that disburses entitlement funds, such as

Social Security, health insurance, public assistance, and unemployment compensation payments—about 48 percent of the federal budget. Spending for entitlement programs is kept separate from the regular appropriations process, which is overseen by the Appropriations Committee. Because the committee effectively sets the agenda for virtually all tax bills and also controls almost half of what the government spends each year, it ranks among the most powerful committees in the House.

(*CAZ*, 427)

(*See 53 What is an entitlement?*)

**Q 386. What is the Consent Calendar?**

**A** The Consent Calendar is a list of noncontroversial bills awaiting floor action in the House. The House usually calls these bills on the first and third Mondays of each month and passes them by unanimous consent. However, if one or more members object to a bill, it is carried over to the next day the House calls the Consent Calendar. Then the bill is considered and usually passed, unless three or more members object. Objections this time force the bill onto another calendar for later consideration.

(*CAZ*, 86, 397)

(*See 297 What is unanimous consent?*)

**Q 387. What is the previous question motion?**

**A** Only a motion to adopt, or "order," the previous question can close debate in the House and bring pending legislation to a vote. The motion cannot be debated and must be voted on immediately, so that sometimes it serves to block attempts at revising or amending a bill. If the House defeats the motion, debate continues and amendments can be proposed. The previous question motion is not allowed when the House sits as the Committee of the Whole. Senate rules make it more difficult for members to close off debate—they can do so in only two ways: by unanimous consent or by a three-fifths vote to invoke cloture.

(*CAZ*, 309)

(*See 360 What is a filibuster, and how can one be ended?; 383 What is the Committee of the Whole?*)

# IV
# CAMPAIGNS & ELECTIONS

## IN GENERAL

**Q 388. How did the two-party system develop?**

**A** The Constitution did not mention political parties, but two national parties emerged soon after its ratification in 1789—the Federalists, who favored strong central government, and the Democratic-Republicans, who wanted limited government. These two parties eventually died out, only to be replaced by the Democratic party (mid-1820s) and the Republican party (1854). Since then, third parties occasionally have sprung up, but most have been short-lived and none has seriously rivalled the two major parties.

*(PAZ, 339–41)*

*(See 10 When has the same party controlled the White House and both houses of Congress?; 429 Which third-party candidates won more than 6 percent of the popular vote?)*

**Q 389. When was the Democratic party founded?**

**A** A split in the Democratic-Republican party gave birth to the Democratic party in the mid-1820s. After 1816, when the Federalist party died out, the Democratic-Republican party was the nation's only political party. But by the mid-1820s it had split into two factions, the National Republicans (favoring economic development projects) and the Democrats (favoring Andrew Jackson and his populist, agrarian outlook). Stung by Jackson's defeat in the 1824 election (decided by the House), Jackson's supporters established their own national political organization to elect him, and after Jackson's victory in 1828, that organization became known officially as the Democratic party. The Democratic party has remained a major political party ever since.

*(PAZ, 340)*

*(See 147 Who was the first Democratic president? The others?; 402 Which presidents have been elected without winning the popular vote?; 403 Which presidential elections were decided by Congress?; 411 How were presidential nominees chosen before conventions?; 416 Which party had the longest series of consecutive presidencies?; 449 Which party has dominated both houses of Congress for the longest series of consecutive Congresses?)*

**Q 390. When was the Republican party founded?**

**A** The Republican party was organized in 1854 after the breakup of the Whig party. Years earlier in 1834, conservative-minded, former Democratic-Republican party members had joined forces with other groups opposed to President Andrew Jackson, forming the Whig party. Whigs vied with Democrats in elections for the next two decades. By the early 1850s, however, the slavery question had broken up the Whig party, with disaffected northern abolitionists and others forming the Republican party. The party won its first presidential election in 1860, led by former Whig Abraham Lincoln. The Republican party has been a leading political party ever since.

(*RD Encyc. of Amer. Hist.*, 938, 1232)

*(See 148 Who was the first Whig president? The other?; 149 Who was the first Republican president? The others?; 416 Which party had the longest series of consecutive presidencies?; 449 Which party has dominated both houses of Congress for the longest series of consecutive Congresses?)*

**Q 391. Why do we vote the Tuesday after the first Monday in November?**

**A** Congress in 1845 considered several factors before deciding on this odd formula for setting election day. November was chosen because, with the harvest over, farmers would be more likely to vote. As to the question of the best weekday, Congress ruled out Monday (the first day) and Friday (the last), bypassed Saturday and Sunday (shopping and church days), and eliminated Thursday (British election day). With just Tuesday and Wednesday remaining, Congress chose Tuesday. But which Tuesday would be best? Congress recognized that scheduling election day on November 1 would disrupt accountants and shopkeepers who had to close out the October books. Therefore, in 1845 it settled on the Tuesday after the first Monday. Prior to 1845, elections had been held in the first week of December, with the day varying between December 1 and December 7.

(*SOW*, 246)

**Q 392. When were voting machines first used?**

**A** Thomas Edison had invented an electric voting machine as early as 1869, but the machine was not used in an election until 1892.

(*Encyc. of Amer. Facts & Dates,* 299)

**Q 393. When the Constitution was ratified, who was eligible to vote in national elections?**

**A** Only about one-half of the adult white males could vote in the first national elections because the electorate was limited to male property owners and taxpayers. Of the original thirteen states, seven required voters to own property, and six required them either to own property or to have paid taxes. Black and Indian slaves (about one-fifth of the population in 1790), women, and white male indentured servants all could not vote. By 1850 most states had dropped remaining restrictions against white male voters, though women and slaves still could not vote.

(*GUSE,* 319, 321–4)

**Q 394. When were blacks allowed to vote in national elections?**

**A** Slaves who had gained their freedom following the Civil War won the right to vote in 1870 in national elections when the Fifteenth Amendment was ratified. Poll taxes, imposed in southern states to discourage poor blacks and white sharecroppers from voting, were banned by the Twenty-fourth Amendment in 1964.

(*SOW,* 14)

(*See 29 What do the amendments to the Constitution say, in brief?*)

**Q 395. When were women allowed to vote in national elections?**

**A** Women won full voting rights in 1920, when a long campaign for woman suffrage culminated in ratification of the Nineteenth Amendment.

(*CAZ,* 435–6; *SOW,* 14)

(*See 29 What do the amendments to the Constitution say, in brief?*)

**Q** **396. When did eighteen-year-olds get the vote?**

**A** Ratified in 1971, the Twenty-sixth Amendment set the voting age in all states at eighteen. Its ratification was faster than any other amendment, just 107 days, or less than half the time any other required. The amendment enabled eighteen-year-olds to vote in the 1972 presidential election. Previously they could vote in just a few states, with most others having a voting age of twenty-one.

(*SOW,* 14–5)

(*See 29 What do the amendments to the Constitution say, in brief?; 30 Which amendment took the longest to ratify?*)

**Q** **397. What have voter turnouts been like over time?**

**A** Voter turnout in presidential elections declined steadily after 1960, dropping from 62.6 percent of eligible voters in that year to a low of 50.1 percent in 1988. Turnout rebounded to 55.1 percent in the 1992 presidential election, however, with the poor economy, the independent candidacy of Ross Perot, and an energized electorate being important factors in the voting surge. Men and women generally vote in proportionally equal numbers. But more whites turn out than either blacks or Hispanics, and voters aged forty-five to sixty-four usually vote in proportionally greater numbers than any other age group. Education is also an important factor—people with more education are more likely to vote.

(*VSAP,* 87–8; *VSC,* 43, 48)

**Q** **398. What has voter turnout been like for eighteen-to-twenty-year-olds?**

**A** In the 1972 presidential election, the first national election in which eighteen-to twenty-year-olds were eligible to vote, an estimated 48 percent of them voted. But their participation in elections has been declining ever since, and only about 39 percent voted in the 1992 presidential election.

(*SOW,* 15; *VSAP,* 87)

**Q** **399. What is the Hatch Act?**

**A** Passed in 1939 to maintain a nonpartisan civil service, the Hatch Act (named after Sen. Carl Hatch, D-N.M.) originally prohibited federal employees from most forms of active participation in election campaigns. But Congress in 1993 approved a sweeping revision, backed by the Clinton administration, allowing many federal employees the freedom to participate in political rallies and campaigns during off-duty hours. Federal employees still cannot solicit campaign contributions from the general public, but they can now publicly endorse candidates and even hold offices in political parties. The new law does not apply to members of the armed forces, who are governed by military rules, and federal employees in sensitive areas, such as the Federal Bureau of Investigation and the Federal Election Commission, who must conform to the original Hatch Act provisions. These include prohibitions against endorsing candidates, working for or against candidates in any way, or even participating in partisan voter-registration drives.

(*CQ Weekly Report,* Nov. 13, 1993, 3146; *PAZ,* 75; *Wash. Post,* Sep.. 22, 1994, A21)

(*See 109 What is patronage?; 274 What is pork-barrel politics?*)

### Q 400. What are PACs?

A Political action committees, or PACs, promote special interests by raising and distributing money for political campaigns. Candidates for president, Congress, and other political offices benefit from PACs either directly (through donated money) or indirectly (through PAC-sponsored ads supporting their candidacy). PACs usually are formed to promote a single issue, such as abortion, or to advance the economic interests of a professional, business, or labor group. They have become a major source of campaign money in recent years, partly because campaign finance reforms have been to their benefit: while individual candidates may receive only $1,000 from any one source, PACs may receive up to $5,000 annually from a single contributor.

(*PAZ,* 339; *SOW,* 252–3)

## PRESIDENTIAL ELECTIONS

### Q 401. What have the results been for presidential elections?

A Fifty-two presidential elections have been held since ratification of the Constitution. No meaningful popular vote figures are available for elections before 1824, largely because many electors were chosen by state legislatures then, not by popular vote.

Popular vote percentages listed below often do not add to one hundred due to rounding and to omission of candidates receiving only a few thousand votes.

| Year | Presidential candidate | Electoral vote | Popular vote | Popular vote (%) |
|------|------------------------|:--------------:|:------------:|:----------------:|
| 1789 | George Washington | 69 | — | — |
|      | John Adams | 34 | — | — |
|      | John Jay | 9 | — | — |
|      | Robert Harrison | 6 | — | — |
|      | John Rutledge | 6 | — | — |
| 1792 | George Washington | 132 | — | — |
|      | John Adams | 77 | — | — |
|      | George Clinton | 50 | — | — |
| 1796 | John Adams, Fed. | 71 | — | — |
|      | Thomas Jefferson, DR | 68 | — | — |
|      | Thomas Pinckney, Fed. | 59 | — | — |
|      | Aaron Burr, DR | 30 | — | — |
|      | Oliver Ellsworth, Fed. | 11 | — | — |
|      | George Clinton, DR | 5 | — | — |
| 1800 | Thomas Jefferson, DR | 73 | — | — |
|      | Aaron Burr, DR | 73 | — | — |
|      | John Adams, Fed. | 65 | — | — |
|      | Charles C. Pinckney, Fed. | 64 | — | — |
|      | *(Election decided by the House, which picked Jefferson.)* | | | |
| 1804 | Thomas Jefferson, DR | 162 | — | — |
|      | Charles C. Pinckney, Fed. | 14 | — | — |
| 1808 | James Madison, DR | 122 | — | — |
|      | Charles C. Pinckney, Fed. | 47 | — | — |
|      | George Clinton, DR | 6 | — | — |
| 1812 | James Madison, DR | 128 | — | — |
|      | George Clinton, Fed. | 89 | — | — |
| 1816 | James Monroe, DR | 183 | — | — |
|      | Rufus King, Fed. | 34 | — | — |
| 1820 | James Monroe, DR | 231 | — | — |

| Year | Presidential candidate | Electoral vote | Popular vote | Popular vote (%) |
|------|------------------------|----------------|--------------|------------------|
| 1824 | Andrew Jackson, DR | 99 | 151,271 | 41.3 |
| | John Q. Adams, DR | 84 | 113,122 | 30.9 |
| | Henry Clay, DR | 37 | 47,531 | 13.0 |
| | William Crawford, DR | 41 | 40,856 | 11.2 |
| | *(Election decided by the House, which picked Adams.)* | | | |
| 1828 | Andrew Jackson, D | 178 | 642,553 | 56.0 |
| | John Q. Adams, Nat.-Rep. | 83 | 500,897 | 43.6 |
| 1832 | Andrew Jackson, D | 219 | 701,780 | 54.2 |
| | Henry Clay, Nat.-Rep. | 49 | 484,205 | 37.4 |
| | William Wirt, Anti-Mason | 7 | 100,715 | 7.8 |
| 1836 | Martin Van Buren, D | 170 | 764,176 | 50.8 |
| | William H. Harrison, Whig | 73 | 550,816 | 36.6 |
| | Hugh L. White, Whig | 26 | 146,107 | 9.7 |
| | Daniel Webster, Whig | 14 | 41,201 | 2.7 |
| 1840 | William H. Harrison, Whig | 234 | 1,275,390 | 52.9 |
| | Martin Van Buren, D | 60 | 1,128,854 | 46.8 |
| | James Birney, Liberty | — | 6,797 | 0.3 |
| 1844 | James K. Polk, D | 170 | 1,339,494 | 49.5 |
| | Henry Clay, Whig | 105 | 1,300,004 | 48.1 |
| | James Birney, Liberty | — | 62,103 | 2.3 |
| 1848 | Zachary Taylor, Whig | 163 | 1,361,393 | 47.3 |
| | Lewis Cass, D | 127 | 1,223,460 | 42.5 |
| | Martin Van Buren, Free Soil | — | 291,501 | 10.1 |
| 1852 | Franklin Pierce, D | 254 | 1,607,510 | 50.8 |
| | Winfield Scott, Whig | 42 | 1,386,942 | 43.9 |
| | John Hale, Free Soil | — | 155,210 | 4.9 |
| 1856 | James Buchanan, D | 174 | 1,836,072 | 45.3 |
| | John Fremont, R | 114 | 1,342,345 | 33.1 |
| | Millard Fillmore, American (Know-nothing) | 8 | 873,053 | 21.5 |

| 1860 | Abraham Lincoln, R | 180 | 1,865,908 | 39.8 |
|---|---|---|---|---|
| | John Breckinridge, | | | |
| | Southern Dem. | 72 | 848,019 | 18.1 |
| | John Bell, | | | |
| | Constitutional Union | 39 | 590,901 | 12.6 |
| | Stephen A. Douglas, D | 12 | 1,380,202 | 29.5 |
| 1864 | Abraham Lincoln, R | 212 | 2,218,388 | 55.0 |
| | George McClellan, D | 21 | 1,812,807 | 45.0 |
| 1868 | Ulysses S. Grant, R | 214 | 3,013,650 | 52.7 |
| | Horatio Seymour, D | 80 | 2,708,744 | 47.3 |
| 1872 | Ulysses S. Grant, R | 286 | 3,598,235 | 55.6 |
| | Horace Greeley, D | | | |
| | *(died before electoral vote)* | — | 2,834,761 | 43.8 |
| | Charles O'Connor, | | | |
| | Straight-Out Democrat | — | 18,602 | 0.3 |
| | Thomas Hendricks | 42* | — | — |
| | B. Gratz Brown | 18* | — | — |
| | *Originally committed to Greeley. | | | |
| 1876 | Rutherford B. Hayes, R | 185 | 4,034,311 | 47.9 |
| | Samuel Tilden, D | 184 | 4,288,546 | 51.0 |
| | Peter Cooper, Greenback | — | 75,973 | 0.9 |
| | *(House named special election commission to award nineteen contested electoral votes; Hayes was awarded the votes.)* | | | |
| 1880 | James A. Garfield, R | 214 | 4,446,158 | 48.3 |
| | Winfield Hancock, D | 155 | 4,444,260 | 48.2 |
| | James Weaver, Greenback | — | 305,997 | 3.3 |
| 1884 | Grover Cleveland, D | 219 | 4,874,621 | 48.5 |
| | James Blaine, R | 182 | 4,848,936 | 48.2 |
| | Benjamin Butler, Greenback | — | 175,096 | 1.7 |
| | John St. John, Prohibition | — | 147,482 | 1.5 |
| 1888 | Benjamin Harrison, R | 233 | 5,443,892 | 47.8 |
| | Grover Cleveland, D | 168 | 5,534,488 | 48.6 |
| | Clinton Fisk, Prohibition | — | 249,813 | 2.2 |
| | Alton Streeter, Union Labor | — | 146,602 | 1.3 |

| Year | Presidential candidate | Electoral vote | Popular vote | Popular vote (%) |
|------|------------------------|----------------|--------------|------------------|
| 1892 | Grover Cleveland, D | 277 | 5,551,883 | 46.1 |
| | Benjamin Harrison, R | 145 | 5,179,244 | 43.0 |
| | James Weaver, Populist | 22 | 1,024,280 | 8.5 |
| | John Bidwell, Prohibition | — | 270,770 | 2.2 |
| 1896 | William McKinley, R | 271 | 7,108,480 | 51.0 |
| | William J. Bryan, D | 176 | 6,511,495 | 46.7 |
| | John M. Palmer, Nat. Dem. | — | 133,435 | 1.0 |
| | Joshua Levering, Prohibition | — | 125,072 | 0.9 |
| 1900 | William McKinley, R | 292 | 7,218,039 | 51.7 |
| | William J. Bryan, D | 155 | 6,358,345 | 45.5 |
| | John Wooley, Prohibition | — | 209,004 | 1.5 |
| | Eugene Debs, Socialist | — | 86,935 | 0.6 |
| 1904 | Theodore Roosevelt, R | 336 | 7,626,593 | 56.4 |
| | Alton Parker, D | 140 | 5,028,898 | 37.6 |
| | Eugene Debs, Socialist | — | 402,489 | 3.0 |
| | Silas Swallow, Prohibition | — | 258,596 | 1.9 |
| 1908 | William H. Taft, R | 321 | 7,676,258 | 51.6 |
| | William J. Bryan, D | 162 | 6,406,801 | 43.0 |
| | Eugene Debs, Socialist | — | 420,380 | 2.8 |
| | Eugene Chafin, Prohibition | — | 252,821 | 1.7 |
| 1912 | Woodrow Wilson, D | 435 | 6,293,152 | 41.8 |
| | Theodore Roosevelt, Progressive | 88 | 4,119,207 | 27.4 |
| | William H. Taft, R | 8 | 3,486,333 | 23.2 |
| | Eugene Debs, Socialist | — | 900,369 | 6.0 |
| 1916 | Woodrow Wilson, D | 277 | 9,126,300 | 49.2 |
| | Charles Hughes, R | 254 | 8,546,789 | 46.1 |
| | Allan Benson, Socialist | — | 589,924 | 3.2 |
| | Frank Hanly, Prohibition | — | 221,030 | 1.2 |
| 1920 | Warren G. Harding, R | 404 | 16,133,314 | 60.3 |
| | James Cox, D | 127 | 9,140,884 | 34.2 |
| | Eugene Debs, Socialist | — | 913,664 | 3.4 |

| | | | | |
|---|---|---|---|---|
| | Parley Christensen, Farmer-Labor | — | 264,540 | 1.0 |
| 1924 | Calvin Coolidge, R | 382 | 15,717,553 | 54.1 |
| | John Davis, D | 136 | 8,386,169 | 28.8 |
| | Robert La Follette, Sr., Progressive | 13 | 4,814,050 | 16.6 |
| | Herman Faris, Prohibition | — | 54,833 | 0.2 |
| 1928 | Herbert Hoover, R | 444 | 21,411,991 | 58.2 |
| | Alfred E. Smith, D | 87 | 15,000,185 | 40.8 |
| | Norman Thomas, Socialist | — | 266,453 | 0.7 |
| | William Foster, Communist | — | 48,170 | 0.1 |
| 1932 | Franklin Roosevelt, D | 472 | 22,825,016 | 57.4 |
| | Herbert Hoover, R | 59 | 15,758,397 | 39.6 |
| | Norman Thomas, Socialist | — | 883,990 | 2.0 |
| | William Foster, Communist | — | 102,221 | 0.3 |
| 1936 | Franklin Roosevelt, D | 523 | 27,747,636 | 60.8 |
| | Alfred Landon, R | 8 | 16,679,543 | 36.5 |
| | William Lemke, Union | — | 892,492 | 2.0 |
| | Norman Thomas, Socialist | — | 187,785 | 0.4 |
| 1940 | Franklin Roosevelt, D | 449 | 27,263,448 | 54.7 |
| | Wendell Wilkie, R | 82 | 22,336,260 | 44.8 |
| | Norman Thomas, Socialist | — | 116,827 | 0.2 |
| | Roger Babson, Prohibition | — | 58,685 | 0.1 |
| 1944 | Franklin Roosevelt, D | 432 | 25,611,936 | 53.4 |
| | Thomas E. Dewey, R | 99 | 22,013,372 | 45.9 |
| | Norman Thomas, Socialist | — | 79,000 | 0.2 |
| | Claude Watson, Prohibition | — | 74,733 | 0.2 |
| 1948 | Harry S. Truman, D | 303 | 24,105,587 | 49.5 |
| | Thomas E. Dewey, R | 189 | 21,970,017 | 45.1 |
| | Strom Thurmond, States' Rights Dem. | 39 | 1,169,134 | 2.4 |
| | Henry Wallace, Progressive | — | 1,157,057 | 2.4 |
| 1952 | Dwight Eisenhower, R | 442 | 33,936,137 | 55.1 |
| | Adlai Stevenson, D | 89 | 27,314,649 | 44.4 |
| | Vincent Hallinan, Progressive | — | 140,416 | 0.2 |
| | Stuart Hamblen, Prohibition | — | 73,413 | 0.1 |

| Year | Presidential candidate | Electoral vote | Popular vote | Popular vote (%) |
|------|------------------------|----------------|--------------|------------------|
| 1956 | Dwight Eisenhower, R | 457 | 35,585,245 | 57.4 |
|  | Adlai Stevenson, D | 73 | 26,030,172 | 42.0 |
|  | Coleman Andrews, Constitution | — | 108,055 | 0.2 |
|  | Eric Hass, Soc.-Labor | — | 44,300 | 0.1 |
| 1960 | John F. Kennedy, D | 303 | 34,221,344 | 49.7 |
|  | Richard M. Nixon, R | 219 | 34,106,671 | 49.5 |
|  | Eric Hass, Soc.-Labor | — | 47,522 | 0.1 |
| 1964 | Lyndon B. Johnson, D | 486 | 43,126,584 | 61.1 |
|  | Barry Goldwater, R | 52 | 27,177,838 | 38.5 |
|  | Eric Hass, Soc.-Labor | — | 45,187 | 0.1 |
| 1968 | Richard M. Nixon, R | 301 | 31,785,148 | 43.4 |
|  | Hubert Humphrey, D | 191 | 31,274,503 | 42.7 |
|  | George Wallace, American Independent | 46 | 9,901,151 | 13.5 |
|  | Henning Blomen, Soc.-Labor | — | 52,591 | 0.1 |
| 1972 | Richard M. Nixon, R | 520 | 47,170,179 | 60.7 |
|  | George McGovern, D | 17 | 29,171,791 | 37.5 |
|  | John Schmitz, American Independent | — | 1,090,673 | 1.4 |
|  | Benjamin Spock, People's | — | 78,751 | 0.1 |
| 1976 | Jimmy Carter, D | 297 | 40,830,763 | 50.1 |
|  | Gerald R. Ford, R | 240 | 39,147,793 | 48.0 |
|  | Eugene McCarthy, Independent | — | 756,691 | 0.9 |
|  | Roger MacBride, Libertarian | — | 173,011 | 0.2 |
| 1980 | Ronald Reagan, R | 489 | 43,904,153 | 50.7 |
|  | Jimmy Carter, D | 49 | 35,483,883 | 41.0 |
|  | John Anderson, Independent | — | 5,720,060 | 6.6 |
|  | Ed Clark, Libertarian | — | 921,299 | 1.1 |
| 1984 | Ronald Reagan, R | 525 | 54,455,075 | 58.8 |
|  | Walter F. Mondale, D | 13 | 37,577,185 | 40.6 |
|  | David Bergland, Libertarian | — | 228,314 | 0.2 |
|  | Lyndon LaRouche, Jr., Independent | — | 78,807 | 0.1 |
| 1988 | George Bush, R | 426 | 48,886,097 | 53.4 |
|  | Michael Dukakis, D | 111 | 41,809,083 | 45.6 |

| | | | |
|---|---|---:|---:|
| | Ron Paul, Libertarian | — | 432,179 | 0.5 |
| | Lenora Fulana, New Alliance | — | 217,219 | 0.2 |
| 1992 | Bill Clinton, D | 370 | 44,908,233 | 43.0 |
| | George Bush, R | 168 | 39,102,282 | 37.4 |
| | Ross Perot, Independent | — | 19,741,048 | 18.9 |

(*CQ Almanac 1992*, 7-A; *GUSE*, 269–313, 329–66; *PAZ*, 510–14)

**Q 402. Which presidents have been elected without winning the popular vote?**

**A** Three presidents—John Q. Adams, Rutherford B. Hayes, and Benjamin Harrison—took office even though they lost the popular vote. Adams's election was decided in the House (1824), Hayes won after an election commission awarded disputed electoral votes to him (1876), and Harrison managed to win enough electoral votes to become president even though he lost the popular vote (1888). In thirteen other elections, the following presidents did not win a majority of the popular vote but nevertheless received more votes than their opponents: Polk, Taylor, Buchanan, Lincoln, Garfield, Cleveland (both victories), Wilson (both victories), Truman, Kennedy, Nixon (first victory), and Clinton.

(*PAZ*, 6, 206; *SOW*, 238)

(*See 84 Which presidents and vice presidents served when?*)

**Q 403. Which presidential elections were decided by Congress?**

**A** Two elections were decided directly by the House—those of Thomas Jefferson and John Q. Adams. The electoral college originally did not distinguish between presidential and vice presidential candidates when voting and in 1800 gave both Jefferson and Aaron Burr the same number of votes. The House decided in Jefferson's favor. The Twelfth Amendment, ratified in 1804, prevented that situation from happening again. During the election of 1824, none of the four candidates—John Q. Adams, Andrew Jackson, Henry Clay, and William Crawford—won a majority of the electoral vote. The House chose Adams, even though he ran second to Jackson in popular and electoral votes. The House also became involved in the 1876 election, a race between Republican Rutherford B. Hayes and Democrat Samuel Tilden. Tilden won the popular vote by a margin of 260,000 but trailed by one vote in the electoral college. The electoral vote in Florida, Louisiana, and South Carolina, however, was in dispute, and two sets of electoral votes were sent from those states. A special election commission was set up to settle the dispute. When it began awarding the votes to Hayes, Democrats objected. After Republicans agreed to withdraw federal troops from the South, southern conservatives allowed the count to continue and Hayes became president. Soon after Hayes took office in 1877, he withdrew federal troops, effectively ending the Reconstruction era.

(*SOW*, 239)

(*See 29 What do the amendments to the Constitution say, in brief?; 405 How does the electoral college work?; 411 How were presidential nominees chosen before conventions?*)

### Q 404. Which vice presidential elections did Congress decide?

A The Senate has decided only one vice presidential election, that of Martin Van Buren's vice president, Richard M. Johnson. The decision fell to the Senate in 1837 after Johnson, a Democrat, missed winning an electoral majority by just one vote. Virginia electors had voted for another candidate to protest Johnson's fondness for slave mistresses. Nevertheless, Senators confirmed his election by a vote along party lines. Johnson was the first vice president not to come from one of the original thirteen states.

(*PAZ*, 258; *SOW*, 239)

(*See 346 What are the special duties of the Senate?*)

### Q 405. How does the electoral college work?

A Whenever one votes in a November presidential election, one actually casts a ballot for a slate of electors from one's state who are pledged to one's candidate. Winning electors then meet in the state capital on the first Monday after the second Wednesday in December to vote for the president and vice president. Similar votes in state capitals nationwide that day constitute what is called the electoral college. Each state sends its vote tally to Congress, which counts the votes and officially declares the winners on January 6. Candidates need a majority of electoral votes to win—in 1992 that was 270 of the total 538 votes. If no candidate receives a majority, the House chooses the president (the Senate chooses the vice president). Each state is allowed as many electors as it has representatives and senators in Congress, plus the District of Columbia has three votes. All but two states have "winner-take-all" systems giving the state's popular vote winner all its electoral votes. Maine and Nebraska allocate electors by the vote in special districts. The Constitution allows electors to vote as they see fit, but nearly all have honored their pledges. The few so-called faithless electors have never altered an election outcome.

(*CAZ*, 114–16; *PAZ*, 151–3)

*(See 402 Which presidents have been elected without winning the popular vote?; 403 Which presidential elections were decided by Congress?; 404 Which vice presidential elections did Congress decide?)*

## 406. How did the election of 1800 change the method of electing the president and vice president?

Prior to ratification of the Twelfth Amendment in 1804, each member of the electoral college voted for two different candidates. The candidate winning the most votes became president; the one winning the second most, vice president. The flaw in this system, set up by the Constitution, revealed itself in 1800 when John Adams and Charles C. Pinckney ran against Thomas Jefferson and Aaron Burr. Jefferson and his vice-presidential running mate wound up with the same number of electoral votes, and the election was thrown to the House (which finally elected Jefferson after thirty-six ballots). The Twelfth Amendment eliminated the problem by ordering separate electoral votes for president and vice president.

(*PAZ*, 143–4, 541)

*(See 29 What do the amendments to the Constitution say, in brief?; 403 Which presidential elections were decided by Congress?)*

## 407. Which states have primaries?

One or both of the major parties held primaries in thirty-eight states before the 1992 presidential election. Since 1960, when presidential candidate John F. Kennedy popularized them as a means to gain the Democratic nomination, primaries have been an important part of the presidential election process. The number of states holding them dipped after reaching thirty-eight in 1980, then rose again to thirty-eight in 1992. The District of Columbia and Puerto Rico also held primaries in 1992. Following is a list of states that had primaries for the 1992 election:

| | |
|---|---|
| Alabama | Nebraska |
| Arkansas | New Hampshire |
| California | New Jersey |
| Colorado | New Mexico |
| Connecticut | New York |
| Florida | North Carolina |
| Georgia | North Dakota |
| Idaho | Ohio |
| Illinois | Oklahoma |
| Indiana | Oregon |
| Kansas | Pennsylvania |
| Kentucky | Rhode Island |
| Louisiana | South Carolina |
| Maryland | South Dakota |
| Massachusetts | Tennessee |
| Michigan | Texas |
| Minnesota | Washington |
| Mississippi | West Virginia |
| Montana | Wisconsin |

(*SOW*, 224–5; *VSAP*, 91–4)

**Q 408. Which states have caucuses?**

**A** In the following states, one or both of the major parties held caucuses to determine party members' preferences for presidential nominee and/or for delegates to the national party convention:

| | | |
|---|---|---|
| Alaska | Maine | Utah |
| Arizona | Minnesota | Vermont |
| Delaware | Missouri | Virginia |
| Hawaii | Nevada | Washington |
| Idaho | North Dakota | Wyoming |
| Iowa | Texas | |

(*PAZ*, 348–9; *VSAP*, 95)

## Q 409. When was the first convention?

**A** National conventions for nominating party candidates developed in reaction to the "King Caucus" system, used to select presidential candidates until the mid-1820s. A third party, the Anti-Masonic party, held the first convention in September 1831 and nominated William Wirt for president. The Whig party held the next one just months later, in December, and nominated its presidential candidate, Henry Clay. The Democrats convened in May 1832 to nominate Andrew Jackson.

(*PAZ*, 315; *SOW*, 222)

(*See 411 How were presidential nominees chosen before conventions?*)


## Q 410. When was the first political convention televised?

**A** Television cameras captured convention proceedings live for the first time in 1940, at the Republican National Convention in Philadelphia. That year the Republicans nominated Wendell Willkie for president and Charles L. McNary for vice president (they lost to the Democrats).

(*SOW*, 223)


## Q 411. How were presidential nominees chosen before conventions?

**A** Party members in Congress met in a caucus to choose most presidential candidates from 1796 until that method died out in the 1820s. Called the "King Caucus" by its detractors, the caucus system was first tried by Democratic-Republicans in 1796. The Federalist party tried the system, too, but dropped it by 1804. The Democratic-Republicans continued to use the caucus to pick party candidates until the divisive election of 1824. Objecting to their party's King Caucus nominee, John Q. Adams, Andrew Jackson, and Henry Clay all ran on their own in 1824 and succeeded in throwing the election to the House. While he had failed to amass a majority, Jackson had nevertheless won the popular vote and the most electoral votes. Still, the House chose Adams as president. The resulting bitter divisions wrecked the party, ended the King Caucus system, and helped bring about party conventions..

(*PAZ*, 93)

(*See 403 Which presidential elections were decided by Congress?*)

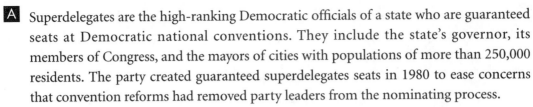

**Q 412. What are superdelegates?**

**A** Superdelegates are the high-ranking Democratic officials of a state who are guaranteed seats at Democratic national conventions. They include the state's governor, its members of Congress, and the mayors of cities with populations of more than 250,000 residents. The party created guaranteed superdelegates seats in 1980 to ease concerns that convention reforms had removed party leaders from the nominating process.

(*PAZ*, 116)

**Q 413. For how long have presidential candidates been nominated on the first ballot at conventions?**

**A** President Andrew Jackson was nominated for a second term on the first ballot at the Democrats' first nominating convention in 1832. Similarly, the newly formed Republican party nominated its first presidential candidate, John C. Fremont, on the first ballot at its first convention in 1856. In all, Republicans and Democrats have each chosen twenty-six presidential candidates on the first ballot. Since Dwight Eisenhower was chosen on the first ballot in 1952, every Republican presidential candidate has been nominated on the first ballot. The Democrats have a similar string of first-ballot nominees dating back to 1956, when Adlai Stevenson ran as the unsuccessful Democratic candidate.

(*FAP*, 367)

**Q 414. When was the longest convention on record?**

**A** The Democratic convention of 1924, which finally nominated John Davis, was the longest. Delegates voted 105 times over 14 days before giving Davis enough votes to clinch the nomination. Davis was later defeated by Republican Calvin Coolidge.

(*FAP*, 365–6; *PAZ*, 510–14)

**Q 415. Has each presidential election since 1960 included televised debates between the candidates?**

**A** After the four Nixon-Kennedy debates in 1960 (the first of which occurred on September 26), televised debates between candidates were not held again until the three Ford-Carter matchups in 1976. The first-ever televised vice presidential debates, between

Sens. Robert Dole and Walter F. Mondale, aired October 15, 1976. Major candidates have debated in every election since 1976: 1980, Carter-Reagan, once; 1984, Reagan-Mondale, twice; 1988, Bush-Dukakis, twice; and 1992, Bush-Clinton-Perot, three times.

(*PAZ*, 57; *SOW*, 244–5; *VSAP*, 76)

(*See 448 Which vice presidential nominees have debated?*)

## Q 416. Which party had the longest series of consecutive presidencies?

A The first opposition party, the Democratic-Republican party, held onto the presidency for seven straight terms from 1801 to 1829. Thomas Jefferson served two terms, James Madison two, James Monroe two, and John Q. Adams one. The Republicans' longest unbroken string amounted to six terms, from 1861 to 1885, and included Presidents Abraham Lincoln, Andrew Johnson, Ulysses S. Grant, Rutherford B. Hayes, James A. Garfield, and Chester A. Arthur. In this century the Democrats enjoyed the longest series of consecutive presidencies—five terms between 1933 and 1953 (served by Presidents Franklin Roosevelt and Harry S. Truman).

(*PAZ*, 503–6)

(*See 10 When has the same party controlled the White House and both houses of Congress?; 84 Which presidents and vice presidents served when?*)

## Q 417. Which tickets of sitting presidents and sitting vice presidents have lost?

A Five such tickets have lost. In 1840 President Martin Van Buren and Vice President Richard M. Johnson became the first to lose. Not until 1912, when President William H. Taft and Vice President James S. Sherman were beaten by the Wilson-Marshall ticket, did another sitting president and vice president fail in their bid for a second term. Herbert Hoover and Charles Curtis fell to the Roosevelt-Garner ticket in 1933, the Carter-Mondale ticket was beaten by Ronald Reagan and George Bush in 1980, and the Bush-Quayle ticket lost to the Clinton-Gore campaign in 1992.

(*PAZ*, 105, 503–6)

## Q 418. How accurate have pollsters been in presidential elections?

A Generally, the closer the polls are to election day, the more accurate they are in relation to the actual election results. Even polls taken after both nominating conventions in the summer before a presidential election can be unreliable. In 1980, for example, summertime polls showed President Jimmy Carter ahead by 1 percent of the vote; in November he lost by 10 percent. The most famous misprediction by pollsters was made before the 1948 election, in which President Harry S. Truman trailed challenger Thomas E. Dewey by as much as 11 percent in the polls and wound up winning by 4.5 percent. Pollsters had taken their last surveys in September and October, and so had missed a late surge for Truman. In other cases, polls immediately after the second convention have predicted the winner but have incorrectly estimated the margin of victory. President Lyndon B. Johnson had a 36 percent lead in polls during the summer of 1964, but actually won by 23 percent in November. Early polls did not fare well in the extremely volatile 1992 presidential election, in which President George Bush seesawed from an early lead to as much as 20 percent behind. However, most polls taken just before the election were within a few percentage points of the actual vote (Clinton 43 percent, Bush 38 percent, and Perot 19 percent). The Harris poll came closest, predicting 44 percent for Clinton, 37 percent for Bush, 17 percent for Perot, and 1 percent other/undecided.

(*CQ Weekly Report*, Aug. 22, 1992, 2515, and Nov. 7, 1992, 3550)

(*See 401 What have the results been for presidential elections?*)

### Q 419. Have exit polls ever influenced an election?

A Exit polls, informal surveys of voter preferences taken as voters leave the polling places, have never directly affected the outcome of a presidential election. But in 1980, basing his decision on network news shows' exit polls predicting a Reagan victory, Jimmy Carter conceded defeat even before the polls had closed in California. As a result many voters still waiting on line simply went home, which cost many other Democratic candidates votes they might otherwise have gotten. Network news shows since then have refrained from declaring winners until after polls have closed everywhere in the United States.

(*SOW,* 246)

### Q 420. What is the coattail effect?

A A presidential candidate whose popularity is strong enough to gain votes for the party's congressional and state office candidates is said to have "long coattails." For example, in 1980 Ronald Reagan's long coattails helped Republicans win a majority in

· the Senate for the first time since 1955. But presidential popularity does not always translate into votes for the party's other candidates, and political analysts tend to downplay its importance.

(*PAZ,* 384)

## PRESIDENTIAL CANDIDATES

**Q** **421. Has anyone run for president unopposed?**

**A** Because of his stature as a national hero, George Washington was unopposed when elected to both his terms (1789 and 1792). However, Washington's vice president, John Adams, faced opponents both times he sought the presidency. The only president besides Washington to run unopposed was James Monroe, a Democratic-Republican running for reelection in 1820. The Federalist party, which had fielded a candidate against him in 1816, died out before the 1820 election.

(*Encyc. of Amer. Hist.,* 145, 149, 192; *PAZ,* 510–14)

**Q** **422. What was the largest presidential landslide?**

**A** Democratic President Lyndon B. Johnson holds the record for largest presidential landslide, having captured an overwhelming percentage of the popular vote in his 1964 race against Barry Goldwater. Johnson polled 61.1 percent to Goldwater's 38.5 percent and won by about 15.9 million votes. Only three other presidents have captured over 60 percent of the popular vote: Republican Warren G. Harding, 60.3 percent for a 6.9 million-vote margin (1920); Democrat Franklin Roosevelt, 60.8 percent for an 11.06 million-vote margin (1936); and Republican Richard M. Nixon, 60.7 percent for a 17.9 million-vote margin (1972). Nixon's margin of victory in the 1972 election was the largest ever.

(*PAZ,* 510–14)

**Q** **423. What was the closest popular vote for president?**

**A** In terms of number and percentage of popular votes, the 1880 contest was closest. Republican President James A. Garfield won by a hair's-breadth margin of 1,898 votes, just one tenth of 1 percent more votes than Democratic challenger Winfield

Hancock received. They had 4,446,158 and 4,444,260 votes, respectively. Other elections won by 1 percent of the popular vote or less were: 1884, Grover Cleveland over James Blaine by 25,685 votes (48.5 percent to 48.2 percent); 1888, Benjamin Harrison over Cleveland in the electoral college, even though Cleveland had 90,596 more popular votes (47.8 percent to 48.6 percent); 1960, John F. Kennedy over Richard M. Nixon by 114,673 votes (49.7 percent to 49.5 percent); and 1968, Nixon over Hubert Humphrey by 510,645 votes (43.4 percent to 42.7 percent).

(*PAZ*, 510–14)

## Q 424. Which incumbent presidents were defeated?

A The eleven incumbent presidents who failed to win reelection are listed below.

| Incumbent president | Defeated by | Year defeated |
| --- | --- | --- |
| John Adams | Thomas Jefferson | 1800 |
| John Q. Adams | Andrew Jackson | 1828 |
| Martin Van Buren | William H. Harrison | 1840 |
| Millard Fillmore | James Buchanan | 1856 |
| Grover Cleveland | Benjamin Harrison | 1888 |
| Benjamin Harrison | Grover Cleveland* | 1892 |
| William H. Taft | Woodrow Wilson | 1912 |
| Herbert Hoover | Franklin Roosevelt | 1932 |
| Gerald R. Ford | Jimmy Carter | 1976 |
| Jimmy Carter | Ronald Reagan | 1980 |
| George Bush | Bill Clinton | 1992 |

* Cleveland was the only president to serve nonconsecutive terms.

(*FAP*, 378)

(*See 141 Who was the only president to have served nonconsecutive terms?*)

## Q 425. Which incumbent presidents decided not to run again?

A Seventeen presidents did not run again, fourteen of them after serving all or part of two terms. The one-term presidents who did not seek renomination were James K. Polk, James Buchanan, and Rutherford B. Hayes. Presidents who served more than one term and then did not run again were George Washington, Thomas Jefferson,

James Madison, James Monroe, Andrew Jackson, Ulysses S. Grant, Grover Cleveland, Theodore Roosevelt, Woodrow Wilson, Calvin Coolidge, Harry S. Truman, and Lyndon B. Johnson. Both Dwight Eisenhower and Ronald Reagan could not run again because of the two-term limit, which became effective in 1951. Earlier presidents who had served two full terms generally abided by the two-term tradition established by President Washington. Franklin Roosevelt broke that tradition in 1940.

(*Encyc. Britannica,* vol. 4, 966, vol. 8, 279; *FAP,* 91; *RD Encyc. of Amer. Hist.,* 294, 568, 576, 674, 737, 879, 970, 1247, 1290)

(*See 84 Which presidents and vice presidents served when?; 125 How long do the president and the vice president serve?; 142 Who was the only president to serve more than two terms?*)

**Q 426. Which presidents were denied their party's nomination?**

**A** Five presidents failed to gain renomination; four of them had succeeded to the presidency. The first president to lose his party's backing was John Tyler. Unpopular with Whigs during his term (1841–1845), he was sidelined when Henry Clay won the Whig nomination in 1844. In 1852 another Whig president, Millard Fillmore, lost his party's nomination to Winfield Scott on the fifty-third ballot. President Franklin Pierce served from 1853 to 1857, but because his handling of the crisis over slavery in Kansas and elsewhere pleased no one, the Democrats dumped him at the 1856 nominating convention. They selected James Buchanan instead. Democrat Andrew Johnson, serving in the Republican administration, finished out President Abraham Lincoln's unexpired term (1865–1869), but in 1868 Republicans passed over him to nominate Horatio Seymour. Republican President Chester A. Arthur (served 1881 to 1885) lost out to James Blaine during his party's 1884 nominating convention.

(*Encyc. Britannica,* vol. 8, 279; *FAP,* 378; *PAZ,* 17–18, 177–8, 253–4, 336–7, 436–8)

**Q 427. Which defeated presidential candidates eventually won?**

**A** Thomas Jefferson, who had finished second in the 1796 race for the presidency, won the election of 1800, which was decided in the House. James Monroe, an also-ran in the 1808 presidential election, easily won the presidency in 1816. Andrew Jackson lost the election of 1824 when the House named John Q. Adams the winner, but he ran again and won in 1828. In 1836 William H. Harrison lost to Martin Van Buren, but he persisted and won when he ran again in 1840 (he died soon after his inauguration, however). Grover Cleveland lost his reelection bid to Benjamin Harrison in 1888, but won a second, nonconsecutive term in 1892 (the only president to do so). The last presidential candidate to lose and run again was Richard M. Nixon. He narrowly lost to John F. Kennedy in 1960 but ran again in 1968 and won.

(*FAP*, 377–8)

(*See 84 Which presidents and vice presidents served when?; 141 Who was the only president to have served nonconsecutive terms?; 403 Which presidential elections were decided by Congress?*)

Q **428. Which candidate has run for president most often?**

A Republican Harold E. Stassen, who became Minnesota's governor at age thirty-one, has run for the presidency ten times, declining to participate in only two elections since his initial bid in 1948. In 1956 and 1972 he decided not to challenge Republican incumbents Dwight Eisenhower and Richard M. Nixon, respectively.

(*SOW*, 219–20)

Q **429. Which third-party candidates won more than 6 percent of the popular vote?**

A Though third-party candidates have run in nearly every election, they have polled 6 percent of the popular vote or better just twelve times (listed below).

| Election year | Third-party candidate | Popular vote (%) |
|---|---|---|
| 1832 | Anti-Mason, William Wirt | 7.8 |
| 1848 | Free Soil, Martin Van Buren (former president) | 10.1 |
| 1856 | American (Know-Nothing), Millard Fillmore (former president) | 21.5 |
| 1860 | Southern Democrat, John C. Breckinridge | 18.1 |
| 1860 | Constitutional Union, John Bell | 12.6 |
| 1892 | Populist, James Weaver | 8.5 |
| 1912 | Progressive, Theodore Roosevelt (former president) | 27.4 |
| 1912 | Socialist, Eugene Debs | 6.0 |
| 1924 | Progressive, Robert La Follette, Sr. | 16.6 |
| 1968 | American Independent, George Wallace | 13.5 |

| 1980 | Independent, John B. Anderson | 6.6 |
| 1992 | Independent, Ross Perot | 18.9 |

(*GUSE*, 23; *SOW*, 217–19)

**Q 430. How many senators have been nominated for president while still in Congress? For vice president?**

**A** Fourteen sitting senators have won their party's nomination for president. Only two, Warren G. Harding and John F. Kennedy, actually have become president, though. Senators have fared much better as potential vice presidential nominees—twenty-seven have been nominated while still in office. Of that number, thirteen have become vice president, including, most recently, Al Gore Jr.

(*The Senate*, 446–7)

(*See 163 What experience have presidents had before being elected?*)

**Q 431. What sitting governors have become president?**

**A** The six sitting governors who have been elected president are listed below. Though not a sitting governor when elected president, Jimmy Carter, Georgia governor from 1971 to 1975, went almost immediately from the governorship to the presidency, holding no other elective office in the interim. He announced his presidential candidacy in 1975 and won the 1976 presidential election.

| President | Sitting governor of (when elected) | Years served as governor |
| --- | --- | --- |
| Rutherford B. Hayes | Ohio | 1868–1872, 1876–1877 |
| Grover Cleveland | Ohio | 1876–1877 |
| William McKinley | Ohio | 1892–1896 |
| Woodrow Wilson | New Jersey | 1911–1913 |
| Franklin Roosevelt | New York | 1929–1933 |
| Bill Clinton | Arkansas | 1978–1980, 1982–1992 |

(*Facts on File 1992*, 1062; *PAZ*, 63–4, 79–80, 289–90, 372–3, 487–8, 507–9; *WHAD*, 217)

**432. Have two governors ever run together on a winning ticket?**

A Two sitting governors, Woodrow Wilson and Thomas Marshall, ran together in 1912 as the Democratic candidates for president and vice president. Wilson had been New Jersey governor since 1911 and Marshall Indiana governor since 1909. The Wilson-Marshall ticket won a three-way race in which former president Theodore Roosevelt split the Republican vote by running against the incumbent president, William H. Taft. Another sitting governor, Grover Cleveland, successfully paired up with former governor Thomas Hendricks to win the presidential election of 1884. Cleveland had been New York's governor since 1883, while Hendricks had served from 1873 to 1877 as Indiana's governor, his last major elective office before the vice presidency.

(*FAP,* 425; *PAZ,* 79, 209, 296, 488–9, 507–9)


Q **433. When did the first woman run for president?**

A Victoria Claflin Woodhull became the first in 1872, when she ran as the Equal Rights Party nominee. The Equal Rights Party fielded women candidates again in 1884 and 1888. In this century women did not appear again as presidential candidates until 1968, but at least one woman candidate (always the nominee of a minor party) has run in every presidential election since then. Neither major party has yet nominated a woman candidate for president, though the Republicans became the first to propose a female nominee, Margaret Chase Smith, at their 1964 national convention.

(*FAP,* 368–70)

*(See 445 Who was the first woman nominated for vice president by a major political party?)*


Q **434. Which blacks have run for president?**

A The first black candidate to mount a serious primary campaign for a major party's presidential nomination was Jesse Jackson. A clergyman and civil rights activist, he tried for the Democratic nomination in both 1984 and 1988, running second behind Michael Dukakis in the latter year. A full century earlier, at the 1888 Republican convention, Frederick Douglass became the first black man ever to receive a vote for the presidential nomination. Benjamin Harrison was named the party's nominee that year.

(*PAZ,* 512; *SOW,* 233)

*(See 260 Which blacks have served in Congress?; 328 Who were the first black, Hispanic, native American, female, Asian, Indian, and Hawaiian representatives and senators?)*

 **435. Who was the first Catholic nominated for president by a major party?**

The first was 1928 Democratic nominee Alfred E. Smith, the grandson of Irish immigrants. Nicknamed "the Happy Warrior" by Franklin Roosevelt, Smith ultimately lost the election to Republican Herbert Hoover. The first Catholic actually elected president, of course, was John F. Kennedy in 1960.

*(PAZ, 385)*

*(See 401 What have the results been for presidential elections?)*

 **436. Has a Democrat ever won the White House while losing Texas?**

Since Texas became a state in 1845, only one Democrat has lost the state and still become president—Bill Clinton in 1992. Clinton lost Texas' 32 electoral votes but won those of most of the other big states to amass a total of 370 electoral votes.

*(SOW, 244, 247)*

*(See 401 What have the results been for presidential elections?)*

## VICE PRESIDENTIAL CANDIDATES

**437. How many vice presidents went on to become president?**

Fourteen vice presidents became president, either by succeeding to the office or by being elected in their own right. They were John Adams, Thomas Jefferson, Martin Van Buren, John Tyler, Millard Fillmore, Andrew Johnson, Chester A. Arthur, Theodore Roosevelt, Calvin Coolidge, Harry S. Truman, Lyndon B. Johnson, Richard M. Nixon, Gerald R. Ford, and George Bush.

*(GUSE, 383)*

**Q** **438. How many vice presidents have been elected to the presidency without first succeeding to it?**

**A** Just five of the forty-five vice presidents to date have been elected to the presidency without first succeeding to it. John Adams was elected in 1796, Thomas Jefferson in 1800, Martin Van Buren in 1836, Richard Nixon in 1968, and George Bush in 1988.

(*PAZ*, 451, 503–6)

(*See 84 Which presidents and vice presidents served when?; 204 Which vice presidents succeeded to the presidency?*)

**Q** **439. Who was the first person elected president in his own right after finishing his predecessor's term in the White House?**

**A** Theodore Roosevelt, who succeeded to the presidency after William McKinley's assassination in 1901, became the first by winning the election of 1904. The four vice presidents before him who had finished their predecessors' terms either did not run afterward or ran and failed to win.

(*PAZ*, 374, 503–6)

(*See 84 Which presidents and vice presidents served when?; 204 Which vice presidents succeeded to the presidency?*)

**Q** **440. Before George Bush in 1988, who was the last sitting vice president elected president?**

**A** The last was Martin Van Buren, elected president over 150 years before Bush. Van Buren served one term as vice president from 1833 to 1837 and then one term as president from 1837 to 1841.

(*PAZ*, 503–6)

(*See 84 Which presidents and vice presidents served when?*)

**Q** **441. Who was the only person elected to two terms as vice president and then two terms as president?**

**A** Richard M. Nixon was elected vice president under President Dwight Eisenhower in 1952 and 1956, and then won presidential elections in 1968 and 1972. He served only about a year and a half of his second term, however, before being forced to resign over the Watergate scandal. John Adams and George Bush both served two terms as vice president but only one as president.

(*PAZ*, 503–6)

(*See 78 What happened in the Watergate scandal?; 84 Which presidents and vice presidents served when?*)

**Q 442. Who was the first vice president who wasn't elected president?**

**A** Thomas Jefferson's first vice president, Aaron Burr, was the first not to be elected president. Both John Adams and Thomas Jefferson before him had been, but four vice presidents after Burr also suffered his fate. The next vice president elected to the presidency was Martin Van Buren, who took office in 1837.

(*PAZ*, 47, 503)

(*See 84 Which presidents and vice presidents served when?*)

**Q 443. Which vice presidents since 1900 tried unsuccessfully for the presidency?**

**A** Seven vice presidents have lost their bids for the presidency since 1900. Woodrow Wilson's vice president, Thomas Marshall, tried unsuccessfully for the Democratic nomination in 1920. Calvin Coolidge's vice president, Charles G. Dawes, failed to get the Republican nod in 1928 and 1932. Franklin Roosevelt's first vice president, John N. Garner, was denied the Democratic nomination in 1940. Henry A. Wallace, Roosevelt's second vice president, ran on the unsuccessful Progressive Party ticket against Harry S. Truman in 1948. Alben W. Barkley, Truman's vice president, failed to get the 1952 Democratic nomination. Lyndon B. Johnson's vice president, Hubert H. Humphrey, lost the 1968 race to Nixon. Lastly, Walter F. Mondale, Jimmy Carter's vice president, lost his race against President Ronald Reagan in 1984. Vice President Richard M. Nixon lost his election campaign against John F. Kennedy in 1960 but finally did win the presidency in 1968.

(*GUSE*, 383)

**444. Has any vice president run against his former running mate?**

A No vice president ever has, though technically every vice president elected before 1804 could have been elected president instead of his running mate. Under the system originally set up by the Constitution, members of the electoral college voted for two candidates and made no distinction between president and vice president. The system worked until 1800, when both presidential candidate Thomas Jefferson and his running mate, Aaron Burr, received 73 electoral votes. The House eventually decided the election in Jefferson's favor. Soon after that, Congress passed the Twelfth Amendment, calling for separate electoral votes for president and vice president. Since then some vice presidents may have wanted to run against their incumbent running mates, but none has ever gotten the chance, either because they could not win their party's nomination or because they were unable to mount a third-party challenge. However, a former president (Theodore Roosevelt) did run as a third-party candidate against his former vice president (William H. Taft), when the latter ran for a second presidential term in 1912.

(*GUSE*, 239–47, 269–77; *PAZ*, 503–6, 510–14)

(*See 401 What have the results been for presidential elections?; 403 Which presidential elections were decided by Congress?; 406 How did the election of 1800 change the method of electing the president and vice president?*)

Q **445. Who was the first woman nominated for vice president by a major political party?**

A The 1984 Democratic vice presidential nominee Geraldine Ferraro was the first. Ferraro, a three-time representative from New York, ran with Walter F. Mondale against Republican incumbents Ronald Reagan and George Bush. Questions about her husband's real estate dealings (he was later convicted on misdemeanor charges) and about her stand on abortion came up during the campaign. The Mondale-Ferraro ticket lost by a landslide to the Reagan-Bush team.

(*PAZ*, 175–80)

(*See 259 How many women have served in Congress?; 328 Who were the first black, Hispanic, native American, female, Asian, Indian, and Hawaiian representatives and senators?; 433 When did the first woman run for president?*)

**Q 446. Who was the first black contender for the vice presidential nomination of a major party?**

**A** Sen. Blanche Kelso Bruce, a Mississippi Republican, became the first in 1880 by winning eleven votes for vice president at the Republican national convention in Chicago. Republicans selected Chester A. Arthur as vice president, however, and the Garfield-Arthur ticket ultimately won the election.

(*FAP*, 417)

(*See 328 Who were the first black, Hispanic, native American, female, Asian, Indian, and Hawaiian representatives and senators?; 434 Which blacks have run for president?; 564 Who was the first black justice?*)

**Q 447. Who was the first vice president to mount a vigorous nationwide campaign?**

**A** In 1900 Theodore Roosevelt became the first to do so, while running with President William McKinley on the Republican ticket. Even though Roosevelt had declared he did not want to be vice president, once nominated he campaigned vigorously and thereby helped President McKinley defeat the Democratic contenders, William J. Bryan and Adlai Stevenson.

(*PAZ*, 375, 453, 512)

(*See 401 What have the results been for presidential elections?*)

**Q 448. Which vice presidential nominees have debated?**

**A** The first vice presidential debate, held October 15, 1976, matched Democrat Walter F. Mondale against Republican Robert Dole. The next vice presidential debate aired during the election campaign of 1984, when incumbent Republican George Bush debated Democrat Geraldine Ferraro. In 1988 Republican Dan Quayle debated Lloyd Bentsen, Jr., and the 1992 campaign featured the first three-sided debate—between Quayle, Democrat Al Gore, and Independent James Stockdale.

(*SOW*, 245; *VSAP*, 76)

(*See 415 Has each presidential election since 1960 included televised debates between the candidates?*)

**Q 449. Which party has dominated both houses of Congress for the longest series of consecutive Congresses?**

**A** The Democrats hold the record, having controlled both houses for thirteen consecutive Congresses from 1955 to 1981 (84th through 96th Congresses). They were the majority party in the House alone for forty consecutive years (1955 to 1995). In 1995 Republicans took control of both houses. The Democratic-Republican party, the country's first opposition party, held majorities in both houses for twelve straight Congresses from 1801 to 1825 (7th through 18th Congresses). The longest unbroken Republican string of majorities in both houses lasted eight straight Congresses from 1895 to 1911 (54th through 61st Congresses). Another Republican streak lasted from 1919 to 1931 (66th through 71st Congresses).

(*CAZ*, 468–70)

(*See 10 When has the same party controlled the White House and both houses of Congress?; 374 Who has served as Speaker?*)

**Q 450. What was the closest popular vote for a senator?**

**A** Only 2 votes separated New Hampshire senatorial candidates Louis Wyman (Republican) and John Durkin (Democrat) in the 1974 election. Wyman won 110,926 votes to Durkin's 110,924. A bitter dispute followed, and the Senate for the first time declared it could not choose a winner. In a special election held in 1975, Durkin finally won the seat by capturing 53.6 percent of the vote. The closest vote to actually determine an election came in the 1912 Nevada Senate race. Democrat Key Pittman won a four-way race by only 89 votes. Pittman had just 7,942 votes, the lowest total in Senate history.

(*SOW*, 250)

(*See 349 When were senators first elected by popular vote?*)

**Q 451. Who was the first senator elected on a write-in vote?**

**A** Sen. Strom Thurmond became the first and only winning write-in candidate for the Senate in 1954. A Democrat and former South Carolina governor, Thurmond polled

143,442 write-in votes to defeat the Democratic party nominee. He has served continuously since 1954, switching to the Republican party in 1964.

(*SOW*, 250)

**Q 452. What is a special election?**

**A** A special election is held when a vacancy occurs in a House or Senate seat. Usually several House seats become vacant during a two-year Congress, and special elections generally are called by the governor of the affected state. In the case of a Senate vacancy, the governor may appoint someone to temporarily fill the vacancy until a special election can be held.

(*GUSE*, 573)

**Q 453. What does it cost to win a Senate seat?**

**A** According to 1992 campaign records, winning Senate candidates spent anywhere from $800,000 to $11.3 million. Incumbent Alphonse D'Amato, a New York Republican, spent the most, while California Democrat Barbara Boxer was not far behind with spending of $10.3 million. New Hampshire freshman senator Judd Gregg, a Republican, spent the least in his campaign.

(*SOW*, 248)

**Q 454. What does it cost to win a House seat?**

**A** House candidates campaign across smaller districts than Senate candidates and generally face less competition, but the cost of getting elected keeps going up. In 1992 fifty House candidates spent over $1 million, with six spending over $1.75 million. In contrast, only fourteen spent over $1 million in 1990. Still, a popular incumbent can occasionally win on a shoestring. Long-time representative William H. Natcher (now deceased) paid just $6,000 for his successful 1992 campaign.

(*SOW*, 249-50)

(*See 327 Who missed the fewest votes?*)

# V

# SUPREME COURT

## IN GENERAL

**Q 455. What does the Supreme Court do?**

**A** The Supreme Court is the highest court and the court of final appeal in the judicial system of the United States. As the ultimate interpreter of the Constitution, the Court has the power to rule unconstitutional acts of Congress, actions of the executive branch, and state laws. The Court has original jurisdiction in a relatively limited area, including cases involving a state and those involving senior foreign diplomats. Most cases come to the Supreme Court on appeal after being heard in the lower courts. If it decides to hear a case, the Court has the power to overrule a lower court decision when sufficient grounds exist. Through this power of judicial review, the Court determines whether laws and actions of government officials are in fact constitutional and thereby establishes legal precedents for the lower courts to follow.

(*SOW,* 177, 182–3)

(*See 485 What is judicial review?*)

**Q 456. How do cases reach the Court?**

**A** Most cases the Court reviews come from lower federal and state courts through writs of certiorari. At least four justices must accept the petition for certiorari review of the lower court's decision. A few cases also come before the Court by means of appeal. Here the Court requires the appellant to file a jurisdictional statement explaining why a review should be granted. The Court often decides these cases summarily—without argument or formal opinion. Another route to the Court, request for certification, is rarely used. An appeals court or other lower court uses this device to request a ruling on questions of law relating to a case.

(*SCAZ,* 64, 276–7; *SOW,* 182–3)

(*See 477 What is certiorari?*)

**Q** **457. What if a case is moot?**

**A** When events or the passage of time alter the circumstances that produced a case or controversy, the case becomes moot and the Supreme Court must refuse to decide it. By the fundamental Case or Controversy Rule, the Supreme Court and other federal courts can decide only cases where legal rights and interests are actually in collision. The Court has recognized exceptions in some moot cases, including criminal and civil cases in which a defendant or plaintiff might continue to suffer legal consequences from the court decision being challenged. Another exception covers situations of such short duration that they necessarily resolve themselves before the case can be heard. In *Roe v. Wade*, for example, the Court ruled even though the plaintiff was no longer pregnant.

(*SCAZ,* 62, 261)

(*See 523 What did the Court rule in* Roe v. Wade?)

**Q** **458. Who writes the Court's opinions?**

**A** A justice voting with the majority writes the Court's opinion on the case. The senior justice siding with the majority actually decides which justice will write it, though the decision may be influenced by the candidate's special knowledge or especially effective arguments. When voting with the majority, the chief justice always assigns the opinion. Any justice may write a concurring or dissenting opinion, which may also be signed by more than one justice.

(*SCAZ,* 24–5, 279)

(*See 466 What does the chief justice do?*)

**Q** **459. What types of opinions are there?**

**A** One type the Court issues is the opinion of the Court, which explains the reasoning behind a decision. The opinion may reflect a unanimous ruling or one reached by a majority of the justices. Another type is the concurring opinion, written when a justice votes with the majority but disagrees with parts of the majority opinion. Concurring opinions sometimes have been nothing more than disguised dissenting opinions. More often, however, a justice opposing the majority writes a dissenting opinion. The Court usually issues *per curiam* opinions in cases involving settled law. *Per curiam* (Latin for "by the court") decisions are usually short and unsigned.

(*SCAZ*, 97, 143, 279, 290–1)

## Q 460. Which justice wrote the most of each type of opinion?

A Justice Oliver Wendell Holmes, Jr. (served 1902–1932) holds the record for writing the most majority opinions—873. But Chief Justice Morrison R. Waite (served 1874–1888) came in a close second with 872. William O. Douglas, a justice from 1936 to 1975, wrote the most dissenting opinions—486. William J. Brennan, Jr. (served 1956–1990) followed with 456. Ironically, Brennan holds the record for most concurring opinions with 258. Harry A. Blackmun (served 1970–1994) had 253 and Byron White (served 1962–1993), 234.

(*SCAZ*, 45, 145, 188–9, 447, 454; *SCC*, 514–20)

## Q 461. Where can you find the opinions in printed form?

A The official record of Supreme Court decisions is the *United States Reports* (U.S. Government Printing Office). Other printed sources of Supreme Court opinions are the *Supreme Court Reporter* (West Publishing Co.); the *United States Supreme Court Bulletin* (Commerce Clearing House); *U.S. Law Week* (Bureau of National Affairs); and the *United States Supreme Court Reports; Lawyers' Edition* (Lawyers Co-Operative Publishing Co.). Electronic sources of information include the LEGAL RESOURCES INDEX (Information Access Corp.), *LEXIS* (Mead Data Central), and WESTLAW (West Publishing Co.).

(*How to Research the Sup. Crt.*, 29, 43–4; *SCAZ*, 280)

## Q 462. Has the Court ever overruled itself?

A The Court has issued over 150 decisions that overturned earlier rulings. Before 1870 the Court decided cases by faithfully applying the rule of precedent known as *stare decisis*, Latin for "let the decision stand." By basing decisions on past rulings, the Court hoped to endow the law with two important features: stability and continuity. After 1870, however, the Court showed less reverence for precedents, and between 1937 and 1969 alone overturned 90 of them. Major cases involving overturned precedents include the 1871 legal tender case, the 1895 decision striking down the federal income tax, the 1937 ruling upholding state minimum wage laws, the 1954 overruling of "separate but equal" facilities for blacks, and rulings in the 1960s protecting criminals' rights.

(*SCAZ*, 302–3, 339–42; *SCC* 129–44)

(*See 493 What did the Court rule in* Brown v. Board of Education of Topeka?; *505 What did the Court rule in* Gideon v. Wainwright?)

**Q** **463. How many acts of Congress have been declared unconstitutional?**

**A** The Court has declared over 125 acts of Congress unconstitutional. It first struck down a congressional act in *Marbury v. Madison* (1803). More recently, in *Immigration and Naturalization Service v. Chadha* (1983), it invalidated Congress' legislative veto.

(*CAZ*, 229; *SCAZ*, 433; *SCC*, 96–9)

(*See 278 What is a legislative veto?; 511 What did the Court rule in* Immigration and Naturalization Service v. Chadha?; *516 What did the Court rule in* Marbury v. Madison?; *527 What did the Court rule in* Scott v. Sandford?)

**Q** **464. What Court decisions were overturned by amendments to the Constitution?**

**A** Five amendments have overturned Supreme Court decisions: the Eleventh (ratified 1798), Thirteenth (1865), Fourteenth (1868), Sixteenth (1913), and Twenty-sixth (1971). The Eleventh Amendment, limiting the jurisdiction of federal courts, overturned the Court's ruling in *Chisholm v. Georgia* (1793). The Thirteenth and Fourteenth Amendments reversed the earlier Dred Scott ruling (1857) in which the Court denied citizenship to blacks. The Sixteenth Amendment negated the *Pollock v. Farmer's Loan and Trust Co.* (1895) decision banning the income tax, and the Twenty-sixth Amendment overturned *Oregon v. Mitchell* (1970), which struck down a federal law lowering the voting age to eighteen.

(*RD Encyc. of Amer. Hist.*, 282–6; *SCAZ*, 144; SCC 550)

(*See 29 What do the amendments to the Constitution say, in brief?; 496 What did the Court rule in* Chisholm v. Georgia?; *527 What did the Court rule in* Scott v. Sandford?)

**Q 465. Has the Court always had nine justices?**

**A** No, Congress has changed the number in the past. Originally, Congress provided for six justices, but that number later varied from five to ten. During the late 1860s, the Republican-dominated Congress temporarily reduced the number of justices to prevent President Andrew Johnson, a Democrat, from filling vacancies on the Court. The current number of nine justices was settled on over one hundred years ago.

*(SOW, 179)*

*(See 473 What was the Court-packing scheme?)*


**Q 466. What does the chief justice do?**

**A** The chief justice presides over the Court during closed conferences and public sessions, and when voting with the majority, he chooses the justice who will write the opinion of the Court. The chief justice also decides which cases will appear on the Court's "discuss list," though any justice may ask that a case be added to it. Cases that do not appear on the list are denied Supreme Court review. In addition, the chief justice administers the oath of office to the president and presides when the president is tried for impeachment. He also supervises the Administrative Office of the U.S. Courts and holds other nonjudicial posts. Like the other associate justices, however, the chief justice has only one vote when the Court accepts and decides cases.

*(SCAZ, 67–8)*

*(See 93 What does the president do?; 249 What does Congress do?)*


**Q 467. How much does a justice get paid?**

**A** Associate justices got $164,100 a year in 1993. In addition to job security—justices are appointed for life—they can retire at full pay once they have served ten years on the bench. The government also pays for four law clerks, two secretaries, and a messenger for each associate justice. The Court has a library, a dining room, an exercise room, and a fleet of cars for the justices' use.

*(SOW, 198–9)*

**468. How much does the chief justice get paid?**

A The chief justice earns slightly more than associate justices—$171,500—and can hire one more secretary, but otherwise has the same staff allotment (See question above). The chief justice receives the same perks as associate justices, except that an official car is designated for the chief justice's use.

(*SOW*, 198–9)

(*See 87 What does the president get paid?; 256 How much does a member of Congress get paid?*)


Q **469. What happens on the first Monday in October?**

A The Court begins hearing arguments scheduled for the new term on that day. Justices hear oral arguments on Monday, Tuesday, and Wednesday during seven two-week sessions that begin in October and end in the last week of April or the first week of May. They recess for two weeks between each of the sessions to consider the cases, and ultimately hear arguments for about two hundred cases during the term. Because so many cases must be heard, each side is allowed only thirty minutes to present orally the highlights of the case, which written briefs cover in detail. Justices may use much of that time to ask questions concerning the case.

(*SCAZ*, 19, 278–9, 354–5)


Q **470. When did the Court first tape arguments, and what happens to the tapes?**

A Oral arguments have been taped since 1955. During the term, justices and their law clerks generally are the only ones allowed to use the tapes, which are kept by the marshal of the Court. When the term is over, the National Archives in Washington, D.C., gets custody of the tapes and makes them available to researchers. The Archives also sells copies of the transcripts.

(*SCAZ*, 20)

(*See 597 What does the marshal of the Court do?*)

**Q 471. How is the federal court system organized?**

**A** The federal court system consists of three levels—district courts, appeals courts, and the Supreme Court. Federal courts, as opposed to state courts, have jurisdiction over cases arising under the Constitution, federal law, or treaties, as well as those involving the United States, a state, or citizens of different states. The ninety-four federal district courts conduct trials and form the lower tier of federal courts. The thirteen appeals courts review district court cases and serve as intermediate-level courts to ease the Supreme Court's caseload. The Supreme Court is the highest federal court. It has the power to review lower court decisions and sets the constitutional standards for the lower courts. Specialized courts, called legislative courts, also operate within the federal court system. These courts hear only those cases within certain specialized areas and include the Federal Tax Court, the Claims Court, and the Veterans' Appeals Court.

(*SCAZ*, 121, 231–5, 479)

(*See 455 What does the Supreme Court do?*)

**Q 472. How much does the judiciary cost to run?**

**A** The federal budget for the entire judicial branch amounted to $2.6 billion for fiscal 1993, or less than two-thousandths of 1 percent of the total federal budget. That figure, which is expected to rise to $3.2 billion by 1995, includes the salaries of Supreme Court justices, judges of lower federal courts, and other employees as well as general operating costs. The federal government budget for the Justice Department is a separate item.

(*Budget of the U.S. Govt., Analyt. Perspectives*, 252)

(*See 52 How was federal money allocated in a recent budget?*)

**Q 473. What was the Court-packing scheme?**

**A** Frustrated by Supreme Court rulings against key New Deal legislation during 1935 and 1936, President Franklin Roosevelt sent his judicial "reorganization" plan to Congress on February 5, 1937. Among other provisions, Roosevelt proposed adding up to six new Supreme Court justices, but Congress and the public saw it for what it was—a scheme to subvert judicial independence by "packing" the Court with justices favoring the New Deal. Public outrage effectively scuttled Roosevelt's plan, though he eventually achieved his underlying objective despite the embarrassing political defeat.

In 1937 two justices broke with the conservative bloc, creating five to four majorities in favor of New Deal legislation.

(*PAZ,* 101–2; *SCAZ,* 349–50)

(*See 120 What was the New Deal?; 465 Has the Court always had nine justices?; 512 What did the Court rule in the* Legal Tender Cases?)

### Q 474. Has the death penalty ever been illegal in the United States?

A During a brief period between 1972 and 1976, Supreme Court rulings rendered capital punishment illegal. The Court had ruled in favor of it in the past, but in *Furman v. Georgia* (1972), critics of laws allowing discretion in imposing the death sentence won a surprising victory. The Supreme Court invalidated every state death penalty law, with two justices condemning the death penalty as cruel and unusual punishment and three noting cases of random (or racist) imposition of capital punishment. Nevertheless, the Court soon reversed itself in *Gregg v. Georgia* (1976), upholding newly written state laws with guidelines for discretionary use of the death sentence.

(*SCAZ,* 58–60)

## DEFINITIONS

### Q 475. What is affirmative action?

A Programs giving preference to previously disadvantaged groups such as blacks are based on the controversial principle of affirmative action. During the 1970s especially, such "race conscious" programs were established in university admissions, employment, and government contracting to compensate for past discrimination and provide a shortcut to achieving integration. But opponents argued affirmative action amounted to reverse discrimination against whites and charged the programs with being a minority-based spoils system. The scope of affirmative action programs was broadened later to include women and other minorities. The Supreme Court charted a confused course through thirteen affirmative action cases between 1974 and 1990, approving some limited plans while striking down others.

(*SCAZ,* 5–6)

(*See 478 Do civil rights apply only to African Americans?*)

**Q 476. What is amicus curiae?**

**A** An *amicus curiae* (Latin for "friend of the court") is someone who, though not directly involved, files a brief relating to a court case. Individuals or groups may act as *amici curiae*, and their amicus briefs may be voluntary or requested by any party in the case, including the judge. The federal government frequently files amicus briefs in Supreme Court cases, as do state governments and special interest groups trying to influence the Court. Controversial issues naturally attract amicus briefs in greater numbers, and in some years the Court has received over 3,000.

(*SCAZ*, 11–12)

**Q 477. What is certiorari?**

**A** Before reviewing a lower court ruling, a higher court issues a writ of certiorari ordering the lower court to forward records of the case. Most cases the Supreme Court reviews are handled in this manner, though only a fraction of the 5,000 petitions for certiorari the Court receives each year ever result in a writ being issued. Generally the Court grants certiorari only when "special and important reasons" justify reviewing the case.

(*SCAZ*, 64–5)

*(See 456 How do cases reach the Court?)*

**Q 478. Do civil rights apply only to African Americans?**

**A** Though considerable legislation has been aimed at ensuring civil rights for African Americans, the civil rights laws bar discrimination against all citizens. Civil rights legislation enacted since 1964 specifically bans discrimination on the basis of national origin, religion, sex, and age. Laws passed since 1990 also have barred discrimination based on physical or mental disability. Civil rights laws have been used in attacks on affirmative action programs, which by design favor blacks, women, and other minorities.

(*SCAZ*, 77; *SOW*, 189)

*(See 475 What is affirmative action?)*

**Q** **479. What is a class action suit?**

**A** When several individuals file a suit on behalf of many others with the same legal interest, it becomes a class action. Proponents believe class actions promote efficiency and economy by trying many claims at once, while critics charge they encourage questionable lawsuits and sometimes effectively force a settlement. Numerous civil rights, environmental, and consumer complaints filed as class action suits have resulted in important rulings, however. In the mid–1970s, the Supreme Court tightened the rules regarding class action suits.

(*SCAZ*, 84–5)

**Q** **480. What is common law?**

**A** Legal principles that have become part of state legal systems through long usage or accepted custom make up what is called common law. Partly derived from early, uncodified English law, common law provides the basis for the states' case law systems, in which earlier cases provide precedents for deciding current litigation. There is no common law at the federal level. When federal courts must rule on suits between citizens of different states (called diversity cases), both the common law and case law of the appropriate state must be followed.

(*SCAZ*, 61–2, 95)

**Q** **481. What is due process?**

**A** First mentioned in the Fifth Amendment, the concept of due process has been steadily expanded through various Supreme Court rulings. The original wording—"No person shall be . . . deprived of life, liberty, or property, without due process of law. . . ."—left substantial room for interpretation. Today, due process underlies Court decisions guaranteeing defendants' rights in criminal, civil, and other government proceedings, and limits government actions infringing on such personal liberties as the right to privacy, to marry, and to have an abortion. Generally speaking, government procedures that follow principles *of essential fairness* are said to exercise due process.

(*Constit. Law*, 667; *SCAZ*, 147–8)

(See 29 *What do the amendments to the Constitution say, in brief?*; 39 *Where is the right of privacy mentioned in the Constitution?*; 483 *What is the incorporation doctrine?*)

**482. What is the exclusionary rule?**

A Created by the Supreme Court in 1914, this controversial rule excludes illegally obtained evidence at criminal trials. Frequently applied to evidence obtained in violation of the Fourth Amendment search and seizure provisions, the rule also prevents prosecutors from using confessions gotten by violating Fifth Amendment rights against self-incrimination or Sixth Amendment rights to legal counsel. Originally the exclusionary rule applied only to federal cases, but the Court extended it to the states in the 1961 *Mapp v. Ohio* ruling.

(*SCAZ*, 157–8)

(*See 29 What do the amendments to the Constitution say, in brief?; 515 What did the Court rule in* Mapp v. Ohio?)

Q **483. What is the incorporation doctrine?**

A The incorporation doctrine requires states to abide by most of the important provisions of the Bill of Rights. Originally the Bill of Rights applied only at the federal level, but between 1925 and 1969 Supreme Court rulings required states to comply with many of its provisions. The Court held that the Fourteenth Amendment's due process clause "incorporated" many of the specific guarantees in the Bill of Rights— at first with regard to First Amendment freedoms and then, selectively, to amendments dealing with criminal law. *Mapp v. Ohio* (1961) and *Gideon v. Wainwright* (1963) were among the many cases involving the incorporation doctrine.

(*SCAZ*, 201–2)

(*See 29 What do the amendments to the Constitution say, in brief?; 505 What did the Court rule in* Gideon v. Wainwright?; *515 What did the Court rule in* Mapp v. Ohio?)

Q **484. What is judicial restraint?**

A A judicial philosophy, it calls for restraint in exercising the Court's judicial powers. Judicial restraint may involve strict procedural requirements for judicial action or may impose a narrow basis for reviewing the conduct of the executive and legislative branches. Generally the Court has emphasized a philosophy of judicial restraint, either through self-imposed restraints or concern for limitations on its jurisdiction.

Judicial restraint is the opposite of judicial activism, which takes an expansive view of the Court's powers.

(*SCAZ,* 214, 216–17)

### Q 485. What is judicial review?

**A** The Supreme Court has the power to review and invalidate any acts of Congress, actions of the executive branch, or state laws it believes conflict with the Constitution. The Constitution makes no specific mention of this power, which is based indirectly on Article III, Section 2 ("The judicial Power shall extend to all Cases . . . arising under this Constitution. . . .") and the supremacy clause, which says that valid federal laws take precedence over state laws. Also, the Judiciary Act of 1789 gave the Court the power to review state laws and court rulings. The Court first struck down a state law in *Ware v. Hylton* (1796). It ruled an act of Congress unconstitutional and also established judicial review over executive actions in its 1803 *Marbury v. Madison* decision.

(*SCAZ,* 217–18)

*(See 19 What does Article III of the Constitution say, in brief?; 36 What is the supremacy clause?; 279 Can a law be overturned?; 463 How many acts of Congress have been declared unconstitutional?; 464 What Court decisions were overturned by amendments to the Constitution?; 516 What did the Court rule in* Marbury v. Madison*?)*

### Q 486. What is the preemption doctrine?

**A** Based on the Constitution's supremacy clause, the Court's preemption doctrine invalidates state laws that conflict with federal law. Chief Justice John Marshall first articulated the doctrine in the Court's 1824 *Gibbons v. Ogden* ruling, and since the 1930s most cases involving the doctrine have addressed federal regulation of commerce and other economic affairs. Determining when a state law actually conflicts with federal law is sometimes difficult, however. In a 1947 decision, the Court adopted standard tests to determine when state laws should be preempted, but has not always applied them consistently.

(*SCAZ,* 303–4)

*(See 36 What is the supremacy clause?; 504 What did the Court rule in* Gibbons v. Ogden*?)*

**Q** **487. What is probable cause?**

**A** Under the Fourth Amendment, police must have proof of wrongdoing before arresting a suspect or conducting a search for evidence. The standard of proof needed is called probable cause. When police seek an arrest or search warrant, a judge determines if there is probable cause. But when acting on their own, police must be able to show probable cause existed. Otherwise, any evidence they obtain may be inadmissible in court (exclusionary rule). The Court has defined probable cause in a variety of ways, depending on the context. Before arresting a suspect, the Court has ruled, police must have "reasonably trustworthy information." The information or evidence need not be admissible at the trial (as in the case of hearsay evidence).

(*SCAZ*, 315–16)

(*See 29 What do the amendments to the Constitution say, in brief?; 482 What is the exclusionary rule?*)

**Q** **488. What does separate but equal mean?**

**A** The 1896 Supreme Court decision in *Plessy v. Ferguson* established the doctrine of separate but equal public facilities for whites and blacks and thereby provided a legal basis for segregation that stood for over a half-century. *Plessy* involved racially segregated seating on a train in Louisiana, but the precedent eventually justified segregation in most aspects of life—from schools to restaurants—especially in the South. Under Presidents Roosevelt and Truman, the federal government began reversing discriminatory policies at the federal level, and in 1946 the Supreme Court struck down state segregation laws affecting interstate carriers. But not until *Brown v. Board of Education of Topeka* (1954) did the Court repudiate the separate but equal doctrine established by *Plessy*.

(*SCAZ*, 294)

(*See 493 What did the Court rule in* Brown v. Board of Education of Topeka?; *522 What did the Court rule in* Plessy v. Ferguson?)

**Q** **489. What is strict construction?**

**A** Originally, strict construction meant taking a narrow view of federal government powers under the Constitution, but more recently it has become a political slogan for less judicial activism, especially in civil liberties cases. The original sense of strict construction figured in debates over congressional powers, and the Supreme Court first favored a broader interpretation of constitutional provisions in *McCulloch v. Maryland* (1819). Particularly with regard to the commerce power, the Court since 1937 has followed what can be called "broad construction" of federal government powers. During the 1960s, the Court also favored wide interpretations of constitutional provisions regarding civil liberties. At that time, President Richard M. Nixon popularized the more modern political sense of strict construction.

(*SCAZ*, 404)

(*See 484 What is judicial restraint?; 514 What did the Court rule in* McCulloch v. Maryland*?*)

## Q 490. What is a test case?

A Lawsuits organized specifically to gain favorable Supreme Court rulings on legal issues are called test cases. The Constitution does not prohibit them, but the Court almost always refuses to hear so–called friendly lawsuits, in which both parties are seeking a mutually desired outcome. Such cases fail the Court's basic "case or controversy rule" requiring an actual dispute between two parties with opposing interests. Many landmark rulings by the Supreme Court have resulted from test cases, among them *Brown v. Board of Education of Topeka* and *Roe v. Wade*.

(*SCAZ*, 419–420)

(*See 457 What if a case is moot?; 493 What did the Court rule in* Brown v. Board of Education of Topeka*?; 523 What did the Court rule in* Roe v. Wade*?*)

## MAJOR CASES

What did the Court rule in the Bakke case? See 536.

## Q 491. What did the Court rule in *Baker v. Carr*?

A Bowing to pressure from rural interests, the Tennessee state legislature had stopped reapportioning seats in 1901. But much of the state's population subsequently had shifted to cities and suburbs, giving rural voters disproportionately greater representation. In 1959 a federal court refused to hear *Baker v. Carr*, which sought reapportionment every ten years in accordance with the state constitution. When the

Supreme Court ruled on *Baker v. Carr* (1962), the justices said only that lower courts could not refuse to hear cases regarding apportionment. The remedy was left up to the district court. However, Supreme Court rulings in *Baker* and related cases ultimately forced reapportionment in every state but Oregon.

(*SCAZ*, 34)

**Q** **492. What did the Court rule in *Barron v. Baltimore*?**

**A** Writing for the Court in 1833, Chief Justice John Marshall refused to extend provisions of the Bill of Rights to the states, setting a precedent that was not reversed until the early twentieth century. The case involved a Baltimore wharf owner who sued the city because its activities had created shoals and shallows around his wharf. He charged the city with violating the Fifth Amendment by "taking" his property without just compensation. The Bill of Rights, Marshall said, was intended to protect citizens against encroachments by the federal government, not by state and local governments.

(*SCAZ*, 38–9)

(*See 483 What is the incorporation doctrine?*)

**Q** **493. What did the Court rule in *Brown v. Board of Education of Topeka*?**

**A** A landmark ruling, this 1954 decision overturned the Court's separate but equal doctrine and brought about desegregation of public schools and other public facilities. The ruling involved five lawsuits—the one against Topeka, Kansas, and four others against school districts in South Carolina, Delaware, Virginia, and the District of Columbia. Writing the Court's unanimous opinion, Chief Justice Earl Warren stated that "separate educational facilities are inherently unequal" and that the plaintiffs and other blacks had been denied their Fourteenth Amendment right to equal protection under the law. The companion case, *Bolling v. Sharpe,* involved the District of Columbia, which was governed by Congress. Warren reached the same result by reading an equal protection requirement into the Fifth Amendment due process clause. In a separate ruling (1955), the Court then remanded the cases to lower courts with directions to effect desegregation "with all deliberate speed."

(*SCAZ*, 49–50)

(*See 488 What does separate but equal mean?*)

**Q** **494. What did the Court rule in *Buckley v. Valeo*?**

**A** The Court in 1976 ruled on challenges to specific provisions of the Federal Election Campaign Act of 1971, which sought to limit campaign contributions and expenditures in federal elections. The Court found in favor of limiting campaign contributions but refused to sanction limits on spending, especially when candidates had decided to spend their own money over and above contributions received. The justices also refused to limit spending by individuals and groups acting independently of the candidate, even though the money might in some way aid the candidate's cause. But they did uphold public financing of the presidential campaign, as well as limits on campaign spending for any candidate who accepted public money.

(*Oxford Companion*, 97; *SCAZ*, 57)

**Q** **495. What did the Court rule in *Champion v. Ames*?**

**A** The Court voted 5–4 in 1903 to uphold a federal law against transporting lottery tickets from one state to another, or from a foreign country to a state. The decision was the first to recognize the so-called federal police power. Congress's power to regulate commerce, the Court said, included the power to ban certain types of interstate commerce that are "offensive to the entire people of the nation."

(*SCAZ*, 129, 296)

**Q** **496. What did the Court rule in *Chisholm v. Georgia*?**

**A** The Court's decision in this case caused an uproar and led to ratification of the Eleventh Amendment (1795), which excluded from the Court's jurisdiction any suits brought against a state by citizens of another state. The case arose from the confiscation of lands belonging to pro-British Loyalists during the American Revolution. Many states had confiscated land during the war, and paying compensation for it might have jeopardized their finances, especially in light of what fighting the war had cost. But the heirs of one Loyalist, George Chisholm, decided to sue anyway. Since the heirs lived out of state in South Carolina, Georgia simply refused to allow itself to be sued. The Supreme Court claimed jurisdiction, however, and in 1793 ruled against Georgia. The decision caused such widespread outrage that by 1794 Congress had passed the Eleventh Amendment. A year later the states ratified it.

(*SCAZ*, 342–3; *RD Encyc. of Amer. Hist.*, 209)

(*See 464 What Court decisions were overturned by amendments to the Constitution?*)

**Q 497. What did the Court rule in *Cooley v. Board of Wardens of Port of Philadelphia*?**

**A** Ruling in 1852, the Court established the dual federalism doctrine, giving states greater power to regulate commerce when uniform national regulation was not required. *Cooley* involved Pennsylvania's right to regulate Philadelphia harbor pilots, but the doctrine effectively created two well-defined spheres with the states and the federal government supreme within their respective areas. The dual federalism doctrine prevented expansion of federal commerce powers into the state sphere until the 1930s, when the Court finally abandoned it.

(*SCAZ*, 91, 185, 396)

(*See 8 What is federalism?*)

**Q 498. What did the Court rule in *Cruzan v. Director, Missouri Department of Health*?**

**A** The Court limited the so-called right to die in this case involving a woman left comatose after an auto accident. All the justices recognized a patient's right to refuse extraordinary life-sustaining treatment. But the five-justice majority ruled states could require "clear and convincing" evidence that the patient had previously expressed the wish to do so in such circumstances.

(*SCAZ*, 315)

(*See 39 Where is the right of privacy mentioned in the Constitution?*)

**Q 499. What did the Court rule in *Dartmouth College v. Woodward*?**

**A** An important early ruling on contracts, the Court's 1819 decision prevented the state of New Hampshire from changing Dartmouth College into a state university. The Court held that Dartmouth's original royal charter, creating the college well before the Union had been established, was a contract between King George III and a private corporation (Dartmouth). Therefore, the state could not change it without violating the Constitution's contract clause. Though later rulings allowed states greater regulatory powers, the Dartmouth College case protected businesses from interference by state governments and so promoted the growth of corporations.

(*Oxford Companion,* 217–18; *SCAZ,* 112, 116–17, 316)

**Q** **500. What did the Court rule in *Elkins v. United States*?**

**A** In 1960 the Court ruled 5-4 to ban the use—in federal courts—of evidence seized illegally by state police and given to federal authorities. The Court held that this so-called silver platter doctrine violated Fourth Amendment rules against illegal search and seizure.

(*Guide to Sup. Ct.,* 911)

(*See 482 What is the exclusionary rule?*)

**Q** **501. What did the Court rule in *Engel v. Vitale*?**

**A** The Court in 1962 ruled 6 to 1 against allowing prayers in public schools. Justice Hugo Black wrote the Court's opinion, finding that school prayers violated the establishment clause of the First Amendment, which requires separation of church and state. Black said that giving students the option of remaining silent or leaving the room during prayers was immaterial and that school prayers amounted to an "indirect coercive effect upon religious minorities."

(*Oxford Companion,* 254–5; *SCAZ,* 357–8)

**Q** **502. What did the Court rule in *Ex parte Milligan*?**

**A** This 1866 ruling limited the jurisdiction of military courts to areas actually in rebellion or under attack. When the Civil War broke out in 1861, President Abraham Lincoln suspended habeas corpus and ordered military courts to try civilians aiding the Confederacy, even though the offenses had occurred outside the war zone. Lincoln broadened the order after 1862 to include draft resisters and anyone discouraging military enlistments. Ultimately thousands of civilians suspected of disloyalty were arrested, imprisoned without trial, and finally released after the emergency ended. The Court avoided the issue while the war was being fought, and didn't hand down its decision until the year after the war was concluded. Though the Constitution authorizes suspension of habeas corpus in "Cases of Rebellion or Invasion," the Supreme Court decided unanimously in *Ex parte Milligan* that civilians should not be tried by military courts in areas where regular courts continue to function.

(*SCAZ*, 204–5, 448)

(*See 67 Has martial law ever been declared in the United States?*)

**Q 503. What did the Court rule in *Fletcher v. Peck*?**

**A** This 1810 decision marked the first time the Court found a state legislative act unconstitutional. The case arose from a disputed land transaction (1795), in which the Georgia legislature sold about thirty-five million acres to land companies for a mere $500,000. Most of the legislators had shares in the land companies, however, and a new legislature the following year voted to rescind the sale because fraud had been involved. But the land companies already had resold much of the land to innocent purchasers, who now held questionable titles, and many lawsuits followed. In *Fletcher v. Peck*, Fletcher sued to recoup money paid Peck for a parcel of the land, but Peck maintained the title was valid. In an opinion written by Chief Justice John Marshall, the Court ruled in Peck's favor, saying the legislature's 1795 land grant was valid, even if fraud had been involved. The legislature in 1796, he said, had acted unconstitutionally because it had impaired the obligation of a contract.

(*RD Encyc. of Amer. Hist.*, 412; *SCAZ*, 116; *WHAD*, 1155–6)

(*See 36 What is the supremacy clause?*)

**Q 504. What did the Court rule in *Gibbons v. Ogden*?**

**A** The Court affirmed the federal government's broad power to regulate commerce in this 1824 ruling. The case stemmed from a dispute between two ferryboat operators, one holding a federal permit (Gibbons) and the other a New York State license granting him a monopoly on serving New York City (Ogden). Writing the Court's opinion, Chief Justice John Marshall ruled New York's law invalid because it conflicted with the federal licensing law. Congress, he stated flatly, had complete power to regulate commerce between the states.

(*SCAZ*, 173–4)

(*See 486 What is the preemption doctrine?*)

**Q 505. What did the Court rule in *Gideon v. Wainwright*?**

**A** An indigent criminal defendant's right to counsel in state courts was guaranteed by this 1963 ruling. Two years earlier, Clarence Earl Gideon had been convicted without legal counsel on a felony burglary charge in Florida. State law there required a court-appointed lawyer only in capital cases (cases involving death or punishment by death). Gideon taught himself enough law to petition the Supreme Court, claiming he had been denied his Sixth Amendment right to counsel. The Court, which had ruled against court-appointed lawyers for most criminal cases in *Betts v. Brady* (1942), agreed to review the case and appointed Abe Fortas to represent Gideon. (Fortas was a well-known Washington attorney who became a Supreme Court justice himself in 1965.) The Court's unanimous ruling upheld Gideon's right to an attorney and also overturned the *Betts* ruling. Granted a new trial, Gideon was acquitted.

(*SCAZ*, 174–5)

**Q 506. What did the Court rule in *Gitlow v. New York*?**

**A** Until the 1900s, the Court had refused to apply at the state level protections guaranteed in the Bill of Rights. While upholding New York State's criminal anarchy law in the 1925 *Gitlow* finding, however, the Court finally declared that states must abide by First Amendment rights to freedom of speech and the press. The Fourteenth Amendment due process clause, the Court said, protected these rights from impairment by the states. The decision laid the basis for the incorporation doctrine, and in subsequent years, the Court ordered states to abide by other parts of the Bill of Rights.

(*SCAZ*, 201–2, 309, 389)

(See 28 What is the Bill of Rights?; 483 What is the incorporation doctrine?)

**Q 507. What did the Court rule in *Griggs v. Duke Power Company*?**

**A** The Court upheld in 1971 provisions of the 1964 Civil Rights Act prohibiting job discrimination against blacks. The case arose from charges that North Carolina's Duke Power Company had unfairly discriminated against blacks by requiring applicants for jobs to have a high school diploma or to pass a general intelligence test before being hired or promoted. The Court ruled in favor of the plaintiffs' arguments that the requirements were not job related and ultimately excluded more blacks than whites. The Civil Rights Act of 1964 specifically prohibits requiring a high school diploma or intelligence test if neither is related to job skills and if both tend to disqualify more black than white applicants.

(*Guide to Sup. Crt.*, 609–10; *SCAZ*, 211–12)

**Q 508. What did the Court rule in *Griswold v. Connecticut?***

**A** The Court's 1965 opinion in *Griswold* marked the first extended discussion of the right to privacy. By a 7–2 vote, the justices struck down a Connecticut law against contraceptive use, even by married couples, based on a right to privacy. Written by Justice William O. Douglas, the majority opinion cited the First, Third, Fourth, Fifth, and Ninth amendments as a basis for the right. Three concurring justices specified the Ninth Amendment, which guarantees that the people retain rights not specifically enumerated in the Constitution.

(*SCAZ*, 146, 314)

(*See 39 Where is the right of privacy mentioned in the Constitution?*)

**Q 509. What did the Court rule in *Heart of Atlanta Motel v. United States?***

**A** The 1964 Civil Rights Act ban against segregated public accommodations was based on a broad interpretation of Congress's power over interstate commerce. The act prohibited racial discrimination if a motel, restaurant, or other public establishment served interstate travelers or if the goods sold somehow involved interstate commerce. The Supreme Court's 1964 decision in *Heart of Atlanta Motel* unanimously upheld this aspect of the 1964 Civil Rights Act, and in later decisions the Court let stand rulings against businesses with even less connection to interstate commerce.

(*SCAZ*, 94, 319)

(*See 488 What does separate but equal mean?; 489 What is strict construction?; 493 What did the Court rule in* Brown v. Board of Education of Topeka?)

**Q 510. What did the Court rule in *Humphrey's Executor v. United States?***

**A** Though the president can legally remove executive branch officials from office, this Supreme Court decision allowed Congress to limit that power where regulatory agencies are concerned. The case stemmed from President Franklin Roosevelt's attempt to remove a Federal Trade Commission official, William Humphrey, in 1933. Humphrey sued and his executors continued the case after his death. Ruling in 1935, the Supreme Court noted that regulatory agencies had "to act independently of executive control" and upheld the right of Congress to define the circumstances under which regulatory officials could be fired.

(*SCAZ,* 18, 375)

(*See 33 Who can appoint and remove officials in the executive branch?*)

## Q 511. What did the Court rule in *Immigration and Naturalization Service v. Chadha?*

A This case challenged the legislative veto, a device used by Congress to overrule certain actions of the federal agencies it creates. The U.S. immigration law contained one such veto provision, allowing either the House or Senate to overrule the Immigration and Naturalization Service (INS) if the agency moved to suspend an alien's deportation. In 1975 the House vetoed an INS decision to stay the deportation of Kenyan Jagdish Rai Chadha, whose student visa had run out. Chadha took the case to court, and in 1983 the Supreme Court ruled against most legislative vetoes, saying the constitutionally mandated separation of powers had been violated. Though the decision invalidated legislative veto provisions in some 200 laws, the overall impact was less sweeping. In many cases agencies continued to abide by veto arrangements informally so as not to alienate Congress.

(*SCAZ,* 236–7, 374)

(*See 31 What is separation of powers?; 278 What is a legislative veto?*)

## Q 512. What did the Court rule in the *Legal Tender Cases?*

A Congress authorized the printing of paper money (greenbacks) in 1862 to help offset the financial strains of the Civil War. Though hard currency advocates opposed the law, the Supreme Court refused to hear legal challenges to the 1862 Legal Tender Act until after the war. The first legal tender case, *Hepburn v. Griswold,* culminated in a highly controversial 4–3 ruling against using greenbacks to pay debts incurred before passage of the 1862 act. Soon after the Court ruled in 1870, however, President Ulysses S. Grant nominated two new justices who critics charged were selected because they favored paper money. With the new justices on the bench, the Court reversed itself in

1871 in two other legal tender cases, *Knox v. Lee* and *Parker v. Davis*. President Grant was accused of "packing the Court," but it is not clear that was the case.

(*SCAZ,* 235–6)

(*See 473 What was the Court-packing scheme?*)

Q **513. What did the Court rule in *Lochner v. New York*?**

A In a controversial decision based on a broad freedom of contract doctrine, the Court voted 5–4 to strike down a New York law limiting hours for bakery employees. The "meddlesome" law interfered with an individual's right to enter into a contract, the Court said in its 1905 ruling. Later, during the 1920s and 1930s, the Court relied on freedom of contract to strike down state minimum wage laws. But the Court reversed itself in 1937, abandoning the doctrine to uphold Washington State's minimum wage law in *West Coast Hotel Co. v. Parrish*. Chief Justice Charles Evans Hughes noted then that the Constitution did not enshrine freedom of contract and that other factors had to be considered.

(*SCAZ,* 118, 147, 185)

Q **514. What did the Court rule in *McCulloch v. Maryland*?**

A While upholding the national bank, this landmark ruling also supported a broad interpretation of congressional powers, giving rise to the doctrine of implied powers. The bank, chartered by Congress in 1816, proved unpopular in many states. Maryland and five other states even tried taxing the bank's branches out of existence, but the Baltimore branch manager, James McCulloch, took Maryland to court. Finally, in 1819, the Supreme Court upheld the bank and overturned state laws taxing it. In defending the bank charter, Chief Justice John Marshall cited the constitutional clause allowing Congress to enact "all Laws which shall be necessary and proper" to execute the powers expressly given it. Thus, the clause "implied" Congress had powers greater than those specifically enumerated in the Constitution.

(*SCAZ,* 184, 246)

(*See 34 What are implied powers?*)

**Q 515. What did the Court rule in *Mapp v. Ohio*?**

**A** In this 1961 decision the Court banned the use of illegally obtained evidence at criminal trials in state courts. Previously the exclusionary rule barring such tainted evidence had applied only to federal courts. But after reviewing the case of Dollree Mapp, convicted of possessing obscene materials found during an illegal search, the Court ruled 6–3 for applying the rule to state courts as well. The Court's majority opinion noted the rule would ensure "the right to be secure against rude invasions of privacy by state officers." *Mapp* was among the cases that established the Court's incorporation doctrine (*Gideon v. Wainwright* and *Miranda v. Arizona* were others.)

(*SCAZ*, 157–8)

(*See 482 What is the exclusionary rule?; 483 What is the incorporation doctrine?; 505 What did the Court rule in* Gideon v. Wainwright?; *518 What did the Court rule in* Miranda v. Arizona?)

**Q 516. What did the Court rule in *Marbury v. Madison*?**

**A** Sometimes ranked the Court's single most important ruling, this 1803 decision established the Supreme Court's right to declare acts of Congress unconstitutional. The case stemmed from outgoing President John Adams's last-minute judicial appointments—all Federalist party members. Appointee William Marbury, who did not receive his commission before Adams's last day, took the new Democratic-Republican administration to court when Secretary of State James Madison refused him the commission. Marbury asked the Court for a writ of mandamus to force Madison to act. (The Court was authorized by the 1789 Judiciary Act to issue such writs to officers of the federal government.) Writing the Court's opinion, Marshall declared Marbury's appointment complete but said the Court could not issue the writ. That provision of the 1789 Judiciary Act, he ruled, was unconstitutional and therefore invalid—even though Congress had passed it. Asserting the Court's right of judicial review, Marshall wrote, "It is, emphatically, the province and duty of the judicial department to say what the law is."

(*SCAZ*, 217–19, 251–2)

(*See 463 How many acts of Congress have been declared unconstitutional?; 485 What is judicial review?*)

**Q** **517. What did the Court rule in *Martin v. Hunter's Lessee*?**

**A** The ruling in 1816 established the Supreme Court's right to hear appeals of state court decisions that conflict with federal statutes and treaties. The Virginia Court of Appeals had upheld the state's confiscation of British-owned land, even though it violated provisions of Jay's Treaty between the federal government and Britain. Denny Martin claimed he had inherited the land from the British owner, while the state of Virginia had given David Hunter the title. The Supreme Court ruled for Martin, and in the Court's opinion, Justice Joseph Story asserted the primacy of the Supreme Court over state courts in areas involving constitutional questions.

(*RD Encyc. of Amer. Hist.*, 685; *SCAZ*, 403; *WHAD*, 1006)

(*See 36 What is the supremacy clause?*)

What did the Court rule in *Miller*? See 533.

**Q** **518. What did the Court rule in *Miranda v. Arizona*?**

**A** The Court's controversial *Miranda* decision forced police to fully inform suspects of their rights before questioning them. Though exceptions have since been allowed, the original 1966 ruling demands that police tell suspects of their right to remain silent, to have an attorney present, to have a court-appointed attorney, and that any statements they make may be used against them. Writing for the 5–4 majority, Chief Justice Earl Warren declared the warnings necessary to counteract the coercive nature of police interrogation. Police and other public officials sharply criticized the ruling.

(*SCAZ*, 258–9)

(*See 505 What did the Court rule in* Gideon v. Wainwright?; *515 What did the Court rule in* Mapp v. Ohio?)

**Q** **519. What did the Court rule in *Near v. Minnesota*?**

**A** *Near* was the first case of prior restraint of the press the Supreme Court ever reviewed. A Minnesota court had issued an injunction closing down a weekly periodical because it violated a state law prohibiting malicious, scandalous, or defamatory publications. By a 5–4 decision, however, the Supreme Court ruled against the injunction in 1931. Chief Justice Charles Evans Hughes declared that suppressing a newspaper as a public nuisance was "the essence of censorship," but acknowledged four possible circumstances in which censorship might be allowed: when publications printed obscene material, revealed important war information, invaded "private rights," or incited violence. The Court has not consistently applied Hughes's guidelines since then.

(*SCAZ*, 194, 309–10)

**Q 520. What did the Court rule in *New York Times Co. v. Sullivan*?**

A This ruling made it extremely difficult for public officials to lodge successful libel suits against individuals and newspapers that criticize them. The case stemmed from an advertisement in *The New York Times* that sought donations for Martin Luther King, Jr.'s defense fund after his arrest in Alabama in 1960. The ad did not characterize the student demonstrations correctly and exaggerated the police response, prompting an elected Montgomery city official, L. B. Sullivan, to sue for libel. The Supreme Court ruled against Sullivan in 1964, though, saying that debate on public issues "should be uninhibited, robust, and wide-open." Public officials, the Court decided, should be able to collect damages in libel suits only when there is proof that "actual malice" prompted the defamatory statement. The "actual malice" requirement was later extended to libel suits filed by public figures.

(*SCAZ*, 264)

**Q 521. What did the Court rule in *Planned Parenthood v. Casey*?**

A In *Planned Parenthood* (1992) the Supreme Court upheld state abortion regulations that did not impose an "undue burden" on women seeking abortions. The majority opinion reaffirmed the earlier landmark ruling in *Roe v. Wade*, but allowed the state to regulate abortions by imposing a mandatory twenty-four-hour waiting period, furnishing women with specific information before an abortion, and requiring parental (or judicial) consent for minors seeking abortions. The Court struck down a further restriction—notification of the woman's husband—because it would have imposed an undue burden on the woman.

(*SCAZ*, 3–5)

(See 523 *What did the Court rule in* Roe v. Wade?)

**Q** **522. What did the Court rule in _Plessy v. Ferguson_?**

**A** By a vote of 8–1 in 1896, the Court upheld legally mandated racial segregation in public transportation, declaring that "separate but equal" facilities for whites and blacks did not violate the Fourteenth Amendment's equal protection clause. Only one justice, John Marshall Harlan, disagreed with this interpretation, writing in his dissent that the Constitution "is colorblind." The separate but equal doctrine was overturned in _Brown v. Board of Education of Topeka_ in 1954.

(_SCAZ_, 185, 294)

(_See 493 What did the Court rule in_ Brown v. Board of Education of Topeka?)

**Q** **523. What did the Court rule in _Roe v. Wade_?**

**A** In a ruling that remains controversial even today, the Court voted 7–2 in 1973 to give women the right to have an abortion. The case revolved around a Texas law banning abortions except to save the mother's life, but the ruling effectively legalized abortion nationwide. Justice Harry Blackmun, writing for the majority, said the right to have an abortion probably stemmed from the "liberty" protected by the Fourteenth Amendment. But he noted that states could limit that right in the interest of protecting health and potential life. The government could ban abortions in the last months of pregnancy, for example. Later rulings allowed some further limitations, but the basic right to an abortion remained intact.

(_SCAZ_, 348)

(_See 39 Where is the right of privacy mentioned in the Constitution?_)

**Q** **524. What did the Court rule in _Roth v. United States_?**

**A** The Court in 1957 upheld an obscenity conviction under a federal statute and a California law, and sought to apply a test for obscenity. Justice William Brennan, Jr., wrote in his opinion that sex is not necessarily obscene, and set forth this obscenity test: "Whether to the average person, applying contemporary standards, the dominant theme of the material taken as a whole appeals to the prurient interest." The Court later devised other tests, including one involving a local standard.

(_Oxford Companion_, 745; _SCAZ_, 270–1)

**Q** **525. What did the Court rule in *Schechter Poultry Corp. v. United States*?**

**A** The Court's ruling in the 1935 "Sick Chicken Case" invalidated a key feature of President Franklin Roosevelt's New Deal, the 1933 National Industrial Recovery Act (NIRA). By way of the NIRA, Congress had delegated to the president the power to approve fair competition codes for various industries. The president could approve an industry code if asked to do so by just one association within that industry. The Schechters, New York poultry wholesalers who had been charged with code violations, asserted, among other things, that Congress had unconstitutionally delegated its legislative powers. The Court agreed and struck down the NIRA in a unanimous decision. One justice described the industry code provisions as a case of "delegation running riot." A shift in the Court's views helped, but Congress avoided a similar ruling on its 1938 Fair Labor Standards Act simply by providing general guidelines for government administrators to follow.

(*SCAZ*, 93–4, 373–4, 436–7)

(*See 120 What was the New Deal?*)

**Q** **526. What did the Court rule in *Schenck v. United States*?**

**A** A case brought under the World War I Sedition Act, *Schenck* involved the distribution of anti-draft-law pamphlets by members of the Socialist party. The Court used the *Schenck* decision to establish its first doctrine for weighing free speech rights against national security. In the 1919 ruling, Justice Oliver Wendell Holmes, Jr., articulated the "clear and present danger" test, a standard the Court used until the 1950s. Holmes reasoned that the government could legally restrict free speech if there was a clear and present danger of its bringing about "evils" that Congress was empowered to prevent.

(*SCAZ*, 189, 364–5, 388–9)

**Q** **527. What did the Court rule in *Scott v. Sandford*?**

**A** In this controversial 1857 ruling, the Court denied citizenship to slaves and freed blacks, barred Congress from outlawing slavery in the territories, and hastened the onset of the Civil War. Popularly called the Dred Scott case, it involved a Missouri slave named Dred Scott who had accompanied his owner to Illinois, a free state, and then to Wisconsin Territory, where slavery had been banned. Aided by his abolitionist owner, Scott sued Missouri for his freedom based on residence in a free state and territory. But Chief Justice Roger B. Taney declared that Scott had no right to sue because slaves and their descendants were not citizens. Taney also ruled that Congress could not outlaw slavery in the territories, which further outraged northern abolitionists. The Dred Scott ruling was overturned by the Fourteenth Amendment, ratified after the Civil War. Scott, whose owner formally granted him freedom in 1857, died of tuberculosis in 1858.

(*SCAZ*, 74–5, 185, 360–1)

(*See 464 What Court decisions were overturned by amendments to the Constitution?*)

**Q** **528. What did the Court rule in the *Scottsboro Cases*?**

**A** Two Supreme Court rulings make up the *Scottsboro Cases,* which expanded the constitutional right to counsel to state criminal cases under certain circumstances and brought about an end to racial discrimination in jury selection. Both cases stemmed from a controversial trial of nine black youths at Scottsboro, Alabama, during which all were found guilty of raping two white women. In the first ruling, *Powell v. Alabama* (1932), the Court voted 7–2 to quash the conviction because the youths had not been allowed "reasonable time and opportunity to secure counsel." This ruling applied only to capital cases, or cases involving punishment by death (but was expanded years later). In the second case, *Norris v. Alabama* (1935), the Court ruled against excluding blacks from the jury for the defendants' retrial. By 1937 four of the original nine defendants had been convicted again. The state dropped charges against the other five.

(*SCAZ*, 359–60, 410–11)

(*See 483 What is the incorporation doctrine?; 505 What did the Court rule in* Gideon v. Wainwright?)

**Q** **529. What did the Court rule in the *Slaughterhouse Cases*?**

**A** These cases, decided in 1873, marked the first test of the just-ratified Fourteenth Amendment. New Orleans slaughterhouse operators sought legal relief in 1869 after Louisiana granted just one slaughterhouse the exclusive right to operate in New Orleans. The operators argued that the state monopoly denied them their rights to privileges and immunities as U.S. citizens, rights guaranteed in a Fourteenth Amendment clause intended to safeguard the liberties of blacks in the South. In 1873, however, the Court voted 5–4 against the operators. The privileges and immunities clause, the Court said, did not restrict the states' jurisdiction over its citizens. The Court's narrow interpretation of the clause, coupled with later rulings, effectively nullified Fourteenth Amendment protections for blacks for over a half-century.

(*RD Encyc. of Amer. Hist.*, 1030; *SCAZ*, 380–1)

**Q  530. What did the Court rule in *Standard Oil Co. v. United States*?**

**A**  In this 1911 decision, the Court upheld the breakup of the Standard Oil Company, calling it an illegal business combination. Writing for the majority, Chief Justice Edward D. White stated that the "rule of reason" must be applied when deciding which companies should be broken up under the Sherman Antitrust Act. Soon after, the Court also ruled against the tobacco trust. But in later instances, notably the 1920 U.S. Steel Corporation case, the Court allowed companies to continue operating as they were.

(*SCAZ*, 14)

**Q  531. What did the Court rule in *Swann v. Charlotte-Mecklenburg County Board of Education*?**

**A**  The Court approved school busing to help desegregate schools in this controversial 1971 decision. While recognizing limits on how far children should be bused, the Court upheld busing as a remedy for de jure segregation—segregation sanctioned by local officials or by laws aimed at maintaining dual school systems for blacks and whites. Three years later in *Milliken v. Bradley*, the Court limited the scope of busing by striking down a plan to bus students between the city of Detroit and its suburbs. As in *Swann*, the Court distinguished between de jure and de facto segregation. The Fourteenth Amendment's equal protection clause, the Court said, did not apply to de facto segregation—segregation resulting from economic status, residence patterns, or similar factors.

(*SCAZ*, 52–3)

(*See 493 What did the Court rule in* Brown v. Board of Education of Topeka?)

**Q** **532. What did the Court rule in *Tinker v. Des Moines Independent School District*?**

**A** Declaring that students do not "shed their constitutional rights . . . at the schoolhouse gate," the Court upheld the case of two students who had protested the Vietnam War by wearing black armbands in school. The 1969 ruling noted that school officials could limit such behavior by students only when it substantially interfered with school discipline. However, three decisions in the 1980s clearly recognized public school officials' authority over students—by upholding their rights to search students' lockers without a warrant (1985), to suspend a student for giving a lewd speech at an assembly (1986), and to censor the student newspaper (1988).

(*SCAZ*, 150–1)

**Q** **533. What did the Court rule in *United States v. Miller*?**

**A** This 1939 ruling dealt with the Second Amendment right to bear arms. The case hinged on a federal regulation—from the 1934 National Firearms Act—requiring that sawed-off shotguns be registered. The justices upheld lower court rulings favoring registration, basing their decision on a fairly narrow interpretation of the Second Amendment. The right to bear arms, the Court said, was linked to the state's need for a militia. But sawed-off shotguns were not "part of ordinary military equipment" and thus could be regulated. Unlike many of the other guarantees in the Bill of Rights, the Second Amendment has not yet been incorporated (recognized by the Court as applying not only at the federal level, but also at the state level).

(*SCAZ*, 20–1; 202–3)

**Q** **534. What did the Court rule in *United States v. Nixon*?**

**A** Rejecting President Richard M. Nixon's claim to absolute executive privilege, the Court in July 1974 ruled unanimously that he must release the "Watergate tapes" to a special prosecutor. In its ruling the Court explicitly recognized, for the first time, the president's right to confidentiality. Executive privilege does relate "to the effective discharge of a President's powers," the Court found, even though the Constitution does not mention it. But the justices ordered the tapes of Oval Office conversations between Nixon and his aides released, citing the overriding need for evidence at his aides' criminal trial. The decision sealed Nixon's fate. Facing certain impeachment, he released the tapes on his own and, having thereby revealed his part in the Watergate coverup, resigned the presidency August 9, 1974.

(*SCAZ*, 159–60, 265–6, 375)

(*See 78 What happened in the Watergate scandal?*; *106 What is executive privilege?*; *146 Which president resigned?*)

**Q** **535. What did the Court rule in** *United States v. Watson?*

**A** According to longstanding practice (common law), police can arrest a suspect without a warrant when the suspect commits a crime in their presence or when they have reason to suspect criminal involvement ("reasonable suspicion"). But the 1976 Watson decision marked the first time the Court explicitly ruled in favor of warrantless arrests, in this case the arrest of a felony suspect in a public place. Once they make an arrest, however, police must promptly show a judge they have probable cause to continue holding the suspect. In 1991 the Court approved delays of up to forty-eight hours between the arrest and hearing.

(*SCAZ*, 22)

(*See 480 What is common law?*; *487 What is probable cause?*)

**Q** **536. What did the Court rule in** *University of California Regents v. Bakke?*

**A** Here the Court ruled 5–4 in 1978 against using racial quotas in the admissions process at state universities. A white student named Allan Bakke challenged quotas after twice being denied admission to the University of California medical school at Davis. He claimed the school's affirmative action program, which reserved sixteen seats each year for minority students, denied his right to equal protection under the law and violated the 1964 Civil Rights Act provision against racial discrimination. The five justices voting for Bakke agreed that racial quotas violated the Civil Rights Act, but only one also found in his favor on the question of equal protection. The Court added that race can be considered as a factor in admissions.

(*SCAZ*, 6)

(*See 475 What is affirmative action?*)

**Q** **537. What did the Court rule in** *Youngstown Sheet and Tube Co. v. Sawyer?*

**A** The Court rejected as unconstitutional President Harry S. Truman's order to seize U.S. steel mills during the Korean War. When steelworkers called a strike in 1952,

Truman feared the shutdown might cause an ammunition shortage for troops fighting in Korea. He could have invoked the 1947 Taft-Hartley Act, which would have allowed him to keep the mills operating during a sixty-day cooling-off period while labor and management kept bargaining. Instead he issued an executive order to seize the mills, based on his general executive authority (under Article II) and his power as commander-in-chief. Steel company owners went to Court, and some weeks later the Supreme Court ruled 6–3 against Truman. Justice Hugo L. Black wrote that only Congress, not the president, had the authority to order seizure of private property. But four concurring justices proved unwilling to so sharply limit future use of the president's emergency powers.

(*SCAZ,* 465)

**Q** **538. What did the Court rule in *Webster v. Reproductive Health Services*?**

**A** This 1989 decision gave states the right to impose important limitations on abortions. By a 5–4 vote the Court upheld key provisions of a Missouri law prohibiting the use of public facilities or public employees for performing abortions. One justice appointed by President Ronald Reagan joined two original dissenters in the *Roe v. Wade* case and stated they would permit restrictions on abortion so long as the limitations had a rational basis; two other Reagan appointees concurred with the majority.

(*Oxford Companion,* 921; *SCAZ,* 3–4)

(See 523 What did the Court rule in Roe v. Wade?)

## BECOMING A JUSTICE

**Q** **539. When did the justices serve?**

**A** The justices, grouped by the president who appointed them, are listed in the order of their confirmation. Names of chief justices are given in boldface, and a (c) after a name identifies an associate justice who later became chief justice (the term as chief justice appears as a separate entry). Years served begin with the year of Senate confirmation or the year of a recess appointment and end with the year of service termination. An * after the years served means the justice died in office.

| NAME | YEARS SERVED |
|---|---|
| *Washington* | |
| **John Jay** | 1789–1795 |
| John Rutledge (c) | 1789–1791 |
| William Cushing | 1789–1810* |
| James Wilson | 1789–1798* |
| John Blair, Jr. | 1789–1796 |
| James Iredell | 1790–1799* |
| Thomas Johnson | 1791–1793 |
| William Paterson | 1793–1806* |
| **John Rutledge** | 1795 |
| Samuel Chase | 1796–1811* |
| **Oliver Ellsworth** | 1796–1800 |
| | |
| *J. Adams* | |
| Bushrod Washington | 1798–1829* |
| Alfred Moore | 1799–1804 |
| **John Marshall** | 1801–1835* |
| | |
| *Jefferson* | |
| William Johnson | 1804–1834* |
| Henry B. Livingston | 1806–1823* |
| Thomas Todd | 1807–1826* |
| | |
| *Madison* | |
| Joseph Story | 1811–1845* |
| Gabriel Duvall | 1811–1835 |
| | |
| *Monroe* | |
| Smith Thompson | 1823–1843* |
| | |
| *J.Q. Adams* | |
| Robert Trimble | 1826–1828* |

| NAME | YEARS SERVED |
|------|--------------|
| *Jackson* | |
| John McLean | 1829–1861* |
| Henry Baldwin | 1830–1844* |
| James M. Wayne | 1835–1867* |
| **Roger B. Taney** | 1836–1864* |
| Philip P. Barbour | 1836–1841* |
| John Catron | 1837–1865* |
| | |
| *Van Buren* | |
| John McKinley | 1837–1852* |
| Peter V. Daniel | 1841–1860* |
| | |
| *Tyler* | |
| Samuel Nelson | 1845–1872 |
| | |
| *Polk* | |
| Levi Woodbury | 1846–1851* |
| Robert C. Grier | 1846–1870 |
| | |
| *Fillmore* | |
| Benjamin R. Curtis | 1851–1857 |
| | |
| *Pierce* | |
| John A. Campbell | 1853–1861 |
| | |
| *Buchanan* | |
| Nathan Clifford | 1858–1881* |
| | |
| *Lincoln* | |
| Noah H. Swayne | 1862–1881 |
| Samuel F. Miller | 1862–1890* |
| David Davis | 1862–1877 |
| Stephen J. Field | 1863–1897 |
| **Salmon P. Chase** | 1864–1873* |

*Grant*

| | |
|---|---|
| William Strong | 1870–1880 |
| Joseph P. Bradley | 1870–1892* |
| Ward Hunt | 1872–1882 |
| **Morrison R. Waite** | 1874–1888* |

*Hayes*

| | |
|---|---|
| John M. Harlan (I) | 1877–1911* |
| William B. Woods | 1880–1887* |

*Garfield*

| | |
|---|---|
| Stanley Matthews | 1881–1889* |

*Arthur*

| | |
|---|---|
| Horace Gray | 1881–1902* |
| Samuel Blatchford | 1882–1893* |

*Cleveland*

| | |
|---|---|
| Lucius Q. C. Lamar | 1888–1893* |
| **Melville W. Fuller** | 1888–1910* |

*Harrison*

| | |
|---|---|
| David J. Brewer | 1889–1910* |
| Henry B. Brown | 1890–1906 |
| George Shiras, Jr. | 1892–1903 |
| Howell E. Jackson | 1893–1895* |

*Cleveland*

| | |
|---|---|
| Edward D. White (c) | 1894–1910* |
| Rufus W. Peckham | 1895–1909* |

*McKinley*

| | |
|---|---|
| Joseph McKenna | 1898–1925 |

| NAME | YEARS SERVED |
|------|--------------|
| *T. Roosevelt* | |
| Oliver W. Holmes, Jr. | 1902–1932 |
| William R. Day | 1903–1922 |
| William H. Moody | 1906–1910 |
| | |
| *Taft* | |
| Horace H. Lurton | 1909–1914* |
| Charles E. Hughes (c) | 1910–1916 |
| **Edward D. White** | 1910–1921* |
| Willis Van Devanter | 1910–1937 |
| Joseph R. Lamar | 1910–1916* |
| Mahlon Pitney | 1912–1922 |
| | |
| *Wilson* | |
| James C. McReynolds | 1914–1941 |
| Louis D. Brandeis | 1916–1939 |
| John H. Clarke | 1916–1922 |
| | |
| *Harding* | |
| **William H. Taft** | 1921–1930 |
| George Sutherland | 1922–1938 |
| Pierce Butler | 1922–1939* |
| Edward T. Sanford | 1923–1930* |
| | |
| *Coolidge* | |
| Harlan F. Stone (c) | 1925–1941* |
| | |
| *Hoover* | |
| **Charles E. Hughes** | 1930–1941 |
| Owen J. Roberts | 1930–1945 |
| Benjamin N. Cardozo | 1932–1938* |

*F.D. Roosevelt*

| | |
|---|---|
| Hugo L. Black | 1937–1971 |
| Stanley F. Reed | 1938–1957 |
| Felix Frankfurter | 1939–1962 |
| William O. Douglas | 1939–1975 |
| Frank Murphy | 1940–1949* |
| **Harlan F. Stone** | 1941–1946* |
| James F. Byrnes | 1941–1942 |
| Robert H. Jackson | 1941–1954* |
| Wiley B. Rutledge | 1943–1949* |

*Truman*

| | |
|---|---|
| Harold H. Burton | 1945–1958 |
| **Fred M. Vinson** | 1946–1953* |
| Tom C. Clark | 1949–1967 |
| Sherman Minton | 1949–1956 |

*Eisenhower*

| | |
|---|---|
| **Earl Warren** | 1954–1969 |
| John M. Harlan (II) | 1955–1971 |
| William J. Brennan, Jr. | 1957–1990 |
| Charles E. Whittaker | 1957–1962 |
| Potter Stewart | 1959–1981 |

*Kennedy*

| | |
|---|---|
| Byron R. White | 1962–1993 |
| Arthur J. Goldberg | 1962–1965 |

*Johnson*

| | |
|---|---|
| Abe Fortas | 1965–1969 |
| Thurgood Marshall | 1967–1991 |

*Nixon*

| | |
|---|---|
| **Warren E. Burger** | 1969–1986 |
| Harry A. Blackmun | 1970–1994 |

| | |
|---|---|
| Lewis F. Powell, Jr. | 1971–1987 |
| William Rehnquist (c) | 1971–1986 |

*Ford*

| | |
|---|---|
| John Paul Stevens | 1975– |

*Reagan*

| | |
|---|---|
| Sandra Day O'Connor | 1981– |
| **William Rehnquist** | 1986– |
| Antonin Scalia | 1986– |
| Anthony M. Kennedy | 1988– |

*Bush*

| | |
|---|---|
| David H. Souter | 1990– |
| Clarence Thomas | 1991– |

*Clinton*

| | |
|---|---|
| Ruth Bader Ginsburg | 1993– |
| Stephen G. Breyer | 1994– |

(*SCAZ*, 471–5; *SCC*, 175–9)

## Q 540. Who are considered the greatest justices?

A Among those usually ranked among the greatest are Chief Justice John Marshall (served 1801–1835), Joseph Story (1811–1845), Chief Justice Roger B. Taney (1836–1864), John M. Harlan (I) (1877–1911), Oliver W. Holmes, Jr. (1902–1932), Charles E. Hughes (1910–1916, chief justice 1930–1941), Louis D. Brandeis (1916–1939), Harlan F. Stone (1925–1946, chief justice 1941–1946), Benjamin N. Cardozo (1932–1938), Hugo L. Black (1937–1971), Felix Frankfurter (1939–1962), and Chief Justice Earl Warren (1954–1969).

(*SCAZ*, 325; *SCC* 336–7; *VSAP*, 300)

(See 85 Who are considered the greatest presidents?)

**Q 541. What are the requirements for becoming a justice?**

**A** The Constitution sets no basic requirements for Supreme Court justices, not even age limits or citizenship requirements. Neither a law degree nor prior experience as a judge is mandatory. Nominees must be confirmed by two-thirds of the Senate, however, so that prior experience—or the nominee's judicial philosophy—ultimately may become a factor. Perhaps because of that, all nominees have been lawyers.

(*SCAZ, 29; SOW, 177*)

(*See 124 What are the requirements for serving as president and vice president?; 348 What are the requirements for being a senator?; 366 What are the requirements for being a representative?*)

**Q 542. Are there different requirements for a chief justice?**

**A** Requirements for the chief justice are the same as those for other justices—none (See above entry).

(*SOW, 177*)

**Q 543. What is the Court's oath of office?**

**A** Justices take two oaths, the constitutional oath and the judicial oath. They are:

*Constitutional Oath:*

"I _____ do solemnly swear that I will support and defend the Constitution of the United States against all enemies, foreign and domestic, that I will bear true faith and allegiance to the same, that I take this obligation freely, without any mental reservation or purpose of evasion, and that I will well and faithfully discharge the duties of the office on which I am about to enter. So help me God."

*Judicial Oath:*

"I _____ do solemnly swear or affirm, that I will administer justice without respect to persons, and do equal right to the poor and to the rich, and that I will faithfully and impartially discharge and perform all the duties incumbent on me as [a justice of the Supreme Court], under the Constitution and laws of the United States. So help me God."

*(SCAZ, 269)*

*(See 86 What is the presidential oath of office?; 257 What is the oath of office for a member of Congress?)*

## Q 544. How long do justices serve?

A Once confirmed by the Senate, a justice has the job for life so long as "good Behaviour" is maintained. The Constitution does not define "good Behaviour," but the phrase has come to include following the law, avoiding scandal, and setting a high moral standard. Only one Supreme Court justice has ever been impeached, and he was acquitted. Another, Abe Fortas, resigned in 1969 under threat of impeachment for unethical behavior.

*(SOW, 177)*

*(See 269 Who has been impeached by Congress?; 569 Who was the only justice to be impeached?)*

## Q 545. How does a justice reach the Court?

A The president nominates Supreme Court justices, subject to Senate confirmation by a majority vote. Presidents routinely consider various factors when selecting a candidate, but party affiliation is a key concern—just thirteen appointees have come from the opposition party. Judicial experience and legal and political ideology also have become important factors. Ethnic background and gender count, too, with a black, an Italian-American, and two women among the most recent appointees. Though it was not always so, the nominee now routinely testifies before the Senate Judiciary Committee prior to a vote of the full Senate. The Senate held the first such hearing in 1925 and, since the 1960s, hearings have become more extensive and sometimes very confrontational. Only a few nominees have ever been rejected or forced to withdraw, however.

*(SCAZ, 101–4, 266–8)*

*(See 547 Who has failed to be confirmed by the Senate?; 561 Who was the first Court nominee to testify before a Senate committee for confirmation?)*

**Q** **546. How many justices have been nominated?**

**A** As of October 1994, there have been 148 nominations. Of them, the Senate has rejected just twelve, four in this century. Eighteen other nominations have been withdrawn, postponed, or otherwise left unresolved by the Senate (See next question).

(*CQ Weekly Report*, May 14, 1994, 1213; *SCAZ*, 101, 471–5; *SCC*, 284–90; *The Senate*, 692–8)

**Q** **547. Who has failed to be confirmed by the Senate?**

**A** Twenty-eight nominations were rejected by the Senate, postponed, not acted upon, or withdrawn. One nomination was submitted twice and still failed to gain confirmation. Three others gained confirmation after their names were resubmitted. A date followed by an * indicates a date of nomination. Otherwise the date represents the day of Senate action.

| Date | Nominee | Action |
| --- | --- | --- |
| Feb. 28, 1793 | William Paterson (Resubmitted and confirmed Mar. 1793) | Withdrawn |
| Dec. 15, 1795 | John Rutledge | Rejected 10–14 |
| Feb. 13, 1811 | Alexander Wolcott | Rejected 9–24 |
| Feb. 12, 1829 | John J. Crittenden | Postponed |
| Mar. 3, 1835 | Roger B. Taney (Resubmitted Dec. 1835 and confirmed as chief justice Mar. 1836) | Postponed |
| Jan. 31, 1844 | John Spencer | Rejected 21–26 |
| Jun. 17, 1844 | Reuben H. Walworth | Withdrawn |
| Jun. 15, 1844 | Edward King | Postponed |
| Feb. 7, 1845 | Edward King | Withdrawn |
| Feb. 7, 1845* | John M. Read | No action taken |

| Date | Nominee | Action |
| --- | --- | --- |
| Jan. 22, 1846 | George G. Woodward | Rejected 20–29 |
| Aug. 16, 1852* | Edward A. Bradford | No action taken |
| Feb. 11, 1853 | George E. Badger | Postponed |
| Feb. 24, 1853* | William C. Micou | No action taken |
| Feb. 21, 1861 | Jeremiah S. Black | Rejected 25–26 |
| Apr. 16, 1866* | Henry Stanbery | No action taken |
| Feb. 3, 1870 | Ebenezer R. Hoar | Rejected 24–33 |
| Jan. 8, 1874 | George H. Williams | Withdrawn |
| Jan. 13, 1874 | Caleb Cushing | Withdrawn |
| Jan. 26, 1881* | Stanley Matthews (Resubmitted Mar. 1881 and confirmed May 1881) | No action taken |
| Jan. 15, 1894 | William B. Hornblower | Rejected 24–30 |
| Feb. 16, 1894 | Wheeler H. Peckham | Rejected 32–41 |
| May 7, 1930 | John J. Parker | Rejected 39–41 |
| Oct. 4, 1968 | Abe Fortas (for elevation to chief justice) | Withdrawn |
| Jun. 26, 1968* | Homer Thornberry | No action taken |
| Nov. 21, 1969 | Clement Haynsworth, Jr. | Rejected 45–55 |
| Apr. 8, 1970 | G. Harrold Carswell | Rejected 45–51 |
| Oct. 23, 1987 | Robert H. Bork | Rejected 42–58 |

(*SCAZ*, 471–5; *SCC*, 284–90; *SOW*, 181–2; *The Senate*, 688–91)

**Q 548. Who declined to serve on the Court?**

**A** The following justices were confirmed for the Court, but did not serve:

| Date | Name | Action |
|------|------|--------|
| Sep. 26, 1789 | Robert H. Harrison | Confirmed for original Supreme Court, but declined |
| Jan. 27, 1796 | William Cushing | Declined chief justiceship |
| Dec. 19, 1800 | John Jay | Declined chief justiceship |
| Jan. 3, 1811 | Levi Lincoln | Declined Cushing's seat |
| Feb. 22, 1811 | John Q. Adams | Declined Cushing's seat |
| Mar. 8, 1837 | William Smith | Confirmed 23–18, but declined |
| Dec. 20, 1869 | Edwin M. Stanton | Confirmed 46–11; died without taking seat |
| Mar. 2, 1882 | Roscoe Conkling | Confirmed 39–12, but declined |

(*SCAZ*, 471–3)

**Q 549. Who was rejected by only one vote?**

**A** President James Buchanan's nominee, Jeremiah S. Black, lost the confirmation by just one vote on Feb. 21, 1861. He was the only nominee ever rejected by such a narrow margin.

(*SCAZ*, 103; *SCC*, 284–90)

**Q 550. Which chief justices were former associate justices?**

**A** Four justices have been elevated to chief justice. The first, Edward D. White, became an associate justice in 1894 and chief justice in 1910 (a Taft appointee). Charles E. Hughes served as an associate justice between 1910 and 1916, when he resigned to run for president. He lost that race but was appointed chief justice in 1930 by President Herbert Hoover. Harlan F. Stone had been an associate justice for sixteen years when President Franklin Roosevelt promoted him to chief justice in 1941. And in 1986 President Ronald Reagan named William Rehnquist chief justice, elevating him after fifteen years' service as an associate justice.

(*SOW*, 205)

## FOR THE RECORD—FIRSTS, ETC.

Whose departure from the Court caused the longest vacancy? See 595.

Who has resigned or retired from the Court for reasons other than health, and why? See 592.

Who served the shortest time on the Court? See 555.

Who is the only president to serve on the Supreme Court after leaving the White House? See 171.

**Q 551. Who was the youngest justice to serve on the Court?**

**A** Justice Joseph Story, thirty-two years and two months when nominated in 1811, was the youngest. The next youngest was Justice William Johnson, thirty-two years and three months when nominated in 1804.

(*SCAZ*, 32; *SCC*, 294–9)

**Q 552. Who was the oldest justice to serve?**

**A** Horace H. Lurton was the oldest associate justice ever confirmed. He was sixty-five when confirmed in 1909. Harlan F. Stone was even older when he was confirmed as chief justice in 1941—sixty-eight—but he had already been serving on the Court since 1925. The oldest justice was Oliver Wendell Holmes, Jr., who retired at ninety in 1932.

(*SCAZ*, 32; *SCC*, 294–9)

**Q 553. Which justice served longest on the Court?**

**A** William O. Douglas served on the Court for thirty-six years and seven months, from April 4, 1939, to November 12, 1975. He beat the previous record of thirty-four years and eight months (set by Stephen J. Field in 1897) by almost two years.

(*SCAZ*, 145–6, 165, 474; *SCC* 300)

**Q 554. Who served longest as chief justice?**

**A** John Marshall served thirty-four years from 1801 to 1835, longer than anyone else who has held the post. Chief Justice Roger B. Taney, Marshall's replacement, came in second with twenty-eight years from 1836 to 1864. The only other chief justice with more than twenty years was Melville W. Fuller, who served twenty-two years from 1888 to 1910.

(*SCAZ,* 68)

**Q 555. Who served the shortest time on the Court?**

**A** Justice James F. Byrnes served the shortest time, resigning after just fifteen months and twenty-one days in office. President Franklin Roosevelt appointed him June 12, 1941 (he was confirmed the same day), but Byrnes resigned October 3, 1942, to take part in the war effort. He became director of the Office of Economic Stabilization. Thomas Johnson, among the first Supreme Court justices, served only about a month longer than Byrnes, between November 7, 1791 and March 4, 1793. In those days justices were required to ride circuit, and the demands of traveling to hearings throughout the South soon forced Johnson to resign for health reasons.

(*SCAZ,* 54–5, 212–13, 471–5)

**Q 556. Who served two separate terms on the Court?**

**A** Charles E. Hughes served first as an associate justice, resigned, and then returned to the Court as chief justice. He is the only justice to have served two separate terms. President William H. Taft appointed him associate justice in 1910, and Hughes remained on the Court until 1916. He resigned that year to run as the Republican presidential candidate, but lost the election to Woodrow Wilson. Years later in 1930, President Herbert Hoover appointed him chief justice, and he served in the post until his retirement in 1941.

(*SCAZ,* 193)

**Q 557. When was the longest time the Court went without a change in membership?**

**A** The Court set this record by going twelve years without a change during the early

1800s. The period began with the appointments of Gabriell Duvall and Joseph Story in 1811 (by Madison) and ended with Justice Henry B. Livingston's death in 1823.

(*SOW,* 180)

(*See 595 Whose departure from the Court caused the longest vacancy?*)

### Q 558. Which president appointed the most justices?

A President George Washington appointed eleven justices during his two terms, more than any other president. Five of those appointees made up the entire panel of the first Supreme Court, and all five were confirmed by the Senate just two days after Washington nominated them in September 1789. The first justices were John Rutledge, William Cushing, James Wilson, John Blair, Jr., and Chief Justice John Jay. The sixth justice, Robert H. Harrison, declined the appointment after the Senate confirmed his nomination, and he was replaced in early 1790 by James Iredell.

(*SCAZ,* 471)

### Q 559. Which full-term president didn't appoint any justices?

A Jimmy Carter is the only president who served a full term without having the opportunity to fill a Supreme Court vacancy. President Andrew Johnson served most of Lincoln's unexpired term and during that time nominated a candidate for a single vacancy. But the Senate took no action on the appointment, leaving the vacancy unfilled. Presidents William H. Harrison and Zachary Taylor died soon after taking office and never made any nominations to the Court. All the other presidents named at least one justice to the Court.

(*SOW,* 180)

### Q 560. Which justice was confirmed the quickest?

A President Harry S. Truman's nominee, Harold H. Burton, was nominated and confirmed the same day, on September 19, 1945. But the record for the fastest confirmation belongs to Justice Samuel F. Miller. A Lincoln appointee, he won confirmation by the Senate in just half an hour on July 26, 1862.

(*SCAZ,* 52, 257, 440–1)

(*See 545 How does a justice reach the Court?*)

**Q 561. Who was the first Court nominee to testify before a Senate committee for confirmation?**

**A** Harlan F. Stone became the first during his confirmation hearing in 1925. The committee subjected him to harsh questioning, in part because as attorney general he had played a role in the investigation of a senator.

(*SCAZ*, 101)

**Q 562. Who was the first woman justice?**

**A** Sandra Day O'Connor, a former Arizona state senator and Court of Appeals judge, became the first woman Supreme Court justice in 1981. In making the appointment, President Ronald Reagan fulfilled a campaign pledge to name a woman to the Court.

(*SCAZ*, 32–3, 272)

*(See 240 Who were the first female, black, and Hispanic members of the cabinet?; 328 Who were the first black, Hispanic, native American, female, Asian, Indian, and Hawaiian representatives and senators?; 433 When did the first woman run for president?; 445 Who was the first woman nominated for vice president by a major political party?)*

**Q 563. Has there ever been more than one female justice on the Court at a time?**

**A** Since the swearing in of Justice Ruth Bader Ginsburg on August 10, 1993, there have been two female justices on the Court.

(*CQ Weekly Report*, Sept. 4, 1993, 2311)

**Q 564. Who was the first black justice?**

**A** Appointed by President Lyndon B. Johnson in 1967, Thurgood Marshall became the first black to join the Supreme Court. Marshall, then U.S. solicitor general, had been part of the legal team that won a reversal of the Court's separate but equal doctrine in the 1954 *Brown v. Board of Education of Topeka* ruling. Marshall served as an associate justice until his retirement in 1991, when he was replaced by another black justice, Clarence Thomas.

(*SCAZ*, 32)

*(See 240 Who were the first female, black, and Hispanic members of the cabinet?; 328 Who were the first black, Hispanic, native American, female, Asian, Indian, and Hawaiian representatives and senators?; 434 Which blacks have run for president?; 488 What does separate but equal mean?; 493 What did the Court rule in Brown v. Board of Education of Topeka?)*

## Q 565. Who was the first Catholic justice?

A President Andrew Jackson appointed the first Catholic justice, Roger B. Taney, who took his seat as chief justice in 1836. Until then justices had always been Protestant. President Grover Cleveland appointed the next Catholic, Edward D. White, in 1894. Other Catholics appointed since then include Joseph McKenna, Pierce Butler, Frank Murphy, William J. Brennan, Jr., Antonin Scalia, and Anthony M. Kennedy.

*(SCAZ, 32; SOW, 203)*

*(See 150 Who was the first Catholic president?; 335 Who were the first Catholics in the House and Senate? The first Jews?)*

## Q 566. Has there ever been more than one Catholic on the Court at once?

A Justices Edward D. White (later chief justice) and Joseph McKenna served together from 1898 until 1921, when White died. McKenna then served with another Catholic justice, Pierce Butler, from 1922 until 1925, when McKenna retired. No more than one Catholic served on the Court after that until 1986. That year, Justice William J. Brennan, Jr., on the Court since 1957, was joined by fellow-Catholic Antonin Scalia. The confirmation of Anthony M. Kennedy in 1988 put three Catholics on the Court at once. That lasted just two years, though, until Justice Brennan retired in 1990.

*(SCAZ, 471–8; SOW, 203)*

## Q 567. Who was the first Jewish justice?

A Louis D. Brandeis became the first Jewish justice when President Woodrow Wilson nominated him in 1916. A proponent of controversial social and economic views, Brandeis's nomination met with stiff, though unsuccessful, opposition from conservatives. Anti-Semitism also figured in the opposition, but a Jewish seat on the Court was maintained until 1969. Other Jewish justices include Benjamin N. Cardozo, Felix Frankfurter, Arthur J. Goldberg, Abe Fortas, Ruth Bader Ginsburg, and Stephen G. Breyer.

(*CQ Weekly Report,* Jun. 19, 1993, 1570; *SCAZ,* 32)

(See 335 Who were the first Catholics in the House and Senate? The first Jews?)

**Q  568. Has there ever been more than one Jewish justice at a time?**

**A**  Two Jewish justices served simultaneously when Louis D. Brandeis and Benjamin N. Cardozo were on the Court together from 1932 until 1938. Cardozo died in 1938. Justice Brandeis resigned in 1939, just weeks after another Jewish justice, Felix Frankfurter, was appointed to the Court. Two Jewish justices, both appointed by President Bill Clinton, are now serving on the Court. Ruth Bader Ginsburg took her seat in 1993, and Stephen A. Breyer began service in 1994.

(*SCAZ,* 471–8; *SOW,* 203)

**Q  569. Who was the only justice to be impeached?**

**A**  A radical Federalist who often pushed his political views from the bench, Justice Samuel Chase went too far one day in 1803 when he denounced the Jefferson administration and so-called democratic "mobocracy." President Thomas Jefferson wrote an angry letter, prodding the House to impeach Chase in 1804 for various statements he had made. At the Senate trial, Chase's attorney argued that his client had not committed any indictable offense, and the Senate vote to acquit Chase in 1805 hinged on just that argument.

(*SCAZ,* 66–7, 198; *SCC,* 326)

(See 269 Who has been impeached by Congress?; 544 How long do justices serve?)

**Q  570. Who wrote the first dissent?**

**A**  Justice William Johnson wrote the first dissenting opinion in the 1805 case *Huidekoper's Lessee v. Douglass.* Dissents did not become common until the twentieth century, though, and some critics argue that the many dissenting and concurring opinions today cloud the Court's intent and weaken its authority. Others argue that they contribute to judicial independence and to the healthy growth of the law. In one recent year, justices filed dissents in almost two-thirds of the cases involving written opinions.

(*SCAZ,* 143)

(See 459 What types of opinions are there?)

**Q 571. Who was the "great dissenter?"**

**A** Justice John M. Harlan (I) earned that title by dissenting 380 times between 1877 and 1911. Probably the most famous opinion of his thirty-four-year career came in *Plessy v. Ferguson* (1896), when he alone opposed the Court's ruling in favor of separate but equal facilities for blacks. "Our Constitution is colorblind, and neither knows nor tolerates classes among citizens," he wrote. The Court's reversal of *Plessy* fifty-eight years later in *Brown v. Board of Education of Topeka* finally vindicated Harlan's dissent.

(*SOW,* 206)

(*See 488 What does separate but equal mean?; 493 What did the Court rule in* Brown v. Board of Education of Topeka?; *522 What did the Court rule in* Plessy v. Ferguson?)

**Q 572. Which justice killed a person in peacetime?**

**A** Henry B. Livingston killed a man in a duel in 1798, eight years before being appointed to the Supreme Court. Livingston was known to have a violent streak; he fought several other duels, though with less serious results.

(*SCAZ,* 242–3)

(*See 214 Which vice president killed a man while in office?; 344 Which members have fought each other in duels?*)

## JUSTICES' BACKGROUNDS

**Q 573. Does Court service run in any families?**

**A**  Among the related Supreme Court justices are: Stephen J. Field (served 1863–1897) and his nephew David J. Brewer (1889–1910), who served together for seven years; John M. Harlan (I, 1877–1911) and his grandson, John M. Harlan (II, 1955–1971); and Lucius Q. C. Lamar (1888–1893) and his cousin, Joseph R. Lamar (1910–1916).

(*SOW,* 202)

(*See 176 Who was the only president whose son also became president?; 177 Which president's grandfather was also president?; 178 Which presidents were distant cousins?*)

**574. Which states have produced the most justices?**

 New York ranks first with sixteen. Ohio had ten, Massachusetts eight, and Pennsylvania and Virginia six each.

(*SCC*, 180–92; *VSAP*, 294–9)

(*See 158 Which state has produced the most presidents?; 217 Which state has produced the most vice presidents?*)


**575. Which colleges graduated the most justices?**

Ten justices attended Yale as undergraduates, making it the most popular college among Supreme Court members. Nine went to Harvard and eight to Princeton.

(*SCC*, 207–21)

(*See 159 Which colleges have produced the most presidents?*)


**576. Which law schools graduated the most justices?**

Thirteen justices got their law degree from Harvard, five from Yale, and four from Columbia. Several other justices attended these schools but did not graduate.

(*SCC*, 207–21)


**577. Who was the last justice not to have a law degree?**

Stanley F. Reed, an associate justice from 1938 to 1957, was the last. He attended the law schools of both the University of Virginia and Columbia University but, like many justices before him, did not complete his studies.

(*SCAZ*, 29)


**578. Who was the last justice never to have attended law school?**

James F. Byrnes, an associate justice from 1941 to 1942, was the last. Byrnes left school at fourteen to work first as a law clerk and then as a court stenographer. While working, he read law in his spare time and passed the bar examination by the time he was twenty-four. Byrnes's route to the bench once was not so unusual. Until the mid-eighteenth century, nearly all aspiring lawyers got their legal training in law offices instead of law schools. In fact, Benjamin R. Curtis, who served from 1851 to 1857, was the first Supreme Court justice to have received his law degree in the United States. He graduated from Harvard in 1832.

(*SCAZ,* 29)

### Q 579. Which justice attended law school classes after being nominated to the Court?

A Though he had served both as a circuit court judge and as U.S. attorney general, Joseph McKenna recognized his need for further legal training after President William McKinley nominated him in 1897. McKenna, who graduated from the Benicia Collegiate Institute law department in 1865, studied law at Columbia University for a few months to bolster his legal training before taking his position on the Court in 1898.

(*SCAZ,* 247–8)

### Q 580. Did any justice fight in a war?

A Thirty-four justices served in the military during U.S. wars. One of them, Justice Frank Murphy, served in two wars, World War I and World War II.

| *American Revolution* | *Civil War* |
| --- | --- |
| Gabriel Duvall | John M. Harlan (I) |
| John Jay | Oliver W. Holmes, Jr. |
| Thomas Johnson | Lucius Q. C. Lamar |
| Henry B. Livingston | Horace H. Lurton |
| John Marshall | Stanley Matthews |
| Alfred Moore | Edward D. White |
| William Paterson | William B. Woods |
| Thomas Todd | |
| Bushrod Washington | *World War I* |
| | Hugo L. Black |
| *War of 1812* | Harold H. Burton |
| | Tom C. Clark |
| John Catron | William O. Douglas |
| James M. Wayne | |

*World War I (cont'd)*

Sherman Minton
Frank Murphy (and World War II)
Stanley F. Reed
Earl Warren

*World War II*

William J. Brennan, Jr.
Arthur J. Goldberg

John M. Harlan (II)
Frank Murphy (and World War I)
Lewis F. Powell, Jr.
William Rehnquist
John Paul Stevens
Potter Stewart
Byron R. White

(*SCC*, 240–1)

(*See 166 Which presidents have fought in which wars?*)

## Q 581. How many justices served in Congress?

**A** Four served in both the House and Senate, thirteen served in the House alone, and eleven served in the Senate alone. David Davis served in the Senate (1877–1883) after resigning from the Court, the only justice to move from the Court to Congress.

(*SCC*, 242–55; *The Senate*, 253)

(*See 163 What experience have presidents had before being elected?*)

## Q 582. Were any members of Congress appointed directly to the Court?

**A** One representative and seven senators went directly from Congress to the Supreme Court. They are listed below by year of confirmation:

*Senators*

1796   Oliver Ellsworth
1837   John McKinley
1846   Levi Woodbury
1894   Edward D. White
1937   Hugo L. Black
1941   James F. Byrnes
1945   Harold H. Burton

*Representative*

1835   James M. Wayne

(*SCC*, 265–72)

## Q 583. How many justices served in the cabinet?

A Listed below are the twenty justices who held cabinet positions before being confirmed as Supreme Court members. Fourteen of them (in bold) went directly from the cabinet to the Court.

| Year of confirmation | Justice | Cabinet post |
|---|---|---|
| 1801 | **John Marshall** | secretary of state, 1800–1801 |
| 1823 | **Smith Thompson** | navy secretary, 1819–1823 |
| 1829 | **John McLean** | postmaster general,* 1823–1829 |
| 1836 | Roger B. Taney | secretary of war (acting), 1831<br>attorney general, 1831–1833<br>treasury secretary,† 1833–1834 |
| 1846 | Levi Woodbury | navy secretary, 1831–1834<br>treasury secretary, 1834–1841 |
| 1858 | Nathan Clifford | attorney general, 1846–1848 |
| 1864 | **Salmon P. Chase** | treasury secretary, 1861–1864 |
| 1888 | **Lucius Q. C. Lamar** | interior secretary, 1885–1888 |
| 1898 | **Joseph McKenna** | attorney general, 1897–1898 |
| 1903 | William R. Day | secretary of state, 1898 |
| 1906 | **William H. Moody** | navy secretary, 1902–1904<br>attorney general, 1904–1906 |
| 1914 | **James C. McReynolds** | attorney general, 1913–1914 |
| 1921 | William H. Taft | secretary of war, 1904–1908 |
| 1925 | **Harlan F. Stone** | attorney general, 1924–1925 |
| 1930 | Charles E. Hughes | secretary of state, 1921–1925 |
| 1940 | **Frank Murphy** | attorney general, 1939–1940 |
| 1941 | **Robert H. Jackson** | attorney general, 1940–1941 |
| 1946 | **Fred M. Vinson** | treasury secretary, 1945–1946 |

| 1949 | **Tom C. Clark** | attorney general, 1945–1949 |
| 1962 | **Arthur J. Goldberg** | secretary of labor, 1961–1962 |

\*The postmaster general was a cabinet post until 1971, when the post office became a quasi-independent corporation.

†Taney served as treasury secretary under a recess appointment, though his nomination for that post eventually was rejected by the Senate.

(*SCC*, 242–55, 265–72)

(*See 171 Who is the only president to serve on the Supreme Court after leaving the White House?; 244 Which presidents once served in the cabinet?*)

**Q 584. Which justices once served as solicitor general?**

**A** Four of them served as solicitor general at some point before being appointed to the Court: William H. Taft (1890–1892), Stanley F. Reed (1935–1938), Robert H. Jackson (1938–1939), and Thurgood Marshall (1965–1967).

(*SCC*, 242–55)

(*See 564 Who was the first black justice?*)

**Q 585. How many justices came directly to the Court from state governorships?**

**A** Three sitting governors have been appointed to the Court—New Jersey governor William Paterson (confirmed 1793), New York governor Charles E. Hughes (1910), and California governor Earl Warren (chief justice, 1954). One other, then New York governor John Jay, was confirmed by the Senate but declined the appointment (1800). Jay, who had been the Court's first chief justice (1789–1795), retired from politics in 1801 after completing his second term as governor.

(*SCAZ*, 471; *SCC*, 265–73)

**Q 586. How many justices came to the Court from lower courts?**

**A** Thirty-one appointees were sitting judges on either a U.S. court of appeals or U.S. district court. Twenty others were state judges when nominated.

(*SCC*, 265–73)

**Q** **587. How many justices had no judicial experience on state or federal courts?**

**A** Thirty-nine of the 108 Supreme Court justices had no prior judicial experience. William Rehnquist—associate justice from 1971 to 1986, when he was named chief justice—was the most recent among them. A Nixon appointee, he had been an assistant U.S. attorney general from 1969 to 1971.

(*SCAZ*, 471–5; *SCC*, 242–64)

**Q** **588. How many justices came directly to the Court from private practice?**

**A** Twenty-one lawyers went from private practice to the Supreme Court. Justice Lewis F. Powell, Jr., confirmed in 1971, was the most recent of them. Abe Fortas, and before him Louis D. Brandeis, also came to the Court from private practice.

(*SCC*, 265–72)

**Q** **589. Who is the only justice who had no political or judicial experience before being nominated?**

**A** Though a prominent Pennsylvania lawyer in private practice, Justice George Shiras, Jr., had no political or judicial experience before President Benjamin Harrison appointed him to the Court in 1892. During his time on the Court, Shiras gained a reputation for his analytical abilities and steadiness.

(*SCAZ*, 378)

**Q** **590. Which of the current justices once clerked on the Court?**

**A** Three current justices once clerked on the Court: John Paul Stevens clerked for Justice Wiley B. Rutledge (1947–1948); William Rehnquist clerked for Justice Robert H. Jackson (1952–1953); and Stephen G. Breyer clerked for Justice Arthur J. Goldberg (1964–1965).

(*CQ Weekly Report*, May 14, 1994; *SCAZ*, 87)

(See 599 What do law clerks do at the Court?)

**Q 591. Who is the only justice to have played professional football?**

**A** Justice Byron R. White played with the former Pittsburgh Pirates professional football team for a year after completing his undergraduate college studies. Nicknamed "Whizzer" for his football skills, White graduated first in his class at the University of Colorado while also excelling at football, basketball, and baseball. After his stint as a pro football player, White attended Oxford University as a Rhodes scholar and then graduated from Yale University law school.

(*SCAZ*, 454–5)

## LEAVING THE COURT

**Q 592. Who has resigned or retired from the Court for reasons other than health, and why?**

**A** Sixteen justices resigned or retired for reasons unrelated to health or age. Eight others cited advanced age but did not mention health problems. All twenty-four are listed below in order of their retirement.

| Justice | Age | Year retired | Reason |
| --- | --- | --- | --- |
| John Rutledge | 51 | 1791 | Became South Carolina chief justice |
| John Jay | 49 | 1795 | Became governor of New York |
| Benjamin R. Curtis | 47 | 1857 | Resigned over low salary, circuit riding, and disagreement over Dred Scott decision |
| John A. Campbell | 49 | 1861 | Loyalty to South |
| David Davis | 61 | 1877 | Became a senator |
| William Strong | 72 | 1880 | Retired before onset of infirmity to set example to others |
| George Shiras, Jr. | 71 | 1903 | Retired to spend time with family |
| Charles E. Hughes | 54 | 1916 | Resigned (first time) to run for president |

| | | | |
|---|---|---|---|
| John H. Clarke | 65 | 1922 | Resigned to promote U.S. entry into League of Nations |
| Oliver W. Holmes, Jr. | 90 | 1932 | Advanced age |
| Willis Van Devanter | 78 | 1937 | Advanced age; improved retirement benefits; opposed New Deal |
| George Sutherland | 75 | 1938 | Advanced age; improved retirement benefits; opposed New Deal |
| Louis D. Brandeis | 82 | 1939 | Advanced age |
| James C. McReynolds | 78 | 1941 | Advanced age; opposed New Deal |
| James F. Byrnes | 63 | 1942 | Resigned to participate in war effort |
| Owen J. Roberts | 70 | 1945 | Resigned to pursue civic interests; served as dean of University of Pennsylvania Law School, without pay |
| Arthur J. Goldberg | 56 | 1965 | Named U.S. ambassador to United Nations |
| Tom C. Clark | 67 | 1967 | Resigned after his son became attorney general |
| Abe Fortas | 58 | 1969 | Resigned because of allegations of unethical behavior |
| Earl Warren | 78 | 1969 | Advanced age |
| Potter Stewart | 66 | 1981 | Retired to spend time with family and to pursue other interests |
| Warren E. Burger | 79 | 1986 | Advanced age; served as chairman of the Bicentennial Commission |
| Byron R. White | 76 | 1993 | Retired to spend time with family and to free seat for younger justice |
| Harry A. Blackmun | 85 | 1994 | Advanced age |

(*SCC*, 327–35)

(*See 555 Who served the shortest time on the Court?*)

**Q** **593. How many justices died while serving on the Court?**

**A** Forty-eight justices have died in office, or just under half the 108 who have served on the Court. The unusually high number of justices who have died while still serving is due to their being appointed for life, and to the fact that in the past judges did not have retirement benefits. Justice James Wilson, who had served nine years on the Court, was the first to die in office (1798). He was nearly fifty-six years old. As of 1994, Justice Robert H. Jackson was the last. Appointed to the bench in 1941, he died at age sixty-two.

(*SCC*, 327–35)

(*See 134 Which presidents died in office of natural causes?; 206 Which vice presidents died in office?; 323 Which members have died in the Capitol?*)

**Q** **594. Has any justice been assassinated?**

**A** No, but one justice narrowly escaped a potentially deadly attack sparked by a court ruling. In 1888, while sitting as a California circuit court judge, Justice Stephen J. Field ruled against a woman seeking her deceased first husband's estate. She threatened to kill Field then, and her new husband, David Terry, attacked Field a year later on his return to California for circuit court duty. A federal marshal assigned to protect Field shot and killed Terry in the melee.

(*SCAZ*, 164–5; *SOW*, 213)

(*See 135 Which presidents were assassinated?*)

**Q** **595. Whose departure from the Court caused the longest vacancy?**

**A** Justice Henry Baldwin's death on April 21, 1844, resulted in a vacancy that lasted a record two years, three months, and thirteen days. Feuding between President John Tyler and Congress accounted for half the delay, though Congress also rejected President James K. Polk's first nominee almost a year after the president took office in March 1845. Polk succeeded in filling the vacancy on August 4, 1846, however, when the Senate finally confirmed Pennsylvania District Court Judge Robert C. Grier—just one day after Polk had nominated him. During the long vacancy, future president James Buchanan three times declined invitations to accept the nomination.

(*SCAZ*, 440–1; *SOW*, 180)

Q **596. What does the clerk of the Court do?**

A The clerk and a twenty-five-member staff manage all the documents connected with cases coming before the Court. The clerk receives and records all briefs, motions, and petitions; administers the Court's dockets and argument calendars; and maintains the record of judgments and mandates. In addition, the clerk advises attorneys and others about the Court's rules and procedures.

(*SCAZ*, 86–7)

Q **597. What does the marshal of the Court do?**

A The marshal is the court's chief security officer, general manager, and paymaster. In addition to overseeing about 200 employees, including about 75 security officers, the marshal plays an important role inside the courtroom. The marshal calls the Supreme Court to order by crying, "*Oyez, Oyez, Oyez*" (French for "hear ye"). When the Court is in session, the marshal is stationed at one end of the bench (the Court clerk is at the other). During oral arguments, the marshal or an assistant operates the white and red lights that warn time for presenting arguments is about to expire.

(*SCAZ*, 254–5)

Q **598. What other administrators work for the Court, and what do they do?**

A Besides the clerk and marshal, the Court employs a reporter of decisions and a librarian. The reporter and a staff of nine assistants edit the Court opinions and supervise their publication. The first two reporters of decisions (journalist Alexander J. Dallas and Judge William Cranch) carried out their duties as a public service, and it was not until 1816 that the Court formally appointed the first reporter. The Court hired its first librarian in 1887, and today the librarian oversees a collection of about 300,000 volumes. The Court curator's office was established in 1974 and takes care of historical papers, offers educational programs for the public, and keeps a historical record of events at the Court. The current curator is Gail Galloway.

(*SCC*, 43)

**Q** **599. What do law clerks do at the Court?**

**A** Clerks assist individual justices by, among other things, reviewing and writing preliminary memoranda on the thousands of cases that come before the Court each year. They also help prepare legal opinions in whatever way the justices want, by doing research or sometimes even writing a first draft. Each justice may have up to four law clerks.

(*SCAZ*, 87)

**Q** **600. Who hired the first law clerk?**

**A** In 1882 Justice Horace Gray hired the first law clerk, a recent Harvard Law School graduate who had finished at the top of his class. For decades the justices had lobbied Congress for the money to hire clerks, without success. Gray paid the new clerk out of his own pocket, but instead of assigning him to legal research, Gray used the clerk mainly as a personal servant and barber.

(*SCAZ*, 88, 177)

**Q** **601. Who can practice law before the Court?**

**A** Any case filed with the Court must be sponsored by a lawyer who has been admitted to the Supreme Court bar, though other lawyers also may work on the case. To be admitted to the bar, a lawyer must have been a member of a state or territory's bar for the previous three years and must submit to the Court a certificate proving this, a personal statement, endorsements by two members of the Court's bar, and an admission fee. About 5,000 lawyers are admitted to the bar each year.

(*SCAZ*, 36–7)

**Q** **602. What are the solicitor general's responsibilities?**

**A** The solicitor general represents the U.S. government before the Supreme Court and decides which cases the government should ask the Court to review. Since the Court reviews most cases requested by the government, the solicitor general has considerable influence over legal issues. The solicitor general also participates in cases as an amicus curiae, giving the government's position on the legal questions involved. The solicitor general's staff includes about twenty-four lawyers, who usually argue the government's positions before the Court. Sometimes, however, the solicitor general or even the attorney general handles an important case. Other duties of the solicitor general's office include monitoring the government's position in lower court cases and reviewing briefs prepared by government agencies.

(*SCAZ*, 384)

(*See 239 What does the attorney general do?; 476 What is amicus curiae?*)

# REFERENCE MATERIALS

## BIBLIOGRAPHIC ABBREVIATIONS

Amer. Cong. Dict.: Kravitz, Walter. *Congressional Quarterly's American Congressional Dictionary.* Washington, D.C.: Congressional Quarterly, 1993.

Amer. Talking: Flexner, Stuart Berg. *I Hear America Talking.* New York: Van Nostrand, 1976.

Book of Chronologies: Wetterau, Bruce. *The New York Public Library Book of Chronologies.* New York: Prentice Hall, 1990.

Budget Baselines: *Budget Baselines, Historical Data and Alternatives for the Future.* Washington, D.C.: U.S. Government Printing Office, 1993.

Budget of the U.S. Govt., Analyt. Perspectives: *Budget of the United States Government: Analytical Perspectives.* Washington, D.C.: U.S. Government Printing Office, 1994.

CAZ: *Congress A to Z: A Ready Reference Encyclopedia.* 2nd ed. Washington, D.C.: Congressional Quarterly, 1993.

CD 1990s: *Congressional Districts in the 1990s: A Portrait of America.* Washington, D.C.: Congressional Quarterly, 1993.

Constit. Law: Epstein, Lee, and Thomas G. Walker. *Constitutional Law for a Changing America: Rights, Liberties, and Justice.* Washington, D.C.: CQ Press, 1992.

CQ Almanac: *Congressional Quarterly Almanac.* 1990, 1991, and 1992 eds. Washington, D.C.: Congressional Quarterly, 1991, 1992, 1993.

CTC: Daniel, Clifton, ed. *Chronicle of the Twentieth Century.* Mount Kisco, New York: Chronicle Publications, 1988.

Dict. of Amer. Hist.: Adams, James Truslow. *Dictionary of American History.* Rev. ed. New York: Scribner's, 1978.

Dict. of Amer. Slang: Wentworth, Harold, and Stuart Berg Flexner. *Dictionary of American Slang*. 2nd ed. New York: T. Y. Crowell, 1975.

Encyc. Americana: *Encyclopedia Americana*. Danbury, Connecticut: Grolier, 1993.

Encyc. Britannica: *Encyclopedia Britannica*. 15th ed. Chicago: Encyclopedia Britannica, 1994.

Encyc. of Amer. Facts & Dates: Carruth, Gorton. *The Encyclopedia of American Facts & Dates*. 8th ed. New York: Harper & Row, 1987.

Encyc. of Amer. Hist.: Morris, Richard B. *Encyclopedia of American History*. 6th ed. New York: Harper & Row, 1982.

Facts on File: *Facts on File Yearbook: The Indexed Record of World Events*. 1992, 1993, and 1994 eds. New York: Facts on File, 1992, 1993, 1994.

FAP: Kane, Joseph. *Facts About the Presidents*. 6th ed. New York: H. W. Wilson, 1993.

Fed. Civ. Workforce Stats.: *Federal Civilian Workforce Statistics: Employment Trends as of July 1993*. Washington, D.C.: U.S. Government Printing Office, 1993.

Guide to Cong.: *Congressional Quarterly's Guide to Congress*. 4th ed. Washington, D.C.: Congressional Quarterly, 1991.

Guide to Pres.: Nelson, Michael, ed. *Congressional Quarterly's Guide to the Presidency*. Washington, D.C.: Congressional Quarterly, 1989.

Guide to Sup. Crt.: *Congressional Quarterly's Guide to the Supreme Court*. 2nd ed. Washington, D.C.: Congressional Quarterly, 1990.

GUSE: *Congressional Quarterly's Guide to U.S. Elections*. 2nd ed. Washington, D.C.: Congressional Quarterly, 1985.

Harvard Encyc.: Thernstrom, Stephan A., et al., eds. *Harvard Encyclopedia of American Ethnic Groups*. Cambridge, Mass.: Belknap Press, 1980.

Hist. Atlas: Martis, Kenneth, and Gregory Elmer. *Historical Atlas of State Power in Congress*. Washington, D.C.: Congressional Quarterly, 1993.

Hist. Tables: *Historical Tables: Budget of the United States Government*. Washington, D.C.: U.S. Government Printing Office, 1990.

How to Research the Sup. Crt.: Martin, Fenton S., and Robert U. Goehlert. *How to Research the Supreme Court*. Washington, D.C.: Congressional Quarterly, 1992.

Legis. Drafter's DR: Filson, Lawrence. *The Legislative Drafter's Desk Reference.* Washington, D.C.: Congressional Quarterly, 1992.

New Columbia Encyc.: Harris, William H., and Judith S. Levey, eds. *The New Columbia Encyclopedia.* New York: Columbia University Press, 1975.

Oxford Companion: Hall, Kenneth, ed. *The Oxford Companion to the Supreme Court of the United States.* New York: Oxford University Press, 1992.

PAZ: Nelson, Michael, ed. *The Presidency A to Z: A Ready Reference Encyclopedia.* Washington, D.C.: Congressional Quarterly, 1994.

People Speak: *The People Speak: American Elections in Focus.* Washington, D.C.: Congressional Quarterly, 1990.

RD Encyc. of Amer. Hist.: *Reader's Digest Encyclopedia of American History.* Pleasantville, New York: Reader's Digest, 1975.

SCAZ: Witt, Elder, ed. *The Supreme Court A to Z: A Ready Reference Encyclopedia.* Washington, D.C.: Congressional Quarterly, 1993.

SCC: Epstein, Lee, Jeffrey A. Segal, Harold J. Spaeth, and Thomas G. Walker. *The Supreme Court Compendium: Data, Decisions, and Developments.* Washington, D.C.: Congressional Quarterly, 1994.

The Senate: Byrd, Robert C. *The Senate 1789-1989.* Washington, D.C.: U.S. Government Printing Office, 1993.

SOW: Moore, John L. *Speaking of Washington: Facts, Firsts, and Folklore.* Washington, D.C.: Congressional Quarterly, 1993.

Stat. Abstract: *Statistical Abstract of the United States, 1993.* Austin, Texas: Reference Press, 1993.

U.S. Govt. Man.: *United States Government Manual, 1993-94.* Lanham, Maryland: Bernan Press, 1993.

VSAP: Stanley, Harold W., and Richard G. Niemi. *Vital Statistics on American Politics.* 4th ed. Washington, D.C.: CQ Press, 1994.

VSC: Ornstein, Norman J., Thomas E. Mann, and Michael J. Malbin. *Vital Statistics on Congress, 1993-1994.* Washington, D.C.: Congressional Quarterly, 1994.

Webster's Biog. Dict.: *Webster's Biographical Dictionary.* Springfield, Massachusetts: G & C Merriam, 1980.

WHAD: Wetterau, Bruce. *World History: A Dictionary of Important People, Places, and Events from Ancient Times to the Present.* New York: Henry Holt, 1994.

World Almanac: Hoffman, Mark S., ed. *World Almanac and Book of Facts, 1993.* Mahwah, New Jersey: The World Almanac, 1992.

## BIBLIOGRAPHY

Adams, James Truslow. *Dictionary of American History.* Rev. ed. New York: Scribner's, 1978.

*Budget Baselines, Historical Data and Alternatives for the Future.* Washington, D.C.: U.S. Government Printing Office, 1993.

*Budget of the United States Government: Analytical Perspectives.* Washington, D.C.: U.S. Government Printing Office, 1994.

Byrd, Robert C. *The Senate 1789-1989.* Washington, D.C.: U.S. Government Printing Office, 1993.

Carruth, Gorton. *The Encyclopedia of American Facts & Dates.* 8th ed. New York: Harper & Row, 1987.

*Congress A to Z: A Ready Reference Encyclopedia.* 2nd ed. Washington, D.C.: Congressional Quarterly, 1993.

*Congressional Districts in the 1990s: A Portrait of America.* Washington, D.C.: Congressional Quarterly, 1993.

*Congressional Quarterly Almanac.* 1990, 1991, and 1992 eds. Washington, D.C.: Congressional Quarterly, 1991, 1992, 1993.

*Congressional Quarterly's Guide to Congress.* 4th ed. Washington, D.C.: Congressional Quarterly, 1991.

*Congressional Quarterly's Guide to the Supreme Court.* 2nd ed. Washington, D.C.: Congressional Quarterly, 1990.

*Congressional Quarterly's Guide to U.S. Elections.* 2nd ed. Washington, D.C.: Congressional Quarterly, 1985.

Daniel, Clifton, ed. *Chronicle of the Twentieth Century.* Mount Kisco, New York: Chronicle Publications, 1988.

*Encyclopedia Americana.* Danbury, Connecticut: Grolier, 1993.

*Encyclopedia Britannica.* 15th ed. Chicago: Encyclopedia Britannica, 1994.

Epstein, Lee, and Thomas G. Walker. *Constitutional Law for a Changing America: Rights, Liberties, and Justice.* Washington, D.C.: CQ Press, 1992.

Epstein, Lee, Jeffrey A. Segal, Harold J. Spaeth, and Thomas G. Walker. *The Supreme Court Compendium: Data, Decisions, and Developments.* Washington, D.C.: Congressional Quarterly, 1994.

*Facts on File Yearbook: The Indexed Record of World Events.* 1992, 1993, and 1994 eds. New York: Facts on File, 1992, 1993, 1994.

*Federal Civilian Workforce Statistics: Employment Trends as of July 1993.* Washington, D.C.: U.S. Government Printing Office, 1993.

Filson, Lawrence. *The Legislative Drafter's Desk Reference.* Washington, D.C.: Congressional Quarterly, 1992.

Flexner, Stuart Berg. *I Hear America Talking.* New York: Van Nostrand, 1976.

Hall, Kenneth, ed. *The Oxford Companion to the Supreme Court of the United States.* New York: Oxford University Press, 1992.

Harris, William H., and Judith S. Levey, eds. *The New Columbia Encyclopedia.* New York: Columbia University Press, 1975.

*Historical Tables: Budget of the United States Government.* Washington, D.C.: U.S. Government Printing Office, 1990.

Hoffman, Mark S., ed. *World Almanac and Book of Facts, 1993.* Mahwah, New Jersey: The World Almanac, 1992.

Kane, Joseph. *Facts About the Presidents.* 6th ed. New York: H. W. Wilson, 1993.

Kravitz, Walter. *Congressional Quarterly's American Congressional Dictionary.* Washington, D.C.: Congressional Quarterly, 1993.

Martin, Fenton S., and Robert U. Goehlert. *How to Research the Supreme Court.* Washington, D.C.: Congressional Quarterly, 1992.

Martis, Kenneth, and Gregory Elmer. *Historical Atlas of State Power in Congress.* Washington, D.C.: Congressional Quarterly, 1993.

Moore, John L. *Speaking of Washington: Facts, Firsts, and Folklore.* Washington, D.C.: Congressional Quarterly, 1993.

Morris, Richard B. *Encyclopedia of American History.* 6th ed. New York: Harper & Row, 1982.

Nelson, Michael, ed. *Congressional Quarterly's Guide to the Presidency.* Washington, D.C.: Congressional Quarterly, 1989.

Nelson, Michael, ed. *The Presidency A to Z: A Ready Reference Encyclopedia.* Washington, D.C.: Congressional Quarterly, 1994.

Ornstein, Norman J., Thomas E. Mann, and Michael J. Malbin. *Vital Statistics on Congress, 1993-1994.* Washington, D.C.: Congressional Quarterly, 1994.

The People Speak: American Elections in Focus. Washington, D.C.: Congressional Quarterly, 1990.

*Reader's Digest Encyclopedia of American History.* Pleasantville, New York: Reader's Digest, 1975.

Stanley, Harold W., and Richard G. Niemi. *Vital Statistics on American Politics.* 4th ed. Washington, D.C.: CQ Press, 1994.

*Statistical Abstract of the United States, 1993.* Austin, Texas: Reference Press, 1993.

Thernstrom, Stephan A., et al., eds. *Harvard Encyclopedia of American Ethnic Groups.* Cambridge, Mass.: Belknap Press, 1980.

*United States Government Manual, 1993-94.* Lanham, Maryland: Bernan Press, 1993.

*Webster's Biographical Dictionary.* Springfield, Massachusetts: G & C Merriam, 1980.

Wentworth, Harold, and Stuart Berg Flexner. *Dictionary of American Slang.* 2nd ed. New York: T. Y. Crowell, 1975.

Wetterau, Bruce. *The New York Public Library Book of Chronologies.* New York: Prentice Hall, 1990.

Wetterau, Bruce. *World History: A Dictionary of Important People, Places, and Events from Ancient Times to the Present.* New York: Henry Holt, 1994.

Witt, Elder, ed. *The Supreme Court A to Z: A Ready Reference Encyclopedia.* Washington, D.C.: Congressional Quarterly, 1993.

# APPENDIX

## CONSTITUTION OF THE UNITED STATES

We the People of the United States, in Order to form a more perfect Union, establish Justice, insure domestic Tranquility, provide for the common defence, promote the general Welfare, and secure the Blessings of Liberty to ourselves and our Posterity, do ordain and establish this Constitution for the United States of America.

### ARTICLE I

**Section 1.** All legislative Powers herein granted shall be vested in a Congress of the United States, which shall consist of a Senate and House of Representatives.

**Section 2.** The House of Representatives shall be composed of Members chosen every second Year by the People of the several States, and the Electors in each State shall have the Qualifications requisite for Electors of the most numerous Branch of the State Legislature.

No Person shall be a Representative who shall not have attained to the age of twenty five Years, and been seven Years a Citizen of the United States, and who shall not, when elected, be an Inhabitant of that State in which he shall be chosen.

[Representatives and direct Taxes shall be apportioned among the several States which may be included within this Union, according to their respective Numbers, which shall be determined by adding to the whole Number of free Persons, including those bound to Service for a Term of Years, and excluding Indians not taxed, three fifths of all other Persons.][1] The actual Enumeration shall be made within three Years after the first Meeting of the Congress of the United States, and within every subsequent Term of ten Years, in such Manner as they shall by Law direct. The Number of Representatives shall not exceed one for every thirty Thousand, but each State shall have at Least one Representative; and until such enumeration shall be made, the State of New Hampshire shall be entitled to chuse three, Massachusetts eight, Rhode-Island

and Providence Plantations one, Connecticut five, New-York six, New Jersey four, Pennsylvania eight, Delaware one, Maryland six, Virginia ten, North Carolina five, South Carolina five, and Georgia three.

When vacancies happen in the Representation from any State, the Executive Authority thereof shall issue Writs of Election to fill such Vacancies.

The House of Representatives shall chuse their Speaker and other Officers; and shall have the sole Power of Impeachment.

**Section 3.** The Senate of the United States shall be composed of two Senators from each State, [chosen by the Legislature thereof,][2] for six Years; and each Senator shall have one Vote.

Immediately after they shall be assembled in Consequence of the first Election, they shall be divided as equally as may be into three Classes. The Seats of the Senators of the first Class shall be vacated at the Expiration of the second Year, of the second Class at the Expiration of the fourth Year, and of the third Class at the Expiration of the sixth Year, so that one third may be chosen every second Year; [and if Vacancies happen by Resignation, or otherwise, during the Recess of the Legislature of any State, the Executive thereof may make temporary Appointments until the next Meeting of the Legislature, which shall then fill such Vacancies.][3]

No Person shall be a Senator who shall not have attained to the Age of thirty Years, and been nine Years a Citizen of the United States, and who shall not, when elected, be an Inhabitant of that State for which he shall be chosen.

The Vice President of the United States shall be President of the Senate, but shall have no Vote, unless they be equally divided.

The Senate shall chuse their other Officers, and also a President pro tempore, in the Absence of the Vice President, or when he shall exercise the Office of President of the United States.

The Senate shall have the sole Power to try all Impeachments. When sitting for that Purpose, they shall be on Oath or Affirmation. When the President of the United States is tried, the Chief Justice shall preside: And no Person shall be convicted without the Concurrence of two thirds of the Members present.

Judgment in Cases of Impeachment shall not extend further than to removal from Office, and disqualification to hold and enjoy any Office of honor, Trust or Profit under the United States: but the Party convicted shall nevertheless be liable and subject to Indictment, Trial, Judgment and Punishment, according to Law.

**Section 4.** The Times, Places and Manner of holding Elections for Senators and Representatives, shall be prescribed in each State by the Legislature thereof; but the

Congress may at any time by Law make or alter such Regulations, except as to the Places of chusing Senators.

The Congress shall assemble at least once in every Year, and such Meeting shall [be on the first Monday in December],[4] unless they shall by Law appoint a different Day.

**Section 5.** Each House shall be the Judge of the Elections, Returns and Qualifications of its own Members, and a Majority of each shall constitute a Quorum to do Business; but a smaller Number may adjourn from day to day, and may be authorized to compel the Attendance of absent Members, in such Manner, and under such Penalties as each House may provide.

Each House may determine the Rules of its Proceedings, punish its Members for disorderly Behaviour, and, with the Concurrence of two thirds, expel a Member.

Each House shall keep a Journal of its Proceedings, and from time to time publish the same, excepting such Parts as may in their Judgment require Secrecy; and the Yeas and Nays of the Members of either House on any question shall, at the Desire of one fifth of those Present, be entered on the Journal.

Neither House, during the Session of Congress, shall, without the Consent of the other, adjourn for more than three days, nor to any other Place than that in which the two Houses shall be sitting.

**Section 6.** The Senators and Representatives shall receive a Compensation for their Services, to be ascertained by Law, and paid out of the Treasury of the United States. They shall in all Cases, except Treason, Felony and Breach of the Peace, be privileged from Arrest during their Attendance at the Session of their respective Houses, and in going to and returning from the same; and for any Speech or Debate in either House, they shall not be questioned in any other Place.

No Senator or Representative shall, during the Time for which he was elected, be appointed to any civil Office under the Authority of the United States, which shall have been created, or the Emoluments whereof shall have been encreased during such time; and no Person holding any Office under the United States, shall be a Member of either House during his Continuance in Office.

**Section 7.** All Bills for raising Revenue shall originate in the House of Representatives; but the Senate may propose or concur with Amendments as on other Bills.

Every Bill which shall have passed the House of Representatives and the Senate, shall, before it become a Law, be presented to the President of the United States; If he approve he shall sign it, but if not he shall return it, with his Objections to that House in which it shall have originated, who shall enter the Objections at large on their Journal, and proceed to reconsider it. If after such Reconsideration two thirds of that

House shall agree to pass the Bill, it shall be sent, together with the Objections, to the other House, by which it shall likewise be reconsidered, and if approved by two thirds of that House, it shall become a Law. But in all such Cases the Votes of both Houses shall be determined by yeas and Nays, and the Names of the Persons voting for and against the Bill shall be entered on the Journal of each House respectively. If any Bill shall not be returned by the President within ten Days (Sundays excepted) after it shall have been presented to him, the Same shall be a Law, in like Manner as if he had signed it, unless the Congress by their Adjournment prevent its Return, in which Case it shall not be a Law.

Every Order, Resolution, or Vote to which the Concurrence of the Senate and House of Representatives may be necessary (except on a question of Adjournment) shall be presented to the President of the United States; and before the Same shall take Effect, shall be approved by him, or being disapproved by him, shall be repassed by two thirds of the Senate and House of Representatives, according to the Rules and Limitations prescribed in the Case of a Bill.

**Section 8.** The Congress shall have Power To lay and collect Taxes, Duties, Imposts and Excises, to pay the Debts and provide for the common Defence and general Welfare of the United States; but all Duties, Imposts and Excises shall be uniform throughout the United States;

To borrow Money on the credit of the United States;

To regulate Commerce with foreign Nations, and among the several States, and with the Indian Tribes;

To establish an uniform Rule of Naturalization, and uniform Laws on the subject of Bankruptcies throughout the United States;

To coin Money, regulate the Value thereof, and of foreign Coin, and fix the Standard of Weights and Measures;

To provide for the Punishment of counterfeiting the Securities and current Coin of the United States;

To establish Post Offices and post Roads;

To promote the Progress of Science and useful Arts, by securing for limited Times to Authors and Inventors the exclusive Right to their respective Writings and Discoveries;

To constitute Tribunals inferior to the supreme Court;

To define and punish Piracies and Felonies committed on the high Seas, and Offences against the Law of Nations;

To declare War, grant Letters of Marque and Reprisal, and make Rules concerning Captures on Land and Water;

To raise and support Armies, but no Appropriation of Money to that Use shall be for a longer Term than two Years;

To provide and maintain a Navy;

To make Rules for the Government and Regulation of the land and naval Forces;

To provide for calling forth the Militia to execute the Laws of the Union, suppress Insurrections and repel Invasions;

To provide for organizing, arming, and disciplining, the Militia, and for governing such Part of them as may be employed in the Service of the United States, reserving to the States respectively, the Appointment of the Officers, and the Authority of training the Militia according to the discipline prescribed by Congress;

To exercise exclusive Legislation in all Cases whatsoever, over such District (not exceeding ten Miles square) as may, by Cession of particular States, and the Acceptance of Congress, become the Seat of the Government of the United States, and to exercise like Authority over all Places purchased by the Consent of the Legislature of the State in which the Same shall be, for the Erection of Forts, Magazines, Arsenals, dock-Yards, and other needful Buildings;—And

To make all Laws which shall be necessary and proper for carrying into Execution the foregoing Powers, and all other Powers vested by this Constitution in the Government of the United States, or in any Department or Officer thereof.

**Section 9.** The Migration or Importation of such Persons as any of the States now existing shall think proper to admit, shall not be prohibited by the Congress prior to the Year one thousand eight hundred and eight, but a Tax or duty may be imposed on such Importation, not exceeding ten dollars for each Person.

The Privilege of the Writ of Habeas Corpus shall not be suspended, unless when in Cases of Rebellion or Invasion the public Safety may require it.

No Bill of Attainder or ex post facto Law shall be passed.

No Capitation, or other direct, Tax shall be laid, unless in Proportion to the Census or Enumeration herein before directed to be taken.[5]

No Tax or Duty shall be laid on Articles exported from any State.

No Preference shall be given by any Regulation of Commerce or Revenue to the Ports of one State over those of another; nor shall Vessels bound to, or from, one State, be obliged to enter, clear, or pay Duties in another.

No Money shall be drawn from the Treasury, but in Consequence of Appropriations made by Law; and a regular Statement and Account of the Receipts and Expenditures of all public Money shall be published from time to time.

No Title of Nobility shall be granted by the United States: And no Person holding any Office of Profit or Trust under them, shall, without the Consent of the Congress, accept of any present, Emolument, Office, or Title, of any kind whatever, from any King, Prince, or foreign State.

**Section 10.** No State shall enter into any Treaty, Alliance, or Confederation; grant Letters of Marque and Reprisal; coin Money; emit Bills of Credit; make any Thing but gold and silver Coin a Tender in Payment of Debts; pass any Bill of Attainder, ex post facto Law, or Law impairing the Obligation of Contracts, or grant any Title of Nobility.

No State shall, without the Consent of the Congress, lay any Imposts or Duties on Imports or Exports, except what may be absolutely necessary for executing it's inspection Laws: and the net Produce of all Duties and Imposts, laid by any State on Imports or Exports, shall be for the Use of the Treasury of the United States; and all such Laws shall be subject to the Revision and Controul of the Congress.

No State shall, without the Consent of Congress, lay any Duty of Tonnage, keep Troops, or Ships of War in time of Peace, enter into any Agreement or Compact with another State, or with a foreign Power, or engage in War, unless actually invaded, or in such imminent Danger as will not admit of delay.

## ARTICLE II

**Section 1.** The executive Power shall be vested in a President of the United States of America. He shall hold his Office during the Term of four Years, and, together with the Vice President, chosen for the same Term, be elected, as follows:

Each State shall appoint, in such Manner as the Legislature thereof may direct, a Number of Electors, equal to the whole Number of Senators and Representatives to which the State may be entitled in the Congress: but no Senator or Representative, or Person holding an Office of Trust or Profit under the United States, shall be appointed an Elector.

[The Electors shall meet in their respective States, and vote by Ballot for two Persons, of whom one at least shall not be an Inhabitant of the same State with themselves. And they shall make a List of all the Persons voted for, and of the Number of Votes for each; which List they shall sign and certify, and transmit sealed to the Seat of the Government of the United States, directed to the President of the Senate. The President of the Senate shall, in the Presence of the Senate and House of Representatives, open all the Certificates, and the Votes shall then be counted. The Person having the greatest Number of Votes shall be the President, if such Number be a Majority of the whole Number of Electors appointed; and if there be more than one who have such Majority, and have an equal Number of Votes, then the House of Representatives shall immediately chuse by Ballot one of them for President; and if no Person have a Majority, then from the five highest on the list the said House shall in like Manner chuse the President. But in chusing the President, the Votes shall be taken by States, the Representation from each State having one Vote; A quorum for this Purpose shall consist of a Member or Members from two thirds of the States, and a Majority of all the States shall be necessary to a Choice. In every Case, after the Choice of the President, the Person having the greatest Number of Votes of the Electors shall be the Vice President. But if there should remain two or more who have equal Votes, the Senate shall chuse from them by Ballot the Vice President.][6]

The Congress may determine the Time of chusing the Electors, and the Day on which they shall give their Votes; which Day shall be the same throughout the United States.

No Person except a natural born Citizen, or a Citizen of the United States, at the time of the Adoption of this Constitution, shall be eligible to the Office of President; neither shall any Person be eligible to that Office who shall not have attained to the Age of thirty five Years, and been fourteen Years a Resident within the United States.

In Case of the Removal of the President from Office, or of his Death, Resignation, or Inability to discharge the Powers and Duties of the said Office,[7] the Same shall devolve on the Vice President, and the Congress may by Law provide for the Case of Removal, Death, Resignation or Inability, both of the President and Vice President, declaring what Officer shall then act as President, and such Officer shall act accordingly, until the Disability be removed, or a President shall be elected.

The President shall, at stated Times, receive for his Services, a Compensation, which shall neither be encreased nor diminished during the Period for which he shall have been elected, and he shall not receive within that Period any other Emolument from the United States, or any of them.

Before he enter on the Execution of his Office, he shall take the following Oath or Affirmation:—"I do solemnly swear (or affirm) that I will faithfully execute the Office of President of the United States, and will to the best of my Ability, preserve, protect and defend the Constitution of the United States."

**Section 2.** The President shall be Commander in Chief of the Army and Navy of the United States, and of the Militia of the several States, when called into the actual Service of the United States; he may require the Opinion, in writing, of the principal Officer in each of the executive Departments, upon any Subject relating to the Duties of their respective Offices, and he shall have Power to grant Reprieves and Pardons for Offences against the United States, except in Cases of Impeachment.

He shall have Power, by and with the Advice and Consent of the Senate, to make Treaties, provided two thirds of the Senators present concur; and he shall nominate, and by and with the Advice and Consent of the Senate, shall appoint Ambassadors, other public Ministers and Consuls, Judges of the supreme Court, and all other Officers of the United States, whose Appointments are not herein otherwise provided for, and which shall be established by Law: but the Congress may by Law vest the Appointment of such inferior Officers, as they think proper, in the President alone, in the Courts of Law, or in the Heads of Departments.

The President shall have Power to fill up all Vacancies that may happen during the Recess of the Senate, by granting Commissions which shall expire at the End of their next Session.

**Section 3.** He shall from time to time give to the Congress Information of the State of the Union, and recommend to their Consideration such Measures as he shall judge necessary and expedient; he may, on extraordinary Occasions, convene both Houses, or either of them, and in Case of Disagreement between them, with Respect to the Time of Adjournment, he may adjourn them to such Time as he shall think proper; he shall receive Ambassadors and other public Ministers; he shall take Care that the Laws be faithfully executed, and shall Commission all the Officers of the United States.

**Section 4.** The President, Vice President and all civil Officers of the United States, shall be removed from Office on Impeachment for, and Conviction of, Treason, Bribery, or other high Crimes and Misdemeanors.

## ARTICLE III

**Section 1.** The judicial Power of the United States, shall be vested in one supreme Court, and in such inferior Courts as the Congress may from time to time ordain and establish. The Judges, both of the supreme and inferior Courts, shall hold their Offices during good Behaviour, and shall, at stated Times, receive for their Services, a Compensation, which shall not be diminished during their Continuance in Office.

**Section 2.** The judicial Power shall extend to all Cases, in Law and Equity, arising under this Constitution, the Laws of the United States, and Treaties made, or which shall be made, under their Authority;—to all Cases affecting Ambassadors, other public Ministers and Consuls;—to all Cases of admiralty and maritime Jurisdiction;—to Controversies to which the United States shall be a Party;—to Controversies between two or more States;—between a State and Citizens of another State;[8]—between Citizens of different States;—between Citizens of the same State claiming Lands under Grants of different States, and between a State, or the Citizens thereof, and foreign States, Citizens or Subjects.[8]

In all Cases affecting Ambassadors, other public Ministers and Consuls, and those in which a State shall be Party, the supreme Court shall have original Jurisdiction. In all the other Cases before mentioned, the supreme Court shall have appellate Jurisdiction, both as to Law and Fact, with such Exceptions, and under such Regulations as the Congress shall make.

The Trial of all Crimes, except in Cases of Impeachment, shall be by Jury; and such Trial shall be held in the State where the said Crimes shall have been committed; but when not committed within any State, the Trial shall be at such Place or Places as the Congress may by Law have directed.

**Section 3.** Treason against the United States, shall consist only in levying War against them, or in adhering to their Enemies, giving them Aid and Comfort. No Person shall be convicted of Treason unless on the Testimony of two Witnesses to the same overt Act, or on Confession in open Court.

The Congress shall have Power to declare the Punishment of Treason, but no Attainder of Treason shall work Corruption of Blood, or Forfeiture except during the Life of the Person attainted.

## ARTICLE IV

**Section 1.** Full Faith and Credit shall be given in each State to the public Acts, Records, and judicial Proceedings of every other State. And the Congress may by general Laws prescribe the Manner in which such Acts, Records and Proceedings shall be proved, and the Effect thereof.

**Section 2.** The Citizens of each State shall be entitled to all Privileges and Immunities of Citizens in the several States.

A Person charged in any State with Treason, Felony, or other Crime, who shall flee from Justice, and be found in another State, shall on Demand of the executive Authority of the State from which he fled, be delivered up, to be removed to the State having Jurisdiction of the Crime.

[No Person held to Service or Labour in one State, under the Laws thereof, escaping into another, shall, in Consequence of any Law or Regulation therein, be discharged from such Service or Labour, but shall be delivered up on Claim of the Party to whom such Service or Labour may be due.][9]

**Section 3.** New States may be admitted by the Congress into this Union; but no new State shall be formed or erected within the Jurisdiction of any other State; nor any State be formed by the Junction of two or more States, or Parts of States, without the Consent of the Legislatures of the States concerned as well as of the Congress.

The Congress shall have Power to dispose of and make all needful Rules and Regulations respecting the Territory or other Property belonging to the United States; and nothing in this Constitution shall be so construed as to Prejudice any Claims of the United States, or of any particular State.

**Section 4.** The United States shall guarantee to every State in this Union a Republican Form of Government, and shall protect each of them against Invasion; and on Application of the Legislature, or of the Executive (when the Legislature cannot be convened) against domestic Violence.

## ARTICLE V

The Congress, whenever two thirds of both Houses shall deem it necessary, shall propose Amendments to this Constitution, or, on the Application of the Legislatures of two thirds of the several States, shall call a Convention for proposing Amendments, which, in either Case, shall be valid to all Intents and Purposes, as Part of this Constitution, when ratified by the Legislatures of three fourths of the several States, or by Conventions in three fourths thereof, as the one or the other Mode of Ratification may be proposed by the Congress; Provided [that no Amendment which may be made prior to the Year One thousand eight hundred and eight shall in any Manner affect the first and fourth Clauses in the Ninth Section of the first Article; and][10] that no State, without its Consent, shall be deprived of its equal Suffrage in the Senate.

## ARTICLE VI

All Debts contracted and Engagements entered into, before the Adoption of this Constitution, shall be as valid against the United States under this Constitution, as under the Confederation.

This Constitution, and the Laws of the United States which shall be made in Pursuance thereof; and all Treaties made, or which shall be made, under the Authority of the United States, shall be the supreme Law of the Land; and the Judges in every State shall be bound thereby, any Thing in the Constitution or Laws of any State to the Contrary notwithstanding.

The Senators and Representatives before mentioned, and the Members of the several State Legislatures, and all executive and judicial Officers, both of the United States and of the several States, shall be bound by Oath or Affirmation, to support this Constitution; but no religious Test shall ever be required as a Qualification to any Office or public Trust under the United States.

## ARTICLE VII

The Ratification of the Conventions of nine States, shall be sufficient for the Establishment of this Constitution between the States so ratifying the Same.

Done in Convention by the Unanimous Consent of the States present the Seventeenth Day of September in the Year of our Lord one thousand seven hundred and Eighty seven and of the Independence of the United States of America the Twelfth. IN WITNESS whereof We have hereunto subscribed our Names,

George Washington,
President and
deputy from Virginia.

**New Hampshire:**
John Langdon,
Nicholas Gilman.

**Massachusetts:**
Nathaniel Gorham,
Rufus King.

**Connecticut:**
William Samuel Johnson,
Roger Sherman.

**New York:**
Alexander Hamilton.

**New Jersey:**
William Livingston,
David Brearley,
William Paterson
Jonathan Dayton.

**Pennsylvania:**
Benjamin Franklin,
Thomas Mifflin,
Robert Morris,
George Clymer,
Thomas FitzSimons,
Jared Ingersoll,
James Wilson,
Gouverneur Morris.

**Delaware:**
George Read,
Gunning Bedford Jr.,
John Dickinson,
Richard Bassett,
Jacob Broom.

**Maryland:**
James McHenry,
Daniel of St. Thomas Jenifer,
Daniel Carroll.

**Virginia:**
John Blair,
James Madison Jr.

**North Carolina:**
William Blount,
Richard Dobbs Spaight,
Hugh Williamson.

**South Carolina:**
John Rutledge,
Charles Cotesworth Pinckney,
Charles Pinckney,
Pierce Butler.

**Georgia:**
William Few,
Abraham Baldwin.

[The language of the original Constitution, not including the Amendments, was adopted by a convention of the states on September 17, 1787, and was subsequently ratified by the states on the following dates: Delaware, December 7, 1787; Pennsylvania, December 12, 1787; New Jersey, December 18, 1787; Georgia, January 2, 1788; Connecticut, January 9, 1788; Massachusetts, February 6, 1788; Maryland, April 28, 1788; South Carolina, May 23, 1788; New Hampshire, June 21, 1788.

Ratification was completed on June 21, 1788.

The Constitution subsequently was ratified by Virginia, June 25, 1788; New York, July 26, 1788; North Carolina, November 21, 1789; Rhode Island, May 29, 1790; and Vermont, January 10, 1791.]

## AMENDMENTS

### Amendment I

*(First ten amendments ratified December 15, 1791.)*
Congress shall make no law respecting an establishment of religion, or prohibiting the free exercise thereof; or abridging the freedom of speech, or of the press; or the right of the people peaceably to assemble, and to petition the Government for a redress of grievances.

### Amendment II

A well regulated Militia, being necessary to the security of a free State, the right of the people to keep and bear Arms, shall not be infringed.

### Amendment III

No Soldier shall, in time of peace be quartered in any house, without the consent of the Owner, nor in time of war, but in a manner to be prescribed by law.

### Amendment IV

The right of the people to be secure in their persons, houses, papers, and effects, against unreasonable searches and seizures, shall not be violated, and no Warrants shall issue, but upon probable cause, supported by Oath or affirmation, and particularly describing the place to be searched, and the persons or things to be seized.

## Amendment V

No person shall be held to answer for a capital, or otherwise infamous crime, unless on a presentment or indictment of a Grand Jury, except in cases arising in the land or naval forces, or in the Militia, when in actual service in time of War or public danger; nor shall any person be subject for the same offence to be twice put in jeopardy of life or limb; nor shall be compelled in any criminal case to be a witness against himself, nor be deprived of life, liberty, or property, without due process of law; nor shall private property be taken for public use, without just compensation.

## Amendment VI

In all criminal prosecutions, the accused shall enjoy the right to a speedy and public trial, by an impartial jury of the State and district wherein the crime shall have been committed, which district shall have been previously ascertained by law, and to be informed of the nature and cause of the accusation; to be confronted with the witnesses against him; to have compulsory process for obtaining witnesses in his favor, and to have the Assistance of Counsel for his defence.

## Amendment VII

In Suits at common law, where the value in controversy shall exceed twenty dollars, the right of trial by jury shall be preserved, and no fact tried by a jury, shall be otherwise re-examined in any Court of the United States, than according to the rules of the common law.

## Amendment VIII

Excessive bail shall not be required, nor excessive fines imposed, nor cruel and unusual punishments inflicted.

## Amendment IX

The enumeration in the Constitution, of certain rights, shall not be construed to deny or disparage others retained by the people.

## Amendment X

The powers not delegated to the United States by the Constitution, nor prohibited by it to the States, are reserved to the States respectively, or to the people.

### Amendment XI (Ratified February 7, 1795)

The Judicial power of the United States shall not be construed to extend to any suit in law or equity, commenced or prosecuted against one of the United States by Citizens of another State, or by Citizens or Subjects of any Foreign State.

### Amendment XII (Ratified June 15, 1804)

The Electors shall meet in their respective states and vote by ballot for President and Vice-President, one of whom, at least, shall not be an inhabitant of the same state with themselves; they shall name in their ballots the person voted for as President, and in distinct ballots the person voted for as Vice-President, and they shall make distinct lists of all persons voted for as President, and of all persons voted for as Vice-President, and of the number of votes for each, which lists they shall sign and certify, and transmit sealed to the seat of the government of the United States, directed to the President of the Senate;—The President of the Senate shall, in the presence of the Senate and House of Representatives, open all the certificates and the votes shall then be counted;—The person having the greatest number of votes for President, shall be the President, if such number be a majority of the whole number of Electors appointed; and if no person have such majority, then from the persons having the highest numbers not exceeding three on the list of those voted for as President, the House of Representatives shall choose immediately, by ballot, the President. But in choosing the President, the votes shall be taken by states, the representation from each state having one vote; a quorum for this purpose shall consist of a member or members from two-thirds of the states, and a majority of all the states shall be necessary to a choice. [And if the House of Representatives shall not choose a President whenever the right of choice shall devolve upon them, before the fourth day of March next following, then the Vice-President shall act as President, as in the case of the death or other constitutional disability of the President.—][11] The person having the greatest number of votes as Vice-President, shall be the Vice-President, if such number be a majority of the whole number of Electors appointed, and if no person have a majority, then from the two highest numbers on the list, the Senate shall choose the Vice-President; a quorum for the purpose shall consist of two-thirds of the whole number of Senators, and a majority of the whole number shall be necessary to a choice. But no person constitutionally ineligible to the office of President shall be eligible to that of Vice-President of the United States.

### Amendment XIII (Ratified December 6, 1865)

**Section 1.** Neither slavery nor involuntary servitude, except as a punishment for crime whereof the party shall have been duly convicted, shall exist within the United States, or any place subject to their jurisdiction.

**Section 2.** Congress shall have power to enforce this article by appropriate legislation.

### Amendment XIV (Ratified July 9, 1868)

**Section 1.** All persons born or naturalized in the United States, and subject to the jurisdiction thereof, are citizens of the United States and of the State wherein they reside. No State shall make or enforce any law which shall abridge the privileges or immunities of citizens of the United States; nor shall any State deprive any person of life, liberty, or property, without due process of law; nor deny to any person within its jurisdiction the equal protection of the laws.

**Section 2.** Representatives shall be apportioned among the several States according to their respective numbers, counting the whole number of persons in each State, excluding Indians not taxed. But when the right to vote at any election for the choice of electors for President and Vice President of the United States, Representatives in Congress, the Executive and Judicial officers of a State, or the members of the Legislature thereof, is denied to any of the male inhabitants of such State, being twenty-one years of age[12] and citizens of the United States, or in any way abridged, except for participation in rebellion, or other crime, the basis of representation therein shall be reduced in the proportion which the number of such male citizens shall bear to the whole number of male citizens twenty-one years of age in such State.

**Section 3.** No person shall be a Senator or Representative in Congress, or elector of President and Vice President, or hold any office, civil or military, under the United States, or under any State, who, having previously taken an oath, as a member of Congress, or as an officer of the United States, or as a member of any State legislature, or as an executive or judicial officer of any State, to support the Constitution of the United States, shall have engaged in insurrection or rebellion against the same, or given aid or comfort to the enemies thereof. But Congress may by a vote of two-thirds of each House, remove such disability.

**Section 4.** The validity of the public debt of the United States, authorized by law, including debts incurred for payment of pensions and bounties for services in suppressing insurrection or rebellion, shall not be questioned. But neither the United

States nor any State shall assume or pay any debt or obligation incurred in aid of insurrection or rebellion against the United States, or any claim for the loss or emancipation of any slave; but all such debts, obligations and claims shall be held illegal and void.

**Section 5.** The Congress shall have power to enforce, by appropriate legislation, the provisions of this article.

### Amendment XV (Ratified February 3, 1870)

**Section 1.** The right of citizens of the United States to vote shall not be denied or abridged by the United States or by any State on account of race, color, or previous condition of servitude.

**Section 2.** The Congress shall have power to enforce this article by appropriate legislation.

### Amendment XVI (Ratified February 3, 1913)

The Congress shall have power to lay and collect taxes on incomes, from whatever source derived, without apportionment among the several States, and without regard to any census or enumeration.

### Amendment XVII (Ratified April 8, 1913)

The Senate of the United States shall be composed of two Senators from each State, elected by the people thereof, for six years; and each Senator shall have one vote. The electors in each State shall have the qualifications requisite for electors of the most numerous branch of the State legislatures.

When vacancies happen in the representation of any State in the Senate, the executive authority of such State shall issue writs of election to fill such vacancies: *Provided,* That the legislature of any State may empower the executive thereof to make temporary appointments until the people fill the vacancies by election as the legislature may direct.

This amendment shall not be so construed as to affect the election or term of any Senator chosen before it becomes valid as part of the Constitution.

### Amendment XVIII (Ratified January 16, 1919)

**Section 1.** After one year from the ratification of this article the manufacture, sale, or transportation of intoxicating liquors within, the importation thereof into, or the exportation thereof from the United States and all territory subject to the jurisdiction thereof for beverage purposes is hereby prohibited.

**Section 2.** The Congress and the several States shall have concurrent power to enforce this article by appropriate legislation.

**Section 3.** This article shall be inoperative unless it shall have been ratified as an amendment to the Constitution by the legislatures of the several States, as provided in the Constitution, within seven years from the date of the submission hereof to the States by the Congress.][13]

### Amendment XIX (Ratified August 18, 1920)

The right of citizens of the United States to vote shall not be denied or abridged by the United States or by any State on account of sex.

Congress shall have power to enforce this article by appropriate legislation.

### Amendment XX (Ratified January 23, 1933)

**Section 1.** The terms of the President and Vice President shall end at noon on the 20th day of January, and the terms of Senators and Representatives at noon on the 3d day of January, of the years in which such terms would have ended if this article had not been ratified; and the terms of their successors shall then begin.

**Section 2.** The Congress shall assemble at least once in every year, and such meeting shall begin at noon on the 3d day of January, unless they shall by law appoint a different day.

**Section 3.**[14] If, at the time fixed for the beginning of the term of the President, the President elect shall have died, the Vice President elect shall become President. If a President shall not have been chosen before the time fixed for the beginning of his term, or if the President elect shall have failed to qualify, then the Vice President elect shall act as President until a President shall have qualified; and the Congress may by law provide for the case wherein neither a President elect nor a Vice President elect shall have qualified, declaring who shall then act as President, or the manner in which one who is to act shall be selected, and such person shall act accordingly until a President or Vice President shall have qualified.

**Section 4.** The Congress may by law provide for the case of the death of any of the persons from whom the House of Representatives may choose a President whenever the right of choice shall have devolved upon them, and for the case of the death of any of the persons from whom the Senate may choose a Vice President whenever the right of choice shall have devolved upon them.

**Section 5.** Sections 1 and 2 shall take effect on the 15th day of October following the ratification of this article.

**Section 6.** This article shall be inoperative unless it shall have been ratified as an amendment to the Constitution by the legislatures of three-fourths of the several States within seven years from the date of its submission.

### Amendment XXI (Ratified December 5, 1933)

**Section 1.** The eighteenth article of amendment to the Constitution of the United States is hereby repealed.

**Section 2.** The transportation or importation into any State, Territory, or possession of the United States for delivery or use therein of intoxicating liquors, in violation of the laws thereof, is hereby prohibited

**Section 3.** This article shall be inoperative unless it shall have been ratified as an amendment to the Constitution by conventions in the several States, as provided in the Constitution, within seven years from the date of the submission hereof to the States by the Congress.

### Amendment XXII (Ratified February 27, 1951)

**Section 1.** No person shall be elected to the office of the President more than twice, and no person who has held the office of President, or acted as President, for more than two years of a term to which some other person was elected President shall be elected to the office of the President more than once. But this Article shall not apply to any person holding the office of President when this Article was proposed by the Congress, and shall not prevent any person who may be holding the office of President, or acting as President, during the term within which this Article become operative from holding the office of President or acting as President during the remainder of such term.

**Section 2.** This article shall be inoperative unless it shall have been ratified as an amendment to the Constitution by the legislatures of three-fourths of the several States within seven years from the date of its submission to the States by the Congress.

### Amendment XXIII (Ratified March 29, 1961)

**Section 1.** The District constituting the seat of Government of the United States shall appoint in such manner as the Congress may direct:

A number of electors of President and Vice President equal to the whole number of Senators and Representatives in Congress to which the District would be entitled if it were a State, but in no event more than the least populous State; they shall be in addition to those appointed by the States, but they shall be considered, for the purposes of the election of President and Vice President, to be electors appointed by a State; and they shall meet in the District and perform such duties as provided by the twelfth article of amendment.

**Section 2.** The Congress shall have power to enforce this article by appropriate legislation.

### Amendment XXIV (Ratified January 23, 1964)

**Section 1.** The right of citizens of the United States to vote in any primary or other election for President or Vice President, for electors for President or Vice President, or for Senator or Representative in Congress, shall not be denied or abridged by the United States or any State by reason of failure to pay any poll tax or other tax.

**Section 2.** The Congress shall have power to enforce this article by appropriate legislation.

### Amendment XXV (Ratified February 10, 1967)

**Section 1.** In case of the removal of the President from office or of his death or resignation, the Vice President shall become President.

**Section 2.** Whenever there is a vacancy in the office of the Vice President, the President shall nominate a Vice President who shall take office upon confirmation by a majority vote of both Houses of Congress.

**Section 3.** Whenever the President transmits to the President pro tempore of the Senate and the Speaker of the House of Representatives his written declaration that he is unable to discharge the powers and duties of his office, and until he transmits to them a written declaration to the contrary, such powers and duties shall be discharged by the Vice President as Acting President.

**Section 4.** Whenever the Vice President and a majority of either the principal officers of the executive departments or of such other body as Congress may by law provide, transmit to the President pro tempore of the Senate and the Speaker of the House of Representatives their written declaration that the President is unable to discharge the powers and duties of his office, the Vice President shall immediately assume the powers and duties of the office as Acting President.

Thereafter, when the President transmits to the President pro tempore of the Senate and the Speaker of the House of Representatives his written declaration that no inability exists, he shall resume the powers and duties of his office unless the Vice President and a majority of either the principal officers of the executive department or of such other body as Congress may by law provide, transmit within four days to the President pro tempore of the Senate and the Speaker of the House of Representatives their written declaration that the President is unable to discharge the powers and duties of his office. Thereupon Congress shall decide the issue, assembling within forty-eight hours for that purpose if not in session. If the Congress, within twenty-one days after receipt of the latter written declaration, or, if Congress is not in session, within twenty-one days after Congress is required to assemble, determines by two-thirds vote of both Houses that the President is unable to discharge the powers and duties of his office, the Vice President shall continue to discharge the same as Acting President; otherwise, the President shall resume the powers and duties of his office.

### Amendment XXVI (Ratified July 1, 1971)

**Section 1.** The right of citizens of the United States, who are eighteen years of age or older, to vote shall not be denied or abridged by the United States or by any State on account of age.

**Section 2.** The Congress shall have power to enforce this article by appropriate legislation.

### Amendment XXVII (Ratified May 7, 1992)

No law varying the compensation for the services of the Senators and Representatives shall take effect, until an election of Representatives shall have intervened.

## NOTES

1.  The part in brackets was changed by section 2 of the Fourteenth Amendment.

2.  The part in brackets was changed by the first paragraph of the Seventeenth Amendment.

3.  The part in brackets was changed by the second paragraph of the Seventeenth Amendment.

4.  The part in brackets was changed by section 2 of the Twentieth Amendment.

5.  The Sixteenth Amendment gave Congress the power to tax incomes.

6.  The material in brackets has been superseded by the Twelfth Amendment.

7.  This provision has been affected by the Twenty-fifth Amendment.

8.  These clauses were affected by the Eleventh Amendment.

9.  This paragraph has been superseded by the Thirteenth Amendment.

10. Obsolete.

11. The part in brackets has been superseded by section 3 of the Twentieth Amendment.

12. See the Nineteenth and Twenty-sixth Amendments.

13. This Amendment was repealed by section 1 of the Twenty-first Amendment.

14. See the Twenty-fifth Amendment.

*Source:* U.S. Congress, House, Committee on the Judiciary, *The Constitution of the United States of America, as Amended,* 100th Cong., 1st sess., 1987, H Doc 100-94.

# INDEX